The Global Future of Higher Edu
Profession

The Global Future of Higher Education and the Academic Profession

The BRICs and the United States

Edited by

Philip G. Altbach
Center for International Higher Education, Boston College, USA

Gregory Androushchak
National Research University, Higher School of Economics, Russia

Yaroslav Kuzminov
National Research University, Higher School of Economics, Russia

Maria Yudkevich
National Research University, Higher School of Economics, Russia

Liz Reisberg
Resiberg & Associates, USA

First published in hardback 2013
Published in paperback 2015 by
PALGRAVE MACMILLAN

Palgrave Macmillan in the UK is an imprint of Macmillan Publishers Limited, registered in England, company number 785998, of Houndmills, Basingstoke, Hampshire RG21 6XS.

Palgrave Macmillan in the US is a division of St Martin's Press LLC, 175 Fifth Avenue, New York, NY 10010.

Palgrave Macmillan is the global academic imprint of the above companies and has companies and representatives throughout the world.

Palgrave® and Macmillan® are registered trademarks in the United States, the United Kingdom, Europe and other countries.

ISBN 978–0–230–36978–8 hardback
ISBN 978–1–137–49361–3 paperback

This book is printed on paper suitable for recycling and made from fully managed and sustained forest sources. Logging, pulping and manufacturing processes are expected to conform to the environmental regulations of the country of origin.

A catalogue record for this book is available from the British Library.

A catalog record for this book is available from the Library of Congress.

Contents

Figures and Tables

Figures

Tables

Preface

The BRIC countries—Brazil, Russia, India, and China—are among the fastest-growing economies in the world. These countries are destined to play a more important global role, joining the United States in shaping a shared economic future. Additionally, with the development of an international higher education market, the BRIC countries will play an increasingly central role in this sphere as well. The BRICs are also likely to compete with each other for prestige and placement in the global rankings, as they work to achieve world-class standing and to strengthen their research universities.

Three of the BRICs—China, Brazil, and India—will continue to experience rapid growth in higher education in the coming years and will absorb more than half of the global growth in enrollments in the next decades. Like the United States, Russia hosts a mature academic system, but spectacular changes in the governing economic model during the last several decades have left the higher education system somewhat adrift. Currently, Russia has excess enrollment capacity and the subsequent challenge of filling seats to sustain budgets—but without compromising quality.

While sheer size does not produce academic superpowers, the academic systems of these four countries will inevitably play a more central role in the global knowledge economy—indeed they are doing so already and all show an upward trajectory in terms of research productivity and expenditure on research and development, with China and Brazil exhibiting the most impressive strength. Additionally, each of the BRIC countries is developing aggressive international strategies to engage foreign partners in new ways.

Yet, all four BRIC countries face serious academic challenges in the quest to serve the needs of their economies and populations, create "world-class" universities, develop a vigorous academic culture, and provide better quality more consistently across the entire sector.

The United States, arguably the world's most influential academic system, is included in our analysis as a point of comparison with the BRIC countries. Although higher education globally reflects many different traditions, the US system is widely emulated in many respects; for the moment it continues to be the primary producer of original basic research. Yet, like the BRICs, the United States currently faces significant challenges, many resulting from having limited sources of revenue while the cost of providing instruction and research continues to increase. An analysis of these issues should prove useful for understanding the challenges that the BRIC nations may confront as they evolve as important international contributors to teaching and research.

The Global Future of Higher Education and the Academic Profession provides an original analysis of the academic systems and challenges of each of the BRIC countries with a comparable analysis of the United States. While there are common elements among these countries, many differences also exist. This book's approach considers all relevant aspects of higher education development in each country, but ultimately focuses on the academic profession.

The academic profession is at the heart of any successful university or academic system, and thus the theme of this book is the professoriate; the challenges face the academic profession in terms of working conditions and how these conditions have changed as each of these economies confronts dramatic change—growth in each of the BRICs and contraction in the case of the United States. The analysis addresses issues relating to salaries, remuneration, and contracts. These central elements determine whether the professoriate can be fully productive and effective.

This book resulted from a related research project concerning academic salaries, remuneration, and contracts (see *Paying the Professoriate: A Global Comparison of Compensation and Contracts*, edited by Philip G. Altbach, Liz Reisberg, Maria Yudkevich, Gregory Androushchak, and Iván F. Pacheco (2012)). The goal here is to expand on the previous study to highlight what is happening in the BRIC countries. Each chapter provides context and analysis that will be useful to policymakers and scholars alike. This is a pivotal moment, as each country considers the relevance of higher education to future economic development in general and the critical importance of cultivating conditions to ensure that the professoriate can flourish. This volume is a multifaceted analysis of some of the challenges, as well as the prospects, facing four of the world's most important emerging academic systems—and a comparison with the United States.

Philip G. Altbach
Gregory Androushchak
Yaroslav Kuzminov
Maria Yudkevich
Liz Reisberg
Boston, USA, and Moscow, Russia

Acknowledgments

This volume has complex origins, and thus we are indebted to many colleagues as well as to our sponsoring organizations. It grew out of a previous study of academic salaries, remuneration, and contracts in 28 countries. We are indebted to all of the researchers who contributed to that project and helped to collect data and analyze this complicated issue. The project reflects collaboration between the National Research University Higher School of Economics' Center for Institutional Studies in Russia and the Center for International Higher Education at Boston College in the United States. Both partners contributed to the funding that made this research possible.

At the Higher School of Economics' Center for Institutional Studies, Elena Shutova provided logistical support. Alexander Novikov and Anna Panova helped us to collect and analyze empirical country data. The World Bank also provided logistical and other assistance.

The Boston College Center is indebted to the Ford Foundation for its support during the early phases of the project. We are also indebted to Edith S. Hoshino, CIHE publications editor, for editing the final manuscript, and to Salina Kopellas for logistical support.

Contributors

Editors

Philip G. Altbach is J. Donald Monan, S. J. University Professor and Director of the Center for International Higher Education at Boston College in the United States. He was the 2004–2006 Distinguished Scholar Leader for the New Century Scholars initiative of the Fulbright program. He has taught at Harvard University, the University of Wisconsin–Madison, and the State University of New York at Buffalo, and has been a visiting scholar at SciencesPo, Paris, France, and the University of Bombay, India. He has also been a guest professor at Peking University, China.

Gregory Androushchak is Adviser to the Rector of the National Research University Higher School of Economics (on topics in economics of education), and a researcher at the Center for Institutional Studies, Russia. His research focuses on college choice and differentiation of returns to higher education by different types of universities, and efficiency of public funding of higher education. He participates in consulting activities with the Ministry of Education and Science of the Russian Federation and the Ministry of Economic Development of the Russian Federation, and regarding policies of public funding of higher education and indicators of efficiency of Russian universities.

Yaroslav Kuzminov is Rector of the National Research University Higher School of Economics, Head of the Department of Institutional Economics, and Academic Supervisor of the Center for Institutional Studies of the Higher School of Economics, Moscow, Russia. In 2001 he initiated the establishment of the Russian Public Council for Education Development (Russian acronym: ROSRO), an independent agency lobbying for education priorities in budgeting. Since 2002 the ROSRO has held open-door discussions on the problems of national education development. He is a member of the Presidential Council for Facilitating the Development of Civil Society Institutions and Human Rights and a member of the Public Council at the Ministry of Education and Science of the Russian Federation. His research interests include economics of education, institutional economics, and economics of culture.

Liz Reisberg is President of Reisberg & Associates, a consulting firm. She was formerly a research associate at the Center for International Higher Education at Boston College in the United States, where she coordinated several grant-funded projects, conducted research, and contributed to center publications. She was the founder and former executive director of the MBA Tour, a company that organizes professional recruitment tours throughout the world to help graduate schools of business meet talented candidates for their MBA programs.

Maria Yudkevich is Vice-rector of the National Research University Higher School of Economics in Moscow, Russia, and an associate professor in its Economics Department. She also chairs the Center for Institutional Studies and Laboratory for Institutional Analysis, a research center for young scholars focusing on both theoretical and applied economic analysis of institutions. Her main areas of interest and research work are contract theory with a special reference to faculty contracts, universities, and markets for higher education.

Authors

Martin J. Finkelstein is Professor of Higher Education at Seton Hall University, South Orange, NJ, United States. He has taught at the University of Denver and Teacher's College, Columbia University, and has served as a visiting scholar at the Claremont Graduate University, the Research Institute for Higher Education, Hiroshima University, Japan, and as a visiting professor at the University of Hong Kong. He is author, with Jack Schuster, of *The American Faculty: The Restructuring of Academic Work and Careers* (2006).

Kevin W. Iglesias is a senior research associate with the Center for College Readiness at Seton Hall University. Prior to joining the center, he served as a human resource manager for the US government. He holds a BA in psychology from La Salle University, an MA in education from Seton Hall University, and a master's in human resource management from Rutgers University. Currently, he is a PhD candidate in higher education research, assessment, and evaluation at Seton Hall University.

N. Jayaram is a senior fellow at the Indian Institute of Advanced Studies, Shimla, India. He is also Professor of Research Methodology at, and former dean of, the School of Social Sciences at the Tata Institute of Social Sciences, Mumbai, India. He has taught sociology in various capacities at Bangalore University (1972–1999) and Goa University (1999–2003). He was the Director of the Institute for Social and Economic Change in Bangalore. He was a visiting professor of Indian studies at the University of the West Indies.

Ma Wanhua is a professor at the Graduate School of Education and Director of the Center for International Higher Education at Peking University, Beijing, China. She has been a visiting professor at the University of California, Berkeley, teaching an undergraduate course on economic reform and education change in China. She has also been a consultant at the East-West Center at Hawaii University and was selected as a Fulbright New Century Scholar, carrying out a research project on the formation of global research universities. In the fall of 2008, she was invited as an Erasmus Mundus professor to Finland and Norway. She has published extensively on reforms of Chinese higher education and the formation of American research universities. Her current research focuses on internationalization of Chinese higher education and capacity building of research universities in both the United States and China.

Simon Schwartzman is President of Instituto de Estudos do Trabalho e Sociedade in Rio de Janeiro, Brazil, and a Fulbright New Century Scholar for 2009–2010. He is a member of the Brazilian Academy of Sciences and a recipient of the Brazilian Order of Scientific Merit. He has also served as the President of the Brazilian Institute for Geography and Statistics, Brazil's census office.

Wen Jianbo is an English lecturer and Vice-director of the College English Department of the School of Foreign Studies, Central University of Finance and Economics, Beijing, China. He is also currently a PhD candidate attending the Graduate School of Education, Peking University, specializing in higher education and comparative education. He was a visiting fellow at the College of Education and Social Services, University of Vermont, from 2008 to 2009. He received his bachelor's and master's degrees in English language and literature.

1
The Prospects for the BRICs: The New Academic Superpowers?

Philip G. Altbach

The BRIC countries—Brazil, Russia, India, and China—are expanding rapidly, and many observers see these countries as dominant economies in the coming decades. When economist Jim O'Neill coined the term BRIC in 2001, those countries accounted for 8 per cent of global gross domestic product (GDP). He predicted that this would increase to 14 per cent by 2011. In fact, the BRICs accounted for almost 20 per cent of GDP in 2012 (Liu and Li 2012). Fareed Zakaria, among others, has commented on a major shift in global influence away from North America and western Europe, and the BRICs are seen at the forefront of this shift (Zakaria 2008). Logic might dictate that academic power will rise along with economic and political expansion (Levin 2010). These four countries do indeed show impressive growth in their higher education systems and promise to expand and improve in the coming decades. Yet, it is by no means assured that the BRICs will achieve the academic prominence that is likely in economic or political spheres. Each, as will be discussed here, faces significant challenges. Some of the systemic factors that impact higher education in the BRICs are analyzed in this chapter; this is followed by an analysis of the most central prerequisite for academic development and excellence—the academic profession.

If the economic destiny of the BRICs is on an upward trajectory, the same cannot be said with certainty for higher education. Just as there are significant variations in the details of economic and political development among the four BRICs, quite different academic traditions, current realities, future plans, and scenarios make it likely that the four countries will proceed along quite different academic paths. Further, the route to global academic dominance is highly complex and depends on much more than patterns of economic growth or the sophistication of a nation's economy or society. All four BRICs are, in different ways, transitional academic systems. Three—Brazil, China, and India—face the challenge of rapid expansion of access and enrollments; at the same time they are attempting to build world-class research universities at the top of the system, to contribute research and top-level training to an increasingly sophisticated economy. Russia, which possesses a mature higher education system and offers a high level of access, faces the challenge of rebuilding its research universities, while improving the quality of the system as a whole.

Centers and peripheries

The BRIC countries find themselves in an unusual paradox. On the one hand, none of them are yet an academic superpower. All lag behind the main academic centers. On the other hand, all except Russia have rapidly expanding academic systems and goals of improving their global standing and building top-ranking universities. Further, all four BRICs are significant regional centers, influencing neighboring countries, and providing academic leadership in their respective areas. Brazil, India, and Russia are by far the most productive academic systems in their regions. In East Asia, Japan remains the dominant academic power, and South Korea is expanding academically, but China has the fastest growth rate and is investing the most resources in higher education.

Russia remains the central academic influence in the former Soviet Union, and Russian is the main language of instruction and research as well. Although countries in Eastern Europe are increasingly looking toward the West and English is replacing Russian a key language of academic communication, Russia retains some influence. India is by far the largest and most influential academic system in south Asia, with some modest impact in the Middle East as well. Brazil is the scientific superpower in Latin America, in terms of research productivity, the production of doctorates, and to other areas. The fact that it uses Portuguese and the other countries are Spanish-speaking limits its influence, however.

Each of the BRICs, because they contain large and self-sustaining academic systems, see themselves as independent academic entities. At the same time, they look to the major academic powers for ideas about higher education development, research paradigms, and other matters. China and Russia are to some extent adapting Western academic organizational and governance ideas. Brazil seems mainly immune from external ideas, while India's academic system, built on the British pattern and influenced by India's own bureaucratic culture, does not look abroad for ideas about change.

English, as the dominant scientific language, has an impact in all of the BRIC countries, and it is a challenge for all but India, which from the beginning of its academic history has used English as the primary language of teaching and research. Following independence in 1947, Indian languages began to be used for teaching in some undergraduate colleges and a few universities. However, a majority of undergraduate courses and almost all graduate-level degrees are taught in English.

English is more problematical in the other BRIC countries. China and Russia have established a small number of courses and degree programs taught in English, in part to attract international students. China in particular has expanded the number of English-medium degrees, and at the top universities some courses are offered in English for domestic students. Brazil seems to lag somewhat behind in embracing English as a major theme in academic development.

The BRICs, with the partial exception of Brazil, are emphasizing the importance of their academics publishing in English, in recognized international scientific journals, and in general participating in the global scientific community. Promotion and prestige are increasingly related to publication, and many Chinese universities offer special payments to their academics who publish in top international journals.

The balance between striving to achieve global recognition, on the one hand, and sustaining a national and regional academic culture on the other remains a dilemma for the BRICs. While they seek to join the academic superpowers, at the same time their own national academic systems require support and their regional influence deserves attention (Altbach and Salmi 2011).

The BRICs remain peripheral in the global knowledge system. China and India send the largest numbers of students in the world overseas for international study. Indeed, those two countries account for close to half of all global student mobility—and their numbers are likely to increase. All of the BRICs have a significant net outflow of students. Students studying in the BRIC countries by and large come from surrounding countries, emphasizing their roles as regional centers. Only China attracts significant numbers of international students, mostly from neighboring East Asian countries.

China, India, and Russia also contribute significantly to the global flow of academic talent, with many PhD graduates from these countries working elsewhere. This brain drain has been quite significant over several decades. Despite modestly improving rates of return and the new trend for some top academics and scientists to hold appointments in several countries, quite significant numbers of academics chose to leave these three countries. The causes are complex and include better working conditions, infrastructure, salaries abroad, academic atmosphere, academic freedom, and other factors.

Interesting variations among the four BRIC countries can be observed. Brazil has not suffered much of a brain drain, and the return rate for Brazilians who study abroad is quite high. An attractive academic environment in the top universities and competitive salaries, no doubt, contribute to the country's higher education. Russia, which has a long and distinguished academic tradition, suffered dramatic financial cutbacks in higher education following the collapse of the Soviet Union in the 1990s. Numerous academics, including many distinguished scientists, left the country, and others quit the universities to start different careers. Only recently has the government recognized the need to rebuild the academic system. Funds have been invested in research universities and in several programs to improve the academic system, although salaries remain largely unattractive. China has implemented several programs to lure back top academics, who returned to China with improved salaries and working conditions. These programs have been modestly successful. India has not recognized its academic brain drain and has no programs in place to lure Indian academics back, although many Indians in various technology fields have returned to the booming high-tech sector—but not to the universities.

The BRIC countries thus occupy an anomalous academic terrain. They are at the same time large, growing, and increasingly powerful academic systems and still striving to occupy a more important global position. In many respects, they remain gigantic peripheries (Altbach 1993).

Massification as the underlying reality

The expansion of enrollments has been the key reality of global higher education in the last half of the 20th and the beginning of the 21st century (Altbach, Reisberg, and Rumbley 2010). The "logic" of massification has affected all countries, resulting in increased access to higher education, greater importance of academic credentials for employment and social mobility, and the centrality of higher education in increasingly knowledge-based economies.

China and India have experienced massive growth in the past two decades and, in fact, will account for more than half the world's

Table 1.1 Total and gross enrollment, 2009

Country	Total enrollment	Gross enrollment ratio
Brazil	6, 115, 138	36[a]
China	29, 295, 841	24
India	18, 648, 923	16
Russian Federation	9, 330, 115	76
United States	19, 102, 814	89

Notes: [a]Gross enrollment ratio for Brazil was not available from UNESCO Statistics. The number was retrieved from Trading Economics, which used data from the World Bank.
Sources: UNESCO Institute of Statistics; Brazil gross enrollment ratio: Trading Economics.

enrollment expansion by 2050. Brazil, which had no universities until 1920, began to rapidly expand its enrollments later than the others. Table 1.1 shows current enrollments for the four BRIC countries and includes the United States for comparison.

In 2012, the BRIC countries and the United States have the five largest enrollments in higher education, and by 2008 the five countries, combined, accounted for 48 per cent of the world's enrollment in higher education (see Figure 1.1). In terms of enrollment, China and India are now among the world's three largest academic systems, and India will soon move into second place. Brazil ranks in fifth position and will no doubt move up the charts in the coming years. Russia will probably experience little enrollment expansion. The reason for the inevitability of expansion in China, India, and Brazil is, of course, the fact that they currently enroll, by international standards, a modest percentage of the relevant age cohort—in the case of India only 16 per cent, while China serves 24 per cent, and Brazil 36 per cent. Russia, in contrast, enrolls 75 per cent—similar to most economically developed countries.

Rapid massification produces some inevitable results—including an overall deterioration in the quality of higher education. This does not mean that the top part of academe becomes worse, but the average quality, measured by virtually any criteria, does go down. For example, 38 per cent of those teaching in postsecondary education in China have only a bachelor's degree, although the proportions of academics with at least a master's degree are much higher in the other BRIC nations. The average quality of students entering postsecondary education declines, at the same time that competition for places in the top universities increases. The phenomenon occurs because a larger number of more modestly qualified students are entering the bottom tier of universities,

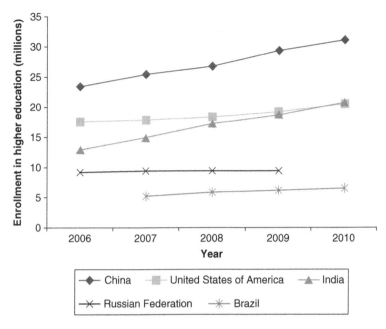

Figure 1.1 Enrollment in higher education, BRICs and the United States, 2006–2010.

Sources: UNESCO Institute of Statistics; Brazil gross enrollment ratio: Trading Economics.

while competition for the limited number of places at the top-ranking universities is greater as applicants are aware of the quality and prestige variations among universities. Per-student funding also declines as numbers increase, and governments do not allocate sufficient funding to maintain quality for larger numbers. Thus, academic systems become more differentiated, either by plan or by the forces of the market— with the emergence of a small top tier of universities, alongside a much larger group of institutions catering to students from a wide range of backgrounds and abilities.

The fact is that none of the BRIC countries provide a reasonable standard of quality to students in the mass sector of postsecondary education. Each underinvests in this sector. As a partial result, the private sector has moved in to provide mass access, and its quality is often low. In China and Brazil, particularly, the academic qualifications of those teaching in the mass sector are inadequate, and part-time instructors are widely used. Dropout rates are high, and many graduates are deemed to be unemployable.

Few countries have been able to develop and sustain a well-defined higher education system that adequately supports mass enrollments and world-class research universities at the same time. The BRIC countries, each in its own way, have been grappling with this key challenge in the era of massification.

The challenge of funding

Postsecondary education everywhere faces significant financial challenges. The cost of catering to a larger and more diverse clientele is at the heart of the problem. Very few governments have the financial resources to fully support a comprehensive mass higher education system. The BRIC countries, due largely to their economic success in recent years, have the ability to provide more funds to higher education. Yet, despite clear needs, public investment remains relatively low when compared to that in developed countries. The average expenditure in education as a percentage of GDP for countries in the Organization for Economic Cooperation and Development (OECD), in general the wealthier nations, is 5.9 per cent (public and private combined); and the United States spends 7.2 per cent of GDP (public and private combined). Table 1.2 shows the BRICs range from 2.1 per cent (China) to 4.3 per cent (Brazil).

Inadequate funding has significant implications throughout the academic system and makes it difficult, if not impossible, for postsecondary

Table 1.2 Expenditure in education and research and development (R&D)

	Expenditure in education			Expenditure in R&D	
	% GDP (2009)	Tertiary education as % of GDP (2008)		Domestic gross expenditure (PPP US$ billions, 2009)	As % of GDP (2009)
		Public	Private		
Brazil	4.3	0.8	n.d.	18.0	0.9
China	2.1	n.d.	n.d.	123.7	1.4
India	4.1	n.d.	n.d.	28.1	0.8
Russia	3.1	0.9	0.5	21.8	1.0
United States	5.7	1.0	1.7	383.6	2.7

Note: n.d. = no data.
Sources: Percentage of expenditure in education as % of GDP: *The Economist's* "Pocket World in Figures." Expenditure in tertiary education as % of GDP: *OECD Factbook*, 2011. Expenditure in R&D: Batelle, *R&D Magazine*. Data from International Monetary Fund and Batelle.

education to fulfill its goals and to serve the needs of individuals and society. The implications include low salaries for the academic profession and others working in higher education, a theme that will be discussed later in this essay. Quality suffers in many ways, with poor and often overcrowded facilities, a lack of support staff, outdated or nonexistent laboratories, substandard libraries and information technology, as well as limited access to internet-based resources, and other problems.

All of the BRIC countries have implemented special funding initiatives for higher education from public resources and have in the past several decades increased financial support for higher education. Yet, in all cases, the amounts allocated have been inadequate. In all four cases, base funding for higher education to pay for the expansion has been especially inadequate—resulting in poor quality of education, denial of access to some who seek to enter postsecondary education, and increasing dropout rates.

R&D and the research universities

Despite the rapidly growing economies of the BRIC countries, and the stated goals of each to emphasize research and development (R&D) as a keystone of economic development, all four countries spend less than the 2008 OECD average of 2.3 per cent of GDP and well under the 2.7 per cent spent by the United States (see Table 1.2 above).

R&D expenditures do not, of course, all go to universities, but there is a correlation between broader R&D expenditures and research support for higher education—and it is clear that the BRICs lag behind the most developed countries. China spends the largest amount and also the greatest proportion of GDP, and India and Brazil do worse. This is also the case for patent applications, another proxy indication of scientific productivity. Most observers note that China's R&D growth— as measured by patents, research expenditures, and facilities—has been impressive; and if current trends continue, China will become a major research power in a decade. The other BRIC nations show less impressive growth, although segments of the higher education systems in each country are impressive.

Two of the BRIC countries, China and Russia, have complex research systems that in many ways weaken the research strength of the universities. In both countries, the apex research organizations are institutes that are part of the Academy of Sciences system. These institutes focus exclusively on research and, by local standards, are better funded by the government than the universities. Perhaps most significant, national policy has long given the universities responsibility mainly for teaching, with research receiving less support. The academy tradition was a central part of Russian, and then Soviet, scientific policy and was adopted in China after the establishment of the People's Republic in 1949. In recent years, both countries have recognized the problems of the academy system and have moved to better integrate the institutes with some of the universities, and also provide more resources to the universities for research. In some cases, academicians have university appointments, and doctoral students work in the institutes. India also has a small number of research institutes, but they are less central to the scientific system.

Research universities are at the pinnacle of any higher education system, and they are central in the efforts of the BRICs to rise to prominence both in higher education and in economic and scientific development (Altbach 2007). Progress has been impressive in three of the BRICs—Brazil, China, and Russia. India lags behind. China, as a result of its two major initiatives aimed at building research universities, the 211 and 985 Projects, invested heavily and now has approximately 100 universities with impressive infrastructures, some of which are developing into globally competitive institutions (Levin 2010). China's government and the top universities aim at establishing the country as a major academic power. China's growing research universities are struggling to build an academic culture to accompany their facilities (Altbach 2009).

Brazil's research universities are, with a few exceptions, concentrated in the state of São Paulo, which allocates a significant part of its tax revenues, by law, to major public research universities and has been able over time to build some of Latin America's top research universities. A few other federal universities have also built a research profile. None of India's universities appear anywhere near the top in any of the international rankings, a surprising fact for a country with the world's third largest academic system. Only the highly respected Indian Institutes of Technology are internationally recognized, and these are small and specialized schools. Russia's traditional research universities, which had significant strength and global respect, declined following the end of the Soviet Union in the 1990s. Rebuilding is now underway, and the government has identified 29 national research universities. Additional funding is provided, and these institutions have a mission of building world-class research universities in Russia. The traditional key universities maintained significant strength, and several new institutions have been established. It is too early to determine if this initiative will result in several Russian universities joining the ranks of the leading global universities.

While the BRIC economies are expanding rapidly, and higher education is recognized as a top priority for each country, none has universities that are in the top ranks of global research universities yet.

A mania for mergers

Two BRIC countries, China and Russia, have frequently used institutional mergers as a means of improving efficiency and enhancing the ranking of universities (indeed, Russian President Vladimir Putin recently announced that another wave of mergers will take place). Perhaps not surprising, since many universities in these two countries were divided into small specialized institutions during the Soviet period in Russia and in the 1950s in China, when the Soviet model was widely followed. But academic mergers are often very difficult to successfully implement. For the most part, they stem from government decisions, rather than the institutions themselves. Often, the goals of mergers are bureaucratic efficiency or a desire to bring together institutions, so that there will be economies of scale—and quick improvement in the global rankings.

Variations in academic culture may also contribute to problems in the successful implementation of mergers: overlapping and conflicting bureaucratic structures, the geographical separation of campuses, entrenched interests of administrators or faculty, the challenges of combining management and other systems, and the simple matter of size. While mergers may not be problematical in all cases, careful attention needs to be paid to both goals and the practical challenges of implementation.

The private sector and the privatization of public higher education

Massification and inadequate public support for higher education have been responsible for the rise of a growing private sector worldwide. Indeed, private higher education is the fastest growing segment worldwide (Levy and Zumeta 2011). Each of the BRIC countries has a growing private sector. In fact, much of the enrollment expansion in the BRICs is in the private sector or in revenue producing segments of the public sector. Brazil's is the largest in terms of the proportion of students attending private universities—about 75 per cent. India has the most complex private sector, since the majority of undergraduate colleges are privately managed, although most receive the bulk of their funding from the government. The growing number of "unaided" (fully privately funded) undergraduate colleges are supervised by a public university and their degrees are awarded by the university. India has a growing segment of private universities—53 out of a total of 496 universities. These private universities are allowed by the government to grant degrees but receive no public funding. Private postsecondary institutions in China and Russia educate a small but growing segment of the student population—0.9 and 17 per cent, respectively. The private sector in the BRIC countries is, with only a few exceptions, for-profit. Brazil and Russia do possess a few high-quality private institutions. In the Brazilian case they are mainly traditional Catholic universities, while in Russia several well-funded private economics and business institutions have emerged in recent years. Neither China nor India has any top-level private universities, although several institutions aspire to achieve excellence. In general, as is common in developing and emerging economies, the private sector caters to students who cannot be admitted to the public universities or to those who have vocational interests served by some of the private institutions. Quality assurance is a challenge in the BRIC countries generally, but it has been particularly problematical for the private sector.

In each of the BRICs the public sector has higher prestige, and students, if they have a choice, will typically choose a public university. This preference is in part changing, as the public sector deteriorates, and a small number of prestigious private institutions have been established. Prestigious private specialized institutions are particularly evident in fields such as management and information technology. As the quality of public higher education deteriorates, the emerging middle classes in the BRICs may be willing to pay for elite private institutions. More wealthy parents are sending their children overseas for undergraduate education as well—particularly in China and India.

There has also been a notable privatization of the public universities in several of the BRIC countries, a phenomenon that is changing the nature of public higher education and affects these four countries in different ways. Public university tuition fees are low in three of the countries (China, India, and Russia) and free in Brazil. In China and Russia, central and provincial authorities allocate budgets for specific numbers of students in each public university, although the amounts are too low to support the full budget of the institution. The universities are permitted to enroll "extra-budgetary" students, who are charged high fees and generally receive the same degree as the regular students. Funds earned from these students provide extra payments to professors and support the budget in general. In this way, public universities function as dual public and private institutions. Indian undergraduate and professional education is increasingly offered by private colleges, which are affiliated to the public universities but receive no funding from public sources. The growing importance of "unaided" colleges is a notable new phenomenon in India.

In all of the BRICs, as in much of the world, universities are asked to earn income from consulting, the sale of intellectual property, and other sources. Some top Chinese universities have been particularly successful in starting companies, such as Peking University's Founder Group, specializing in information technology products, which contribute to the institutional budgets. Many Chinese universities have invested in "technology parks"—some of which have spawned innovative industries and other commercial ventures. The Brazilian public universities seem least affected by the pressure to privatize, as Brazil has, at least so far, retained its commitment to fairly generous public support for its public universities. However, it should be kept in mind that 80 per cent of Brazilian students attend private higher education institutions.

These factors have, without question, produced significant change in the nature of public universities worldwide and have brought market forces to academe as never before.

Corruption and the creation of an academic culture

Universities in all of the four BRIC countries face the challenges of solidifying academic cultures that are at the same time meritocratic, collaborative, and competitive. The need is particularly acute at the top of the system in the research universities, if they are to aspire to world-class status, but it is relevant throughout the system. The culture within an academic institution is central to fulfilling the mission of the university and significant to the academic staff as well.

This discussion mainly concerns public universities in the BRIC countries. Most of the growing private sector has little semblance of academic culture. As noted, most institutions are run for profit, offering vocationally popular qualifications and with no aspirations to conduct research. Most of the teachers are part-time, and few, if any, have long-term or permanent employment arrangements. There is no shared governance; top managers control all aspects of the institutions. There are, of course, a few exceptions to these general patterns. The older Catholic universities in Brazil, several new and well-funded business schools in Russia, and Manipal, Symbiosis, and several other institutions in India are among these exceptions.

An effective institutional culture includes a system of shared governance in which the academic staff has effective control over the key elements of curriculum, hiring and promotion of staff, awarding of degrees, and related aspects at the core of any university. At the same time, academic leaders must hold the power to lead the institution and not be subject either to strict governmental control or to the "anarchy" of professorial (or sometimes student) participation in each decision. An appropriate mix of faculty autonomy and administrative leadership is necessary for effective governance.

The BRIC countries vary in their arrangements. China's highly bureaucratic academic structures are formed by a combination of academic governance and the parallel administrative authority of Communist Party groups in each department and at the top university level, creating a highly bureaucratic and sometimes politicized academic culture. Both India and Russia have substantial degrees of bureaucratic controls. Brazilian universities are typically governed by elected administrators at all levels, with academic and other staff and often students voting. This arrangement encourages a politicization of academic decision making and often makes needed but difficult decisions impossible to implement. It is fair to say that aspects of university internal organization and university–government relationships create problems in the BRIC countries.

Academic freedom is also a central value for higher education worldwide. All of the BRIC countries have faced some challenges to academic freedom, which in some cases continue. China's situation is the most problematic. Many observers have commented on problems of access to information in some disciplines, and restrictions (sometimes self-imposed) on certain kinds of research or on the interpretation of findings. Publishing certain results or interpretations may create problems. Sanctions for violating norms can be either subtle or severe and are on the minds of many academics, especially in the social sciences. The fact that political authorities are an integral part of the university administration, through the Communist Party secretary, underlines the concern for ideological conformity.

Academic freedom issues are more subtle in the three other BRIC countries, and in general all three offer a high degree of academic freedom. Although academic freedom was severely compromised in Brazil during the military dictatorship between 1964 and 1985, it now has a very strong record of academic freedom, with no restrictions on information access and publication, or barriers to the faculty's political expression or involvement. Russia continues to be affected by the legacy of the Soviet Union in many aspects of its society and economy, including in higher education. This tradition includes a certain amount of self-censorship of perceived controversial ideas, while academic freedom, at least in terms of the freedom to speak out and publish in areas of relevant expertise, seems to be reasonably well-protected in Russia at present. The situation in India, as in many areas, is complex. Academic freedom is in general well-entrenched and protected. Yet, in some parts of the country, there are informal constraints on publishing controversial findings in areas such as religious conflicts, interpretations of aspects of Indian history, intercaste and ethnic relations, among others. From the legal perspective, however, academic freedom is protected.

Academic corruption is not a topic that lends itself to careful research or open discussion (Heyneman 2009). Yet, that issue exists to some extent in many academic systems. Three of the BRIC countries have been, and to some extent continue to be, affected by serious malfeasance. Only Brazil seems not to have any entrenched corrupt practices although, as is the case everywhere, there is occasional corruption that may involve an individual or institution. In the other three countries, elements of corruption have affected many universities, and in some cases remain a problem. It is not possible to accurately measure the phenomenon, and this discussion will simply mention aspects of the problem that have been noted by observers. It has not been suggested that any of these countries face systemic and endemic malfeasance in the academic system, but China and India in particular face sufficient issues to create problems for the success of an effective national higher education system.

In the aftermath of the collapse of the Soviet Union, Russian higher education experienced a multiplicity of crises, many stemming from drastic cutbacks in funding from the government. Among these problems was a dramatic increase in corrupt practices. Professors, unable to support themselves with their deteriorating salaries, charged students for "tutoring," which resulted in good grades, sold course materials, and charged money for admission to some faculties and institutions. In recent years, improvements in salaries—although salaries are still quite low by international standards, better working conditions, and enforcement of rules by both government and academic authorities have decreased corrupt practices dramatically. The implementation of a national entrance examination for the universities, for example, eliminated payments for admission to departments or institutions.

Corruption in India varies by institution and region. Practices that are frequently highlighted in the Indian media include "selling" academic posts—by asking for bribes for appointments, awarding posts to people from specific regional or caste groups or for political reasons, widespread cheating by students in examinations, and many others. It is possible that the media exaggerates the extent of the problem, and there is no accurate data. It is the case that the top institutions, such as the Indian Institutes of Technology and others, operate with complete probity; and national examinations for entry to these institutes and for other purposes seem to be free of problems.

Numerous reports of plagiarism of academic work by students and professors have been noted in the Chinese media and are widely discussed. Many observers have commented on widespread falsification of data in research, manipulation of the journal publication process, and other shady practices. The pressure to publish research articles is immense, and many have commented that a generally understood set of academic ethics has not been widely accepted in China. The all-important national entrance examination, the *gaokao,* is widely regarded as entirely fair and efficiently managed. While the extent of actual corruption cannot be measured, it is mainly agreed that the development of an academic culture with probity as a key element is slow to be implemented in China.

Corruption is, thus, an issue of some importance in three of the BRICs, and is, in some ways, a detriment to the development of a world-class academic system. Basically, all of the BRICs need to foster an academic culture that supports the essential missions of higher education. While such a culture takes time to mature, it also requires an adequately funded higher education system, clear rules that are enforced by governmental and academic authorities, and working conditions that foster high quality.

National challenges

The foregoing discussion has highlighted some of the key factors affecting the BRIC nations as they participate in the rapidly changing global higher education environment of the 21st century. It is also useful to

examine some of the specific challenges affecting each of the countries. National academic development is affected by global trends and
national circumstances and policies. This discussion only highlights
some of the most significant national elements shaping the country.

Brazil

Brazil has significant advantages in its higher education environment,
particularly when compared to other Latin American countries. The
country's public universities, although they account for only 20 per cent
of enrollments, are Latin America's research powerhouses. They produce
more than half of Latin America's doctorates and a high percentage
of the continent's research. They also mainly employ full-time faculty
and pay relatively attractive salaries. Yet, there are only a few internationally competitive universities—three in the state of São Paulo and
a few other federal institutions. The majority of the public universities
and all but a few of the growing private sector are of mediocre to poor
quality. The system as a whole is poorly coordinated, with the largely
anarchic for-profit private sector dominating Brazilian higher education.
The public universities are sponsored by several different governmental
entities, with little coordination among them.

The governance of the private institutions tends to be in the hands
of the owners and their appointed administrators, with little chance
for an independent academic culture to emerge. The public institutions
all operate with the traditional Latin American concept of autonomy
from government control and with internal "democracy." This unwieldy
arrangement makes academic leadership difficult or unachievable and
contributes to academic paralysis. The fact that public universities
cannot charge for tuition and are restricted from generating much
income from intellectual property and other entrepreneurial activities also makes it difficult for the universities to engage in innovative
programs.

While Brazil's federal governments and some of the state governments
provide relatively generous support for public universities, only the
three main public universities in the state of São Paulo and a few other
federal universities have achieved prominence as research universities
of an international standard. There is no national strategy for higher
education, other than a commitment to expand access. The powerful
state governments have no specific plans for their universities, although
the generous funding arrangements in São Paulo, where the three main
public universities receive a set percentage of state tax revenues, have
permitted these institutions to develop impressively into key research

universities. One of the few federal efforts is a large scholarship scheme to send Brazilian students abroad, in the hope to build up skill levels.

Brazil, in common with many countries, has a serious problem of access and degree completion for some racial and ethnic groups and for lower-income groups in society, and it is currently experimenting with an innovative program offering funding and support for students.

On average, Brazil's universities are among the best in Latin America. Brazil does not suffer from the Latin American problem of an academic profession that is largely part-time, and the country produces many more advanced degrees than its neighbors. Yet, its higher education system is inadequate to serve Brazil's rapidly growing and increasingly sophisticated economy.

Russia

Russia's challenges are, in general, of a different nature than in the other BRICs. Russia is a mature economy with a population that is contracting. Its access rate is high: 76 per cent of the age cohort attends postsecondary institutions, and the academic system will not expand. Quality throughout the system is considered to be a major challenge, and it is recognized that Russia needs to rebuild its once impressive research universities. While many problems faced higher education during the Soviet period, the top universities were recognized for their high quality in the sciences. Following the end of the Soviet Union, funds were dramatically cut, morale collapsed, many of the top academics left for other countries, and many of those who stayed left the academic profession. Low salaries necessitated moonlighting and, as noted earlier, contributed to rising corruption. Facilities deteriorated, and laboratories quickly became outdated.

Like China, Russia has an "academy system," in which much of the research is conducted by the relatively well-funded and prestigious Academy of Sciences. The system faces the challenge of integrating the universities and the academies, in order to maximize the effectiveness of research and to make the most efficient use of available human and financial resources.

Internationalization lags far behind in Russia. While the country is host to over 90,000 international students, almost all of them are from the former Soviet Union. Only a few courses are offered in English, at places such as the Higher School of Economics, the Peoples Friendship University, and a few others. Few international students are prepared to undertake studies in Russian. Relatively few Russian students study abroad, and many of those do not return home.

Like many countries, non-elite postsecondary institutions face severe resource constraints, low morale, overcrowded facilities, and an influx of students who may not be well-qualified for higher education. As a result, dropout rates are high, and many graduates cannot easily find employment. Improving these institutions presents a significant challenge: how to better integrate them into a more coherent academic system and ensure that the quality of instruction is adequate. At the top of the system, rebuilding the research universities has already begun. The government has identified 29 research universities and has provided them with significant, but still inadequate, additional resources. National policy aims at enabling these universities to join the top ranks of world universities and to score well in the global rankings.

Russia still faces the challenge of building an academic culture that stresses productivity, academic freedom, teaching excellence, and a commitment by the academic staff to their universities and to the highest standards of scholarship. To achieve these goals, salaries will need to be significantly improved, along with the internal governance and ethos of many universities.

India

India faces the greatest challenges of all of the BRIC countries (Altbach 2009). Its access rate is significantly lower, at 13 per cent, than the others, and its population is growing more rapidly than any of the others. Thus, the key reality in the coming decades will be providing access for millions of new students (Agarwal 2009).

India has no world-class universities. The Indian Institutes of Technology, a few of which appear on the global rankings, are small and are not universities, since they offer a limited number of disciplines. A few of the traditional universities, such as the Jawaharlal Nehru University in New Delhi, are recognized as having several distinguished departments and some top professors but are nonetheless largely unranked. India may be the only large country with no top universities.

Indian higher education is inadequately funded, and a surprising amount of the financial resources spent are paid to the academics, whose salaries, when compared to other developing and middle-income countries, are surprisingly high. Very little public funding is available for research. The state governments, which are mainly responsible for funding the universities and many of the colleges, seldom provide adequate resources and have no consciousness of the importance of the research function of the universities. However, a number of schemes aimed at improving the capacity at the top of the academic system have been proposed by the central government. The funds allocated are largely inadequate, and in any case most government resources in the coming period will necessarily be spent on coping with the expansion of student numbers and access.

Structurally, the Indian system is also the most problematical. The current arrangements in undergraduate colleges affiliated to universities that have responsibility for examinations, awarding of degrees, and certain aspects of quality assurance are no longer effective. India's 32,000 colleges are overwhelming the 496 universities, many of which are responsible for hundreds of colleges, often located far from the main campus. The system has proved over decades to be immune to efforts to reform it and has grown even more unwieldy. When India has successfully implemented change in higher education, it has had to ignore the established universities and start entirely new institutions, such as the Institutes of Technology. Further, although there is a quality-assurance agency, it is inadequate and has been unable to evaluate more than a small minority of institutions.

In recent years, the private sector has expanded dramatically. There are now more than 100 private universities—called "deemed universities." There are thousands of "unaided," mainly private, colleges in all fields that are subject to the authority of the affiliating universities but are somewhat loosely controlled. Many of these colleges are for-profit, sponsored by local politicians, or by nonprofit religious or ethnic societies. Most of the private universities focus on high-demand subjects—such as management studies, information technology, and the like. Many are for-profit. A few are nonprofit.

India's system of providing special advantages for students from disadvantaged caste, ethnic, and income groups, commonly referred to as reservations, now accounts for close to half the places allocated in many colleges and universities. Reservations also govern who may be appointed to teaching and research positions. While there are significant historical, political, and sociological reasons for the reservation policies, they have come under much criticism in recent years and certainly have an impact on the academic system as a whole.

It is difficult to envisage a practical strategy for India to overcome these structural, political, and financial challenges and build a globally competitive academic system or, for that matter, to produce the talent needed for India's rapidly growing and increasingly high-tech economy.

China

China's academic progress in the past several decades has been remarkable, especially since the nation emerged from the Cultural Revolution of 1966–1976 with its academic system largely destroyed (Organization for Economic Cooperation and Development 2007). The 211 and 985 Projects, aimed at supporting about 100 research universities, succeeded in adding infrastructure and creating an impressive group of research universities—a dozen of which are achieving international stature. Even more impressive has been the growth of enrollments. China has increased its access rates from a few percent to 24 per cent.

Yet, serious challenges persist. While China has invested heavily in the top of its academic system and has achieved impressive results, academic institutions (public and private) at the bottom of the hierarchy are often of low quality and produce graduates unable to find appropriate employment. The gulf between the top and the bottom of the system, as is the case in many countries, has grown. China seems to have no strategy in place for improving the mass sector of its higher education system.

The practice in many Chinese universities of enrolling additional students on campus or in affiliated colleges—in order to earn additional income, increase access, and provide opportunities for academic staff to supplement their salaries—has many negative aspects, including distracting academics from their basic tasks, quality control, and others.

The private (*minban*) institutions are typically focused on vocational subjects and are often of poor quality. They are typically uncoordinated and have few links to the rest of the higher education system. Quality assurance is problematical. Many of the private institutions use academic staff employed in the public universities, thus taking them away from their core responsibilities. Ensuring that the "private sector serves the public interest" is a significant challenge.

The Chinese academic profession is under significant strain. Academics are underpaid and must earn extra income. Only 13 per cent hold doctoral degrees and 35 per cent have earned only a bachelor's degree. They are subject to tight bureaucratic and, in some cases, political controls. Many have only a rudimentary grasp of academic culture.

The Chinese academic system exhibits some significant contradictions. On the one hand, it has accomplished much in the past several decades, and the best universities are close to achieving a world-class status. Substantial resources have been invested, and there have been significant improvements in research output and impact, patents, and other measures of productivity. On the other hand, much of the system remains on quite shaky ground and in need of major improvement. The problem of continued enrollment growth, as China moves from the current access rate of 22 per cent to double that figure, will create additional strains on the system.

The national challenges described here are quite significant for each of the BRIC countries. While there are some common threads among them, each country faces its own reality. And each has different ways of coping with problems. Some are likely to be more successful than others. One of the central requirements of a successful academic system is the academic profession. Thus, a consideration of the challenges facing the professoriate in the BRIC nations is of special importance.

The academic profession

The academic profession is at the heart of the university. No institution of higher education can be successful without a well-qualified, highly motivated, and effective professoriate. Yet, too often the academics are forgotten in discussions of the problems of universities—or sometimes demonized as creators of the university's difficulties. The academic profession in the BRIC countries, as in the rest of the world, faces significant challenges in the 21st century. Indeed, in many countries salaries are inadequate and in some cases deteriorating, and conditions for teaching and research are inadequate. In general, the "best and brightest" are not attracted to the universities.

As a general rule, the overall academic qualifications and working conditions of the professoriate decline in a mass higher education system. Not surprisingly, the proportion of academic staff with doctoral degrees declines, as do overall salaries, working conditions, and most likely the quality of teaching. The proportion of part-time staff increases, as does the number of full-time professors who moonlight in other teaching or research positions or in non-academic work.

If there ever was an academic community, it is weakened by the circumstances of mass higher education. The differences in salaries, working conditions, and prestige between the minority of academics with positions at the top in the research universities and the very large majority of those with appointments elsewhere are huge.

An examination of the status of the academic profession in the BRIC countries—particularly the terms and conditions of academic appointments, remuneration, and contracts—is of central relevance because the future of the academic systems of these key countries will depend, in large degree, on the health of the academic profession.

Unlike the professoriates in many other parts of the world, including the United States and, dramatically, in developing countries with rapidly expanding enrollments, none of the BRIC countries are overwhelmed by part-time academics. Brazil is particularly notable since the rest of Latin America relies on part-time faculty for a large majority of teaching. There are part-time teachers in the BRIC countries, and their numbers seem to be growing, but they do not dominate. A pattern, however, which is evident in China and Russia, is that regular faculty members often teach extra classes to students who are admitted "above the state allocation," in order to earn extra salary for themselves and income for the university, or "moonlight" in private postsecondary institutions.

Salaries and remuneration

Our research reveals some surprising patterns in salaries among the four BRIC countries (Altbach et al. 2012). Surprisingly, in the public colleges and universities, India and Brazil score best on academic salaries, when measured according to purchasing power parity (see Table 1.3).

Indeed, both India and Brazil compare reasonably favorably with the United States and other developed countries. Full-time academics in these countries can live on their academic salaries, without earning significant extra income. Russia and China compare less favorably. At average levels, their salaries are only one-fifth of those in the other two countries and dramatically less than salaries in developed countries.

These basic salary comparisons have great significance for the academic profession. Chinese and Russian academics cannot live on their

Table 1.3   Academic salaries comparison

	Salaries (US$ PPP)			Top/Average ratio
	Entry	Average	Top	
Brazil	1,858	3,179	4,550	2.4
China	259	720	1,107	4.3
India	3,954	6,070	7,433	1.9
Russian Federation	433	617	910	2.1
United States	4,950	6,054	7,358	1.5

Source: Altbach, Reisberg, Yudkevich, Androushchak, and Pacheco (2012).

academic salaries and must earn additional funds from other sources, from within or outside the university (Ma 2009). The need for additional income means that they cannot devote full attention to their academic work, and both research and teaching suffer as a result.

The comparisons also show inequalities among academic ranks. China is the most unequal, with senior professors earning more than four times the salaries of junior academic staff. The other three countries show an approximate doubling between the most junior and the top ranks. The United States and other developed countries show less variation between the ranks and thus a flatter academic salary structure.

While there is relatively little data on the total compensation earned by academics in the four countries, it is clear that in all of them academics typically earn more from their universities than the basic salaries reported here. In China, especially, academics are paid extra for publication, research, and other academic activities; and the most productive staff can earn significant additional income. In both China and Russia, as noted earlier, many academics earn extra income by teaching more classes. These practices seem to be less evident in Brazil and India, although Indian academics earn added income through special allocations—due to cost of living in cities, and other categorical increments.

Somewhat surprisingly, Indian academic salaries, when measured by purchasing power parity, are highest among the four BRIC countries, largely as a result of recent across-the-board salary increments implemented by India's University Grants Commission and funded by the central and state governments. Current salary scales place Indian academics in the burgeoning middle class, and provide a reasonable standard of living. However, these relatively attractive salaries are not accompanied by any performance measures, and are incrementally increased on the basis of length of service and not according to any evaluation. Brazilian salaries are also relatively attractive and permit most Brazilian academics with full-time appointments to enjoy a middle-class lifestyle. In both China and Russia, academics do not earn enough from their basic academic salaries to enjoy a middle-class existence and thus must earn additional income—with consequences for academic productivity, morale, teaching quality, and institutional commitment.

In all four BRIC countries, the basic pattern of allocation of salary increments is largely based on length of service and other bureaucratic elements, rather than on productivity or merit. Generally, it is possible to estimate the salary of a member of the academic staff, based on his or her rank and length of service, with other variables playing little role.

The lack of a merit system for salary allocation removes a key measure of productivity among academic staff.

In common with most countries, the salary structures available in the BRICs are not competitive with those of similarly qualified professionals in other fields, nor are salaries competitive internationally. Even Indian and Brazilian academic salaries do not compare favorably, when measured in direct terms with salaries in developed countries—even if it is possible for academics in India and Brazil to enjoy a middle-class local lifestyle. For Russia and China, salaries are dramatically below global norms. These disparities contribute to a significant brain drain and nonreturn rates from all of the BRIC countries, particularly from Russia, China, and India.

Academic appointments

The terms and conditions of academic appointments are central to creating a career structure and measuring the productivity of academic staff. Academic freedom is, in part, dependent on the nature of academic appointments. Without an effective means of hiring, evaluating, and promoting the academics, it is difficult to attract and retain the best minds for the profession.

In all four BRIC countries, there is a significant degree of academic inbreeding—hiring faculty members who received their degrees from the university hiring them. Most agree that inbreeding limits the diversity of the professoriate and mobility among institutions, reduces the possibilities of hiring the best talent, and creates a more hierarchical structure in departments and faculties. On the other hand, there are often reasons for this practice, including a lack of appropriate talent outside the university that is hiring and, of course, a tradition of inbreeding.

With the exception of a few universities at the top of the academic hierarchy in each of the BRIC countries, there is no national market for hiring and little possibility of employing internationally—India in fact has legal restrictions on hiring permanent foreign staff. Some of the top universities in China and Russia do hire internationally and offer distinguished professors salary packages significantly higher than national averages. China's top universities also place a premium on hiring Chinese with foreign doctorates as a way of building a high-quality faculty and reducing inbreeding.

Appointment processes at the top institutions in the BRIC countries are well established and reasonably transparent, and positions are typically advertised publically and open to all applicants. At many institutions, however, appointment processes are less clear and often subject to favoritism and other irregularities. The appointment processes in the private higher education sector is often problematical, with few controls.

Most academics are appointed at entry level, and over time are promoted up the hierarchy. In some countries there are quotas on the number of full professors, and thus not everyone can achieve the top rank. Only rarely are openings available for senior professors.

Security of employment

None of the BRICs have formal tenure arrangements similar to the system in the United States or civil service appointments as are common in western Europe. These arrangements provide security of employment after a period of probation and, in the American case, a careful evaluation of the individual prior to promotion and awarding of a tenured position. Tenure and civil service appointments protect academic freedom, and at the same time provide significant but not completely guaranteed security of employment (Chait 2002).

For most public universities, in all four BRICs, as is the case for most countries, academic staff have considerable "de facto" job security. Once appointed at the bottom rank, few are ever fired. Although a variety of formal employment arrangements exist—including renewable contracts, periodic reviews, and others—there is little evaluation of academic work and an expectation among both the employer and the faculty member that jobs are permanent until retirement. There are some exceptions to this generalization—for example, many of China's top universities have instituted rigorous internal evaluation processes for contract renewals and promotions.

The de facto job-security arrangements mean significant disadvantages for the universities and some drawbacks for individual academics: first, a significant security of tenure for most academics; second, no firm guarantee of job protection relating to academic freedom. In all four BRIC countries, academic salaries are by and large related to rank and longevity of service—and not related to job performance or market conditions (Altbach and Jayaram 2006). Only in China are some academics at the top universities judged and rewarded based on academic performance.

Conclusion

The higher education systems of the BRIC countries, because of the growing economic importance of these four key nations, are now global players. They have received a great deal of attention and are seen as on their way to the top ranks of the world's academic systems. All four countries see higher education as a key ingredient to future economic development, and all have developed impressive plans for their universities. All have goals of improving the status of their top universities in the global rankings, as they provide increased access to underserved populations. Observers worldwide—pointing to impressive plans and, especially in China, increased spending on higher education and improved performance in research, patents, and publications—are optimistic about the future prospects of the BRICs.

This analysis shows that BRIC countries face quite significant challenges in their efforts to build world-class higher education systems. Among these challenges are:

- building a "system" of postsecondary education that accommodates both research universities at the top and mass access at the bottom— with appropriate articulation for students;
- ensuring that the private higher education sector serves a broader public interest and that quality is maintained;
- adequately funding the postsecondary sector to ensure both quality and access;
- ensuring that the academic profession is appropriately trained and adequately paid;
- supporting effective internal governance and management of universities so that the academic profession has appropriate authority and at the same time complex academic institutions are effectively managed;
- providing appropriate institutional autonomy, so that the key academic decisions can be made by the academic community, while at the same time there is effective overall supervision by government or other relevant authorities.

The higher education success of the BRICs is by no means assured— the stakes are quite high because these four key countries need effective higher education systems to support their impressive economic growth. Just as important, universities are central to the civil societies of countries that will inevitably play global leadership roles in the coming decades.

Acknowledgement

I am indebted to Iván F. Pacheco for comments.

References

Agarwal, Pawan. 2009. *Indian higher education: Envisioning the future.* New Delhi: Sage.

Altbach, Philip G. 1993. Gigantic peripheries: India and China in the world knowledge system. *Economic and Political Weekly,* June 28, 1220–1225.

———. 2006. Tiny at the top. *Wilson Quarterly,* Autumn, 49–51.

———. 2007. Peripheries and centers: Research universities in developing countries. *Higher Education Management and Policy* 19, no. 2: 2–24.

———. 2009. One-third of the globe: The future of higher education in China and India. *Prospects,* 15–27.

Altbach, Philip G., and N. Jayaram. 2006. Confucius and the guru: The changing status of the academic profession in China and India. *Journal of Educational Planning and Administration* 20 (October 2006): 395–410.

Altbach, Philip G., Liz Reisberg, and Laura E. Rumbley. 2010. *Trends in global higher education: Tracking an academic revolution.* Rotterdam: Sense.

Altbach, Philip G., and Jamil Salmi, eds. 2011. *The road to academic excellence: The making of world-class research universities.* Washington, DC: World Bank.

Altbach, Philip G., Liz Reisberg, Maria Yudkevich, Gregory Androushchak, and Iván F. Pacheco, eds. 2012. *Paying the professoriate: A global comparison of compensation and contracts.* New York: Routledge.

Brazil gross enrollment ratio: Trading Economics, http://www.tradingeconomics .com/brazil/school-enrollment-tertiary-percent-gross-wb-data.html (accessed August 8, 2012).

Chait, Richard P., ed. 2002. *The questions of tenure.* Cambridge, MA: Harvard Univ. Press.

Heyneman, Stephen P., ed. 2009. *Buying your way into heaven: Education and corruption in international perspective.* Rotterdam: Sense.

Levin, Richard. 2010. Top of the class: The rise of Asia's universities. *Foreign Affairs,* May–June.

Levy, Daniel, and William Zumeta. 2011. Public policy for private higher education: A global analysis. *Journal of Comparative Policy Analysis: Research and Practice* 13, no. 4: 383–396.

Liu, Cecily, and Fangchao Li. 2012. BRIC key for sustained growth. *China Daily USA Weekly,* February 3, 24.

Ma, Wanhua. 2009. The prospects and dilemmas of Americanizing Chinese higher education. *Asia Pacific Education Review* 10 (March): 117–124.

Organization for Economic Cooperation and Development. 2007. *Thematic reviews of tertiary education: China.* Paris: OECD.

UNESCO Institute of Statistics. Table 3B. Enrollment by ISCED level, enrollment in total tertiary, full and part-time, total (male and female). http://stats.uis .unesco.org/unesco/TableViewer/tableView.aspx (accessed August 8, 2012).

Zakaria, Fareed. 2008. *The Post-American World.* New York: Norton.

2

Higher Education, the Academic Profession, and Economic Development in Brazil

Simon Schwartzman

With 192 million inhabitants and more than two trillion dollars of gross domestic product in 2010, Brazil has one of the largest economies in the world and, with about US$11,000 per capita, is an upper-middle-income country. In the last ten years, the country has benefited from the expansion of international trade and is a major exporter of agricultural, mineral, and also manufactured products. Most of the population lives in large urban settlements, such as São Paulo, Rio de Janeiro, Recife, Belo Horizonte, and Salvador. Social and economic inequality, still one of the highest in the world, is improving; and absolute poverty is being reduced. Brazil is a federation, with 27 states and more than 5,000 municipalities, with the central government playing a major role in tax collection and distribution of social services and benefits. Taxes amount to about 37 per cent of the gross domestic product—the highest percentage in Latin America and similar to that of developed welfare states—without, however, providing similar types of services. Most of the tax revenue supports an oversized public bureaucracy, social security, and the service of public debt.

Public education started late and higher education later still. By 1950, 57 per cent of the population of five years and older, was illiterate; and only 56,000 attended some kind of a higher education institution, in a population of 41 million. By 2000, all children had access to education, but many still drop out when reaching puberty; and the quality of education, as measured by the Organization for Economic Cooperation and Development Program for International Student Assessment (OECD 2009) and other national and international assessments, is low. At age

15, most students entering high school do not have the minimum competencies in reading and mathematics for their levels, and many others have already dropped out of school. Higher education has been expanding continuously—6.3 million students for a population of 191 million in 2009. Yet, there are still serious shortcomings of quality and coverage. With recent economic growth, shortages of qualified manpower became a serious problem. In 2011, a survey among Brazilian industrialists found that 69 per cent of them revealed difficulties in finding qualified workers and that this was affecting their ability to compete. In recent years, education has become a major issue in public debate. The public sector already spends 5 per cent of gross domestic product on public education (with an additional 2% spent by families), and there is a proposal to extend public expenditure to at least 7 per cent (Confederação Nacional da Indústria 2011).

Higher education in Brazil

Until the early 19th century, Brazil was a Portuguese colony. The first higher education institutions—two schools of law, two medical schools, and one polytechnic and military school—were created around 1810. Other institutions were created later on, but the first university, the Universidade de São Paulo, was only established in 1934—bringing together the pre-existing schools of engineering, medicine, law, agriculture, and some others, in the state of São Paulo. They were supposed to be integrated by a new Faculty of Philosophy, Sciences, and Letters, modeled presumably on the Italian legislation, conceived to prepare academics for secondary education, and doing research, which at the time only existed in schools of agriculture and medicine and in some institutes dealing with tropical diseases and plagues (Stepan 1971). To staff the new institution, professors from Germany, Italy, and France were hired in the areas of chemistry, physics, biology, and the social sciences, and some of them remained in Brazil. In 1937, the national government created the Universidade do Brasil (currently the Federal University of Rio de Janeiro, which existed on paper since 1920), also around a Faculty of Philosophy and with invited professors from abroad. In the early 1940s a Catholic university was established in Rio de Janeiro, and since the 1950s a network of federal universities was created throughout the country, together with public and private non-university higher education institutions (Schwartzman 1991). In 1991, Brazil had about 893 higher education institutions, enrolling about 1.5 million students. Of these institutions, 99 had university status—half of them public—while 794 were non-university, small, mostly private higher education schools—teaching evening courses in areas such as law, administration, and accounting (Instituto Brasileiro 1993).

This typology of institutions—university and non-university, public and private—summarizes the way the higher education sector was shaped from the beginning and still remains, to a large extent, today. The main purpose of all institutions, university or otherwise, has been to provide students with a legally and nationally valid professional certification. This certification is particularly valued in the more traditional learned professions—law, medicine, engineering, and dentistry—which are regulated by law and have a legal minimum curriculum established by the Ministry of Education, in partnership with legally established professional councils. This same model was extended to other fields. In 2004, Brazil had 43 legally regulated higher education professions—including statisticians, chemists, public-relation specialists, journalists, economists, sociologists, meteorologists, nurses, musicians, and football coaches (Nunes and Carvalho 2007). All these course programs last four to six years. There are no general education, college-type undergraduate courses and few two-year, postsecondary vocational programs.

From a legal point of view, professional degrees—granted by a university, non-university institutions, or faculties—are the same, which creates a permanent problem for government and professional corporations of trying to prevent (unsuccessfully, in most cases) the proliferation of low-quality diploma mills.

According to the legislation, universities are institutions that, besides providing professional degrees, also offer graduate education, do research, and include the social, biological, and physical sciences, and professions. Universities are autonomous and free to decide how many students to admit and what programs to offer. However, they have to abide to the minimum legal syllabus for the regulated professions. Non-university institutions require authorization from the Ministry of Education to open new course programs and change the number of places being offered, and are subject to closer oversight. In practice, only a few universities actually do research and graduate education in a significant way. In 1968, new legislation introduced several features of North American higher education, including regular master's degree and doctoral programs, the credit system, the replacement of chairs by academic departments, and strengthening the role of the university central administration. In the new model, academics would be affiliated not to a faculty but to a department, according to their field of knowledge, and be assigned to teach in professional or graduate-course programs, as needed. However, the most traditional faculties maintained their autonomy, and, in the public perception, the main role of higher education institutions is still to provide degrees in the learned professions.

Public institutions are fully funded by the national or state budgets, while private institutions are funded either by private endowments or, in most cases, by tuition. In the past, private institutions were supposed to be nonprofit, and this was indeed the case for the Catholic universities and other denominational institutions (such as Universidade Mackenzie in São Paulo, established by the Presbyterian Church in 1870 as a high school), and also some community-supported institutions in the southern states, populated largely with descendants of German, Italian, and Japanese immigrants. However, as demand for higher education expanded, for-profit institutions began to appear, and the legislation now allows higher education institutions to function as privately owned, for-profit companies.

The 1968 reform led to two diverging trends. Until the 1960s, teaching in a public university was mostly a secondary activity for prestigious professionals, who would earn most of their income from their practice as lawyers, medical doctors, dentists, or engineers and would teach for the prestige and networking opportunities provided by the university. After the reform, teaching in public universities became a career in the civil service, with competitive salaries and other benefits of full-time employment. Besides lecturing, higher education academics were supposed to do research and service activities and graduate education programs were created to grant the advanced degrees required for their careers (Balbachevsky and Schwartzman 2010). These trends were followed by the creation or expansion of several research-support agencies, by both national and state governments, which provide additional resources and income for academics in public universities. They include the National Council for Scientific and Technological Development, an agency within the Ministry of Science and Technology which provides fellowships and research grants; the Financing Agency for Studies and Projects, also within the Ministry of Science and Technology, which provides support to large-scale projects and industrial innovation; and the Coordination for the Advancement of High Level Personnel, an agency within the Ministry of Education which provides fellowships for postgraduate studies and performs the assessment of postgraduate course programs. In the state of São Paulo, the State Foundation for Science and Technology provides both fellowships and research support of various kinds, and many other states have similar institutions. Most of this professionalization of academic careers took place in the federal universities and in the state of São Paulo, the largest and richest state in the Brazilian federation. Later, other states also created their own academic careers for their institutions.

This public sector, however, did not grow fast enough to accommodate the expanding demand for higher education, which was mostly absorbed by private institutions. The limited growth of the public sector can be explained by two factors: its high cost, due to the relatively high academic salaries; and selective admission of students, based on *numerus clausus* (closed numbers) and competitive entrance examinations for the various course programs in each university. This differed from policies in most other Latin American countries, where the rule has been open admissions and a lack of well-paid careers for academic staff in public institutions.

Today, about 78 per cent of enrollment in higher education in Brazil takes place in private institutions. Private institutions could not adopt the same organization model and career patterns of the public ones. Public institutions are fully supported with budgetary resources and legally forbidden to charge tuition; private institutions, with few exceptions, cannot receive public subsidies and depend on tuition to survive. Since public institutions attract the best-qualified students, coming usually from richer families, private institutions need to cater to low-income sectors unable to pay much. Most of their students must work and, because of that, most of their courses are provided in the evenings. The private institutions cannot afford to hire many full-time academics or provide the conditions for academic research. It is difficult for the private sector to teach in fields requiring technical facilities; so, it tends to concentrate on the social professions—administration, accounting, law, and teacher education—instead of medicine, dentistry, engineering, and other technically based fields.

Brazilian legislation still assumes that all higher education provision should be organized within a university or, eventually, evolve into one—centered on high-quality academic research and Wilhelm von Humboldt's ideal of integration between research and teaching. Yet, in practice, few institutions, even in the public sector, can meet the standards related to a research university. A recent study found that only ten universities in Brazil could be classified as comprehensive research universities, providing doctoral education and doing research in a wide variety of subjects: the three state universities of São Paulo (Universidade de São Paulo, Universidade Campinas, and Universidade Estadual Paulista) and seven federal universities in the states of Rio de

Janeiro, Minas Gerais, Pernambuco, Rio Grande do Sul, Brasilia, and Santa Catarina (Steiner 2005); other institutions may provide advanced education and research in selected areas.

Twenty-one per cent of the country's population and 33 per cent of the national gross domestic product is concentrated in the state of São Paulo. It is the country's industrial, agricultural, and financial hub; and the metropolitan area around the city of São Paulo, with about 20 million people, is one of the largest in the world. Politically, the state has a strong tradition of autonomy regarding the national government. Besides the three state universities, which are among the best in the country, São Paulo has a well-endowed Science Foundation, which provides support for graduate education and research in the state.

Currently, Brazilian legislation allows the existence of three main types of institutions: fully autonomous universities, with graduate education and research; autonomous university centers, with no graduate education and research but, supposedly, good-quality teaching in different fields; and isolated faculties, with limited autonomy to create new programs and to expand admission. There are also a small number of technical institutes supported by the federal government, but Brazil never developed an extended system of technical, shorter higher-education programs—such as the French Institutes Universitaires de Technologie.

In recent years, this picture has been changing in many ways. In the public sector, the federal government has been pressing public institutions to admit more students and to open evening courses. One program gives additional resources for federal universities willing to expand. Many institutions are introducing quotas for low-income or minority students. Private universities are granted tax exemption, if they admit a certain number of low-income students without fees. The quality of public higher education is uneven, with some observers believing it is declining. Some private institutions are starting to compete with the public ones, by providing high-quality and expensive education—in fields such as business administration, law, and economics. In the past, most private institutions were small, family-owned institutions. Today, some private institutions have opted to provide high-quality, expensive education in fields such as business administration, economics, and law. Yet, most of the private sector has developed into large for-profit institutions, offering low-cost evening courses for older and less-qualified students, who would not be admitted or could not manage the course loads at public institutions in the most demanding fields. A recent merger of two large private universities created the Universidade de

Anhanguera, in São Paulo, probably the second largest higher education institution in the world—after the University of Phoenix in the United States—with more than 400,000 students. Some of the large for-profit universities attract money from national and international investment funds, and their shares are negotiated in the stock exchange.

As the Brazilian economy grows and the country seeks to compete more strongly in the international economy, the issues of quality and coverage of Brazilian higher education become more pressing. The percentage of young people, of the age 18–24 years attending higher education is still very low, about 15 per cent, with half of the students older. This limits the number of students who finish secondary education and are able to continue to study for a postsecondary degree. The priority of the national government in the last several years has been to expand access by all means, without considering its implications in terms of quality. Except for the Universities of São Paulo and Campinas, no Brazilian institution appears in the different international rankings of higher education institutions. Quality control in graduate education and research has been traditionally much stronger but is still limited, in terms of the requirements of a mature, knowledge-based economy.

According to the Ministry of Education,[1] in 2009, there were 2,314 higher education institutions in Brazil—90 per cent private—and 5.1 million students in regular, first-degree courses, 75 per cent of which are in private institutions. Of the institutions, only 186 had university status. The size of these institutions varies enormously. A small, isolated faculty would have about 1,700 students, on average; a university, 15,000. The largest private university, based in São Paulo and with locations scattered in many cities, had 213,000 first-degree students in 2008; the largest public university, the University of São Paulo, had about 55,000 first-degree and 25,000 graduate students in 11 locations.

Data on graduate education are collected by a different agency in the Ministry of Education, the Coordination for Improvement of Higher Education Personnel (see Table 2.1). In 2009, there were 88,286 students in master's degree programs, 53,237 students in doctoral programs, and 9,122 students in professional master's degree programs. Of the 150,000 graduate students, 80 per cent were in public universities, one-third of them in the state of São Paulo. Also, some graduate programs are granted by public research institutes, which are not usually classified as higher education institutions—such as the Institute of Applied and Pure Mathematics in Rio de Janeiro, the Brazilian Center for Physics Research, or the Oswaldo Cruz Institute in the field of public health.

Table 2.1 Postgraduate education in Brazil: students and degree programs, by level and type of institutions

Institutions	Students			
	Master's	Doctoral	Professional master's	Total
Federal	46,628	28,569	3,234	78,431
State	23,522	19,486	1,396	44,404
Private	17,585	5,163	4,253	27,001
Municipal	551	19	239	809
Total	88,286	53,237	9,122	150,645

	Degree programs				
	Master's	Doctoral	Master's/ Doctoral	Professional master's	Total
Federal	568	22	792	97	1,479
State	210	18	416	33	677
Private	262	0	172	109	543
Municipal	14	n.a.	2	4	20
Total	1,054	40		243	1,337

Note: n.a. = not applicable.
Source: Ministry of Education, Coordination for the Advancement of High-Level Personnel 2009. http://www.capes.gov.br (accessed August 26, 2010).

These data from the Ministry of Education do not fully coincide with those of the National Household Sample Survey. The 2008 survey identified 6.2 million first-degree students, 1.1 million more than the Ministry of Education; and 326,000 graduate students, half of them in private institutions, about twice as many as those reported by the education authorities. The larger number of graduate students is probably due to the inclusion of students in non-degree, specialization, or master of business administration-type programs, which are not regulated and do not enter the Ministry of Education official statistics.

The academic profession and its subcultures

Public and private, university and non-university, and nonprofit and for-profit institutions have different institutional cultures, deal with certain kinds of students, and arrange various working contracts with their staff; and these differences affect, necessarily, the characteristics of the academic staff in each of these contexts. In public universities, most academics have full-time contracts, earn most of their income, and spend most of the time at their institution. This varies somewhat, by fields and generation. Older lawyers, medical doctors, and dentists may maintain a private practice, while younger professors of mathematics, physics, or economics would not. Although all academics are supposed to have a doctoral degree and to engage in research, in practice only some of them meet these requirements. Those who do research have access to funds from science and technology agencies, are affiliated with scientific societies, travel to participate in scientific events, and can do consulting or technical assistance work. Those with lesser academic credentials may get more involved with local professional networks and with the academics' unions, which are present and active in all institutions. In both cases, academics have a sense of ownership regarding their university and participate directly or indirectly in commissions, councils, and other governance bodies.

The situation is quite different in the private sector and, particularly, in the new, large, for-profit universities that have emerged in recent years. In these institutions, the teacher is just an employee. Some of them may have full- or half-time contracts; but most work with part-time contracts—based on the number of classes taught in each semester, with no job stability or prospects for a career. These large universities have adopted quality controls that are typical of large service companies, controlling the time the teacher enters and leaves the classroom and the fulfillment of prescribed teaching curricula. Another approach is to make sure that the teachers are not too severe or too lenient with their students, who are asked to respond to consumer satisfaction surveys. If a concern exists regarding quality control, a teacher can be reprimanded or replaced. The teachers usually teach in the evenings, work in their main jobs during the day, and may teach in different institutions at the same time, with no particular loyalty to any of them.

Table 2.2 gives the main figures for the academic profession in Brazil, based on the 2008 higher education census carried out by the Ministry of Education. The census counts the number of teaching posts per institution but does not say whether the same person holds posts in different places. There were, in 2008, 338,890 higher education teaching posts in the country, or about 15 first-degree students per teacher, with large variations among sectors: 10.6 students per teacher-post in the public sector and about 17.3 in the private sector. Besides, 76 per cent of the academics in public institutions had full-time contracts, against just 18 per cent in the private sector.

Table 2.2 Academic posts[a] in higher education institutions

	Full-time	Part-time	Per hour	Total
Private	40,774	50,431	128,317	219,522
Public	91,608	18,756	9,004	119,368
Total	132,382	69,187	137,321	338,890

Note: [a]The same person can have two or more part-time posts.
Source: Ministry of Education, Higher Education Census 2008.

It is possible to summarize the features of the academic profession in Brazil, in terms of four clearly differentiated groups of people (Schwartzman and Balbachevsky 1996). The more traditional and smaller group is formed by people in prestigious professions—lawyers, medical doctors, engineers—who earn most of their income from their private practice or outside jobs and for whom teaching in higher education is a secondary activity. They may teach in private institutions but also work part-time in public institutions, as happens with many of the professors in the more prestigious public law schools. A second small group is formed by academics, who were able to complete their doctoral studies in a prestigious institution, often abroad, and consider themselves, in the first place, to be academic researchers. The third group, which makes up the bulk of the teaching staff in public institutions, is composed of people who depend wholly on their university job, have a specialization or a master's degree (seldom a doctorate), and see themselves mostly as public employees. Most of them have full-time contracts and enjoy the benefits of civil service employment—including job stability, reasonable salaries, and early retirement. The fourth group is made up of staff whose main source of income comes from teaching part-time in private institutions, without stable contracts and often working in one or more places.

The political organization and mobilization of the third group display many of the features of the teaching profession in public institutions in Brazil. The staff are organized in powerful unions, both at national and regional levels—such as the National Docent's Union of Higher Education Institutions and the Docent's Association of the University of São Paulo. These unions are associated with Brazil's Laborers' Party, of former president Luis Ignácio Lula da Silva, and can influence and have veto power on the legislation and actions from the education authorities that may affect the interests of their affiliates. They oppose anything that they may consider the "privatization" of public universities (including charging tuition for students, individual salary negotiations, or competing in the market for research grants) or that can threaten the stability and the contract benefits of their members. The unions are opposed to any policy that may differentiate the academics' income in terms of their performance, except through seniority or formal academic credentials. For instance, in 1998 (during the government of Fernando Henrique Cardoso), the Ministry of Education introduced an additional premium to the teachers' salaries, according to the number of classes taught each month. This was a "gratuity," in the sense that it was a temporary payment that could be stopped if the teacher taught fewer classes or upon retirement. In 2005, the unions demanded, and achieved, the transformation of this additional payment into a permanent part of their salaries.

For academics in the third group, with doctoral degrees and engaged in research, who can get additional benefits from research grants, affiliation with their academic association is more relevant than affiliation with the unions; but their interests usually coincide, except when the unions try to curtail the freedom the researchers have to administer their grants or earn additional income from consulting. The National Council for Science and Technology provides about 6,000 research productivity grants every year, which can add up to R$2,800 (Brazilian reais, equivalent to US$1,600) a month, tax free, for university professors who apply for it with a research plan—not usually accessible to the other three groups.

The fourth group is made up mostly by academics who work in private institutions. They work more, earn less, and have less political clout. One would expect that the staff in such working conditions would be unhappy with their situation, but in fact they are mostly satisfied with their jobs (Balbachevsky and Schwartzman forthcoming), which is probably explained by the low expectations regarding their situation. They do not identify much with the institution where they work, either because they teach in different places or because teaching is a secondary activity for them. They are also unionized, but the unions in the private sector are less politicized and militant than those in the public institutions. One important difference is that unions in the public sector can strike without risking job stability and loss of income, while in the private sector they cannot.

Qualifications

In federal universities, an academic career comprises five ranks— auxiliary, assistant, adjunct, associate, and full professor (*auxiliar, assistente, adjunto, associado, titular*). Each of these ranks, up to full professor, is divided into four levels. In principle, access to a university career track should require a doctoral degree and passing and winning an open formal contest (*concurso*). These contests are formal procedures for each track to which anyone can apply, requiring a written and oral examination and a formal lecture, plus an evaluation of the applicant's qualifications by a committee of internal and external examiners.

However, in federal institutions, a doctoral degree is not required for the first two ranks. In the past, many academics with just a graduate (undergraduate) degree were hired through provisional contracts, which were later transformed into permanent appointments. Promotion up to associate level is done by seniority and also by the acquisition of postgraduate degrees; promotion to full professorship, in principle, should also depend on passing an open competition. Admission is usually at the assistant level, but individuals can present themselves in a formal contest for full professorship, if they have the proper formal qualification.

In the state universities of São Paulo, the ranks are auxiliary, assistant, doctor professor, associate, and full professor (*auxiliar, assistente, professor doutor, associado, titular*). A doctoral degree is required for the doctor professor's rank. To be promoted to associate professor, it is necessary to pass a *livre docência* exam, reminiscent of the German *Privatdozent* qualification[2]; to be promoted to full professorship, it is necessary to be approved in an open competitive exam. Other states have similar career paths, except for the *livre docência*, which is a peculiarity of the São Paulo institutions. Most private institutions do not have career ladders, instead salaries are paid according to the academic degree owned by the faculty member. The Ministry of Education collects information on formal degrees, but not on academic ranks.

Table 2.3 gives the distribution of Brazilian academics by academic qualification and type of institution. Although, in principle, it is necessary to have a doctoral degree to teach in higher education, only 22 per cent of academics actually have that degree, ranging from 48.1 per cent in public universities to 17 per cent in a public faculty. The best situation is found at the public universities in the state of São Paulo, where 86 per cent of the academic staff have a doctorate. At present, lesser degrees—such as master's, specialization, and training certificates—are accepted by many institutions as academic credentials. Specializations are programs that provide a teaching load of at least 360 hours of instruction to the students, and are given by a recognized institution; and training certificates are similar programs with a teaching load of 180 hours

Table 2.3 Academic qualifications of faculty members in institutions

Institution and faculty	With no university degree (%)	First degree (%)	Specialization (%)[a]	Master's degree (%)	Doctoral degree (%)	Total
Public university	0.02	11.9	12.8	27.1	48.1	103,607
Private university	0.00	7.9	20.3	29.4	14.3	103,607
Public university center	0.00	9.5	37.2	36.9	16.3	975
Private university center	0.00	9.9	34.1	43.2	12.8	35,212
Public faculty	0.04	7.8	36.8	38.3	17.0	6,729
Private faculty	0.01	9.2	44.4	38.0	8.3	109,770
Public technological center	0.65	15.8	30.7	38.4	14.4	8,057
Total (*N*)	97	36,012	100,419	121,548	80,814	367,957

Note: [a]Specialization is one of the lesser degrees—a program with a teaching load of at least 360 hours, provided by an institution.
Source: Ministry of Education, Higher Education Census (2008).

of instruction. Currently, Brazilian universities graduate about 11,000 students with PhDs each year—a significant number, but still a small proportion compared with the need to fill the 287,000 teaching positions still staffed by underqualified personnel. Moreover, since private, low-cost teaching institutions are not able to pay for full-time staff with advanced degrees, this picture is not likely to change in the foreseeable future.

Academic contracts

Public universities in Brazil are part of the civil service, and both academics and administrative staff are subject to national rules and regulations relating to the civil service. All academic hiring in public universities requires a public posting of positions; and the applicants must submit their curriculum vitae, provide a formal lecture, and go through a written examination—assessed by a committee of people from within and outside the department. This is a formal procedure; there are no search committees and no possibility of choice by the university authorities. Anyone can apply, and those with higher grades obtain the jobs. University departments can exert some discretion in the selection of the examiners (with at least one coming from an outside institution); and the examiners can confer among themselves, before grading the candidates according to their formal qualifications and performance in the written and oral examination and public lecture. But, at the end, each examiner issues their verdict, and the applicant with the higher grade gains the job. For federal universities, the Ministry of Education establishes the number of postings available for each institution. Beyond that, the universities are free to carry out the selection process. Once admitted, an academic gets a full-time contract and becomes a civil servant of the national or state government, depending on the university affiliation.

To be a civil servant in Brazil has many advantages—including additional benefits for academics. Once hired as a civil servant, it is impossible for a person to be dismissed; except due to gross misbehavior, which requires a complex procedure and final approval at the ministerial level, although it can be overruled by the courts. This means that, in practice, all academics entering public institutions are tenured, regardless of their future performance. Salaries tend to be higher than those in the private job market. The retirement age in the country is 65 years for men and 60 years for women, but, for those in education, including university professors, it is five years earlier—60 and 55. It is also possible to retire earlier from public service after ten or more years of work, with proportional earnings, and to get another job in another university, combining the two salaries.

In public universities, up to an associate professor rank, promotion takes place regularly, based on seniority and the acquisition of additional academic credentials. It is a bureaucratic procedure that does not depend on assessments of any kind. Salaries are the same, according to the rank, in all federal universities; and there is no allowance for individual salary negotiations. Benefits include 45 days of paid vacations, health coverage, and generous retirement benefits. Until recently, academics could retain their full salary after retirement. However, some changes have been introduced in recent years, reducing this value—depending on the time the person occupied the position, his or her age, and other factors. The universities can also grant extended leaves for academics to complete their master's or doctoral degrees in other institutions, as well as sabbatical leaves every five years.

Besides the basic salary, actual remuneration may include benefits related to academic degrees and current or past administrative activity. Full-time, exclusively dedicated academics cannot have other regular employment but may receive research fellowships and additional payment for research and technical activities done within the university. Many public universities have established autonomous foundations, which are used to sign research and technical assistance contracts with public and private agencies, and firms that pay additional money for researchers involved in their projects. This practice is not allowed in other branches of the civil service but has been tolerated in the universities.

Most private higher education institutions work with part-time or hourly contracts for their academic staff, with a core group of full-time employees as well. The minimum qualification is an undergraduate degree, but the institutions need to hire a certain number of lecturers with specialization and master's or doctoral degrees to meet the requirements of the Ministry of Education. There are no formal procedures for hiring the staff. An institution needing a lecturer in a given subject can place an advertisement in a newspaper or on the internet, and the decision to hire is made by the person in charge. In both cases, contracts are regulated by Brazilian legislation for private labor contracts. Even if the payment is made according to the number of hours taught, it is necessary to have a formal working contract if it is not an occasional job. This legislation requires a one-month vacation and an additional "Christmas" salary for all labor contracts in the country. Both the employer and employee must contribute about 10 per cent of the salary to the national social security fund, which allows for retirement after 30 years of work for women and 35 years for men, or at ages 60 and 65—at most about R$3,000 a month (US$1,700) or less, depending on the previous income. Moreover, employers have to make a monthly deposit for each employee in a government fund ("working time warranty fund"), which can be used if the person loses the job, retires, or faces some other special circumstances. The employer is free to dismiss the employee at any time—with payment of an indemnity that is proportional to the duration of the contract. There is no tenure, and the employee does not lose retirement benefits. So, mobility is much easier in the private than in the public sector, both from the employer's and the employee's points of view. In some institutions, academics have access to a private health plan, but this is not mandatory. Those working in the private sector are also entitled to 13 salaries (13 paychecks a year), 30 days of paid vacation, and early retirement, if they teach; but otherwise, the benefits are much smaller. They can be dismissed at any time, receiving a small compensation in proportion to the working time—there is no tenure. There is a ceiling for retirement payments equivalent to about US$2,000 a month, or less, depending on the salary earned while active, the person's age, and the number of years contributing to social security. For greater retirement benefits, it is necessary to join a private retirement fund.

Salaries and other revenues

Table 2.4 gives the range of monthly salaries for academics in full-time, exclusive dedication contracts in federal universities. It goes from about US$20,000 to 87,000 a year. State universities have their own payment scale. In the state of São Paulo, the corresponding range is from R$3,435.00 to R$10,216.96 per month, or between US$25,000 and US$76,000, a year. Salaries in poorer states can be lower. The admission procedures, promotion rules, and benefits in state universities are similar to those of the federal government.

Although the pay scales are the same in all federal universities, each person is attached to the institution where she/he works and not to the national civil service, which means that one cannot move to another institution with the same job, except in exceptional situations. One consequence of this system is the minor mobility of academics from one institution to another and the lack of mechanisms for public universities to compete for talent in the country or abroad. There are

Table 2.4   Academic salaries in federal universities in Brazil, 2010 (R$)

	First degree	Training[a]	Specialization[b]	Master's degree	Doctoral degree
Full professor	4,786.62	5,221.96	5,580.63	7,818.69	11,755.05
Associate 4	3,662.97	3,945.91	4,241.00	5,793.14	7,913.30
Adjunct	3,662.97	3,945.91	4,241.00	5,793.14	7,913.30
Assistant	3,201.62	3,444.85	3,643.99	4,874.54	
Auxiliary 1	2,762.36	2,949.68	3,120.08		

Notes: Values in Brazilian reais (US$1.00 = R$1.75).
[a]Training is a lesser programs, similar to specialization, with a teaching load of 180 hours.
[b]Specialization is a lesser programs, with a teaching load of at least 360 hours.
Source: Ministry of Education; the full source of the information is Presideñcia da Reput'blica Casa Civil Subchefia para Assuntos Jurit'dicos LEI No 11.784, DE 22 DE SETEMBRO DE 2008. http:www.planalto.gov.br/ccivil_03/_ato2007-2010/2008/lei/l11784.htm (accessed April 6, 2011).

resources to pay visiting professors for short periods, but a public university finds it difficult to hire a foreign-born academic for its permanent staff.

Most private institutions do not publish data on their salary levels and career paths. However, an informal enquiry among several private institutions showed that they pay between R$20 and R$50 per hour taught, depending on the academic's formal degree. This means that a 20-hour, part-time job receives between R$455 and R$1,032 (US$260 and US$590) per month. Yet, many academics work only 12 or fewer hours per week in an institution, which means that they have to work in different institutions or must combine teaching with other professional activities to earn a reasonable income.

Table 2.5 presents the main data on university academics' income, based on the National Household Survey for 2008. The figures refer to monthly income in Brazilian reais in 2008. The estimated number of academics in the survey is much smaller than the figures reported by the higher education census—96,000 in the public sector against 119,000 in the census and 112,000 in the private sector against 219,000 in the census. One possible explanation for the differences is that the census gives information on posts, while the household survey gives information on people who may hold one or more teaching posts; and there may also be sampling errors. As one could expect, this difference is much higher in the private sector, where part-time contracts are the rule.

Table 2.5 Mean income of teachers in higher education

	Main work (R$)	All activities (R$)	Main work (%)	Number of cases
Public sector, civil servant	2,564.00	2,921.98	87.7	65,756.00
Private sector, regular contract	2,025.13	2,471.29	81.9	98,835.00
All public sector	2,213.37	2,512.83	88.1	96,000.00
All private sector	1,887.77	2,301.15	82.0	112,026.00
Total	2,027.75	2,389.71	84.9	208,026.00

Notes: R$1.75 = US$1.00.
Source: National Household Survey (PNAD) (2008).

The data also show that, although most academics in public institutions are civil servants and most of those in the private sector have private working contracts, many exceptions occur regarding these rules. About 17 per cent of those working in the public sector do not have a regular job, and 12.6 per cent are hired according to private law legislation. While only limited information is available about the kind of jobs held, these academics may be, for instance, graduate students working as research or teaching assistants or replacement academics with temporary contracts. In the private sector, about 9 per cent of the academics do not have a regular working contract. Incomes of those in the public sector are higher than those in the private sector, and incomes of those with regular contracts are higher than those without these contracts. For the civil servants in the public sector, their main salary represents 87.7 per cent of their income from all activities. For those with regular contracts in the public sector, their main salary is only 82 per cent, with another 18 per cent coming from other sources. One-fourth of the academics holding civil servant status earn additional income from a secondary job and for those with private law contracts, 32 per cent do. This proportion is likely to be still higher, given people's propensity to not fully report the income earned outside their main job.

Figure 2.1 compares the distribution of earnings for higher education teachers in public institutions, with civil service contracts, and for those in the private sector, with labor-market contracts. Each column corresponds to one-fifth of the income distribution for the academics. For the lowest 20 per cent, the mean monthly income is R$898.54 (US$511.16); for the upper 20 per cent, the mean monthly income is R$7,320.54 (US$4,183.16). Of the academics in the private sector, 43 per cent are

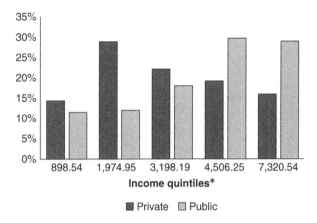

Figure 2.1 Income distribution of teacher earnings (R$).
Notes: The data are monthly incomes. *Five salary levels.
Source: National Household Survey (PNAD) (2008).

in the first two of the five levels, while 58.4 per cent of those in the public sector are in the two highest groups.

Higher education teachers in Brazil tend to have incomes above the average for persons in other careers with similar qualifications. For those in the public higher education sector, income is not as good as salaries of medical doctors, top-level engineers, and those in business—but is better than in other, less prestigious occupations. Earnings for those in the private higher education sector are closer to the average for persons with higher education—similar to architects, civil engineers, and data-processing specialists. Thus, higher education teachers, particularly those working in the public sector, are part of the country's upper-middle class—that is, likely to live in upper-middle-class neighborhoods, own a house or an apartment, have a car, and send their children to private schools.

Academics' working conditions

More detailed information on the working conditions of Brazilian academics can be obtained from the International Comparative Survey on the Academic Profession, carried out in Brazil, in 2007 (Balbachevsky and Schwartzman 2009; Balbachevsky et al. 2008). The sample of 1,200 respondents included academics in public and private institutions, as well as in non-university scientific research centers and institutes. For the analysis, the respondents were divided into five strata, based on the characteristics of the institutions in which they work—public, research-intensive universities; other public universities; private, elite institutions; other private institutions; and research institutes.

Table 2.6 shows that, in a typical 40-hour week, for half of the time academics are devoted to teaching and related activities, with the heaviest teaching load taking place in private institutions. Research-related activities consume half of the time in research centers but less than 6 per cent in private institutions. The third activity is administrative work, about 5 per cent of the time; and other activities take another 2–3 per cent of the time.

In public universities, full-time contracts assume that academics spend half of their time in research. As Table 2.6 shows, the percentage reported by academics is closer to ten hours, or 25 per cent of the time, except in research institutes. Still, there are many indications that only a fraction of those claiming to do research are actually engaged in research activities. In the private sector, most academics have a secondary job; and even among those in the public sector, 18.3 per cent have an additional job, either in another teaching institution, a non-governmental organization, or working in private practice.

Given the expectation that all academics should do research and publish, the number of persons reporting to have done research and been published is relatively high in all groups. However, Table 2.7 shows large differences in the nature of the research activity of various groups. In the research centers and research-intensive universities, research is done with outside funding, more articles are published in international publications and in peer-review journals, and international collaboration is more frequent. In non-research public and private institutions, external funding is much more limited, most of the publications are in Portuguese, and international cooperation is less active. In the private sector, the teaching load tends to be large, and little time is allocated for research. This is not necessarily the practice in public universities, where the teaching load is not related to one's performance in research. The 2007 Academic Profession Survey found that, on average, academics in public, research-intensive institutions spend 16.7 hours a week in teaching activities, compared with 18.9 hours in other public institutions and 21 hours in the private sector. Most academics in the public sector have full-time contracts, while very few do in the private sector. In 1988, the federal government introduced legislation providing an additional payment for higher education teachers, according to the number of classes given; but this policy was abolished in 2006, with the additional payment becoming part of the regular salary.

Table 2.6 Hours worked per week in different activities, by type of institution, 2007

Type of institution	Intensive public research	Other public	Elite private	Other private	Research institutes	Total
Teaching (preparation of instructional materials and lesson plans, classroom instruction, advising students, reading and evaluating student work) in hours	17.11	19.82	21.17	22.76	12.03	19.87
Research (reading literature, writing, conducting experiments, fieldwork) in hours	12.84	9.14	9.3	5.86	20.41	9.36
Extension (services to clients and/or patients, unpaid consulting, public or voluntary services) in hours	2.78	2.6	3.55	2.17	1.09	2.53
Administration (committees, department meetings, paperwork) in hours	5.41	4.77	6.34	3.24	6.09	4.64
Other academic activities (professional activities not clearly attributable to any of the categories above) in hours	3.03	2.36	2.17	2.73	2.24	2.54
Total respondents in the survey	195	614	60	270	53	1,192

Source: Changing Academic Project. 2007. http://www.open.ac.uk/cheri/pages/CHERI-Projects-CAP.shtml (accessed April 8, 2012).

Table 2.7 International publication patterns, 2007

Characteristics of research	Types of institution				
	Public, research intensive	Public, other	Private, elite	Private, others	Research institutes
Academic articles published in the last three years	6.51	4.19	2.46	3.28	7.43
Research with outside funding (%)	59.2	29.9	24.9	13.1	40.0
Only published the language of instruction at your current institution (%)	28.5	57.9	29.7	71.9	19.6
Never co-authored with colleagues located in other (foreign) countries (%)	71.8	85.5	91.9	94.2	51.0
Never published in a foreign country (%)	37.2	68.1	45.9	84.3	25.5
Never published in a peer-reviewed journal (%)	41.6	54.0	40.5	75.9	19.6

Note: % within the type of institution.
Source: Changing Academic Project. 2007. http://www.open.ac.uk/cheri/pages/CHERI-Projects-CAP.shtml (accessed April 8, 2012).

Dispersed centers of research

A better account of the effects of higher education on economic development requires an analysis of the scope of research. Research in Brazil is not only conducted at research universities. Several ministries support research at non-university institutions.

The best contribution to economic development in Brazil, in terms of research, was probably in agriculture. Agricultural research takes place mostly in an institution associated with the Ministry of Agriculture, the Brazilian Enterprise for Agricultural Research, which has provided a long history of developing new-plant varieties and technologies to make use of impoverished soil, enabling Brazil to become one of the largest agricultural producers in the world. This institution works in partnership with several universities and benefits from researchers graduated from Brazilian institutions and abroad, but is not a higher education institution.

A century ago, research in tropical medicine in non-university institutions, such as the Oswaldo Cruz Institute in Rio de Janeiro, was important to identify the nature and to reduce or eliminate the devastating effects of Chagas disease, malaria, yellow fever, and other diseases. The Oswaldo Cruz Institute remains an important research center within the Ministry of Health, and tropical medicine remains one of the strongest fields of research in Brazil (Glänzel, Leta, and Thijs 2006; Leta, Glänzel, and Thijs 2006).

The creation of the National Council of Research and the Brazilian Institute for Physics research in the 1940s were part of an effort to develop nuclear capabilities in the country, which was not successful. In the late 1970s, the science and technology sector was reorganized by the military government to realign it with the drive for economic development; several ambitious high-technology projects were started, in the areas of computer science, semiconductors, and space technology. Some of these projects have not succeeded or are lingering; but there was a substantial increase in the volume of resources dedicated to science, technology, and research, which led to the creation of a Ministry for Science and Technology in 1985. Embraer—the Brazilian Agency for Space Research and one of the world's largest manufacturers of mid-size planes—grew from the Technological Institute of the Air Force in the city of São José dos Campos and was considered the best engineering school in the country. Petrobrás, Brazil's oil company, has partnerships with many universities to develop all kinds of technologies related to deep-sea oil drilling. Other examples could be listed (Schwartzman 2008).

Still, overall, the productivity of Brazilian science is not so high. In 2009, 32,100 articles were published by Brazilian authors, indexed by Thomson Reuters Scientific INC, corresponding to 54 per cent of the publications in Latin America and 2.69 per cent worldwide. This was a significant increase compared to 2000—with 10,521 publications, 1.35 per cent worldwide. The number of patents registered at the US Patent Office was quite small, 148 in 2009, compared with 9,556 for South Korea.[3] The number of citations of scientific publications by Brazilian authors was 8.91 for the period 1996 to 2009, above Russia and India (4.48 and 6.2), but well below the United Kingdom, Canada, or Belgium (in the 14–15 range).[4] This index may be biased in favor of English-speaking countries (the highest ranks are those of the United States and the United Kingdom) but is nevertheless a rough indication of the relevance and impact of a country's scientific output.

Conclusions

To what extent do higher education and the academic profession contribute to Brazil's social and economic development? The link between education, as human capital, and economic development, is well established in the economic literature (Becker 1964; Schultz 1994). But, also, the expansion of education is strongly influenced by movements of social groups, to gain prestige and access to privileged jobs and market niches, which do not necessarily generate wealth and increased productivity to society as a whole. Several authors have analyzed this by looking at education as a "positional good," and interpreting education expansion in terms of the search for credentials, rather than the search for increasing knowledge and competencies (Brown 2003; Collins 1979; Hirsch 1977; Schwartzman 2011). These two interpretations do not need to be considered as mutually exclusive, since, to some extent at least, the drive for education credentials leads also to the increase in competencies. But the drive for higher credentials leads also to a redistribution of existing wealth in favor of some groups (Bourdieu and Passeron 1990). Distinguishing these two aspects of education development helps when discussing its impact on broader economic development and well-being.

In Brazil, the expansion of higher education was clearly not driven by sustained public policies for economic growth but, instead, by a demand for greater social mobility—which governments, at different points in time and with limited resources and policies, tried to steer. The creation of a public university sector was linked to a broader process of urbanization and the expansion of the public sector, as well as to the ability of professional corporations to enact legislation protecting their market niches—already present in the 19th century (Coelho 1999), it became stronger as the country modernized. A recent example of this trend was the successful drive of sociologists' and philosophers' unions and associations to make the teaching of sociology and philosophy mandatory in secondary education, creating a large job market for themselves, justified by the need to increase the students' critical thinking.

Another issue is the competencies produced by the higher education system. About 43 per cent of all first-degree students are in the fields of the social sciences, business, and law professions, which do not require much in terms of previous qualifications and limited investments in equipment by the institutions. This proportion is highest in the private sector. The second largest segment is in education, provided mostly by state and private institutions. Most of these courses take place in the evening, and a large part of the students are schoolteachers, working to earn a formal qualification, allowing them to be promoted in the public schools where they work. At the other extreme, only 8.4 per cent of the students are in the field of engineering and production. The large agricultural and mining companies in Brazil are capital intensive and do not employ many people. Industry is more productive today than in the past, but employs fewer people and makes use of imported machinery. The most complex industries—in areas like automobile manufacturing, industrialized food, metallurgy, and appliances—are either foreign-based or in partnership with foreign companies that do their research abroad. Industrialists complain of the lack of qualified middle-level technicians, but do not require many specialists with higher education degrees. The most demanding fields, in terms of manpower, are services of different kinds—commerce, transportation, education, health care, and also construction work. In that sense, one could say that the profile of the students coming out of higher education institutions is adjusted to the country's economy. Evidentially, a higher education diploma in Brazil leads to higher income, even if the person ends up working in activities requiring only secondary education skills. This status quo has to do with the relative scarcity of people with higher education degrees in the country. In 2009, only 11 per cent of the population aged 25–40 years had a higher education degree, according to the National Household Survey. Moreover, with the legal knowledge, people with diplomas are able to circumvent protective legislation, particularly in public jobs.

Finally, how good is higher education produced in Brazil? If one judges from international rankings, it is apparent that no institution in the country appears in the top 100, in any of the most influential rankings. This is probably unfair to the University of São Paulo, which appears as the best in the Latin American region in international comparisons and has strong research departments, graduate programs, and professional schools in medicine, engineering, law, economics, agriculture, and other fields (Schwartzman 2007). This university and some other public institutions—such as the University of Campinas and the Federal University of Minas Gerais—also appear at the top in the national rankings of degree programs, carried out regularly by the Brazilian Ministry of Education. These rankings, however, only report which programs are better or worse and do not include standards to distinguish among the excellent, good, acceptable, and unacceptable. Yet, law students need to pass a bar exam carried out by the lawyers' professional association, before being allowed to practice; and only about 20 per cent of the applicants pass, which is either an indication of the quality of the education provided by most Brazilian law schools or a reflection on the quality of the examination.

It is possible to summarize by saying that some of the higher education provided by Brazilian institutions is good but that most of it is bad. While most of the low-quality programs in business administration, law, and economics—provided in large scale by private institutions—do not form specialized study, they do provide students general competencies they would not receive otherwise. Since these programs are not subsidized, the fact that they respond to demand and that their graduates earn higher salaries in the job market constitutes their value. The issue is more serious in low-quality programs provided by public universities that are heavily subsidized by the government and do not charge students tuition. There are good reasons to argue that public universities should be required to show that they are using public resources effectively and providing skills in areas of higher priority for society. However, it is difficult politically for governments to implement such policies, particularly if they are associated with changes that might restrict access to public subsidies.

Brazilian higher education, as well as the working conditions and competencies of its academic profession, is uneven—as are most things in the country, with large social and regional imbalances. Development of the higher education sector needs to be conceptualized as part of a broader process of social change, which is neither harmonious nor efficient and is subject to periods of rapid expansion and retraction. The experience of the last several decades has been mostly of expansion and growth, and it is hoped that this enhancement will continue.

Notes

1. There are two main sources of information on Brazilian education. One is the National Institute for Education Research of the Ministry of Education in Brasilia, which performs regular censuses of basic and higher education, collecting data from the institutions, and is also in charge of the main assessment systems for basic, secondary, and higher education. The second is the Brazilian Institute for Geography and Statistics, Brazil's census office. Besides the decennial demographic census and other statistics, this institute carries out a yearly National Household Sample Survey, which collects education, employment, and other information from a sample of about 100,000 households. The data of these two sources diverge somewhat, but since they bring different types of information, both will be used in the text that follows.
2. "Privatdozent (abbreviated PD, P.D. or Priv.-Doz.) or Private lecturer is a title conferred in some European university systems, especially in German-speaking countries, for someone who pursues an academic career and holds

all formal qualifications (doctorate and habilitation) to become a tenured university professor. With respect to the level of academic achievement, the title compares to associate professor (North America) or something between senior lecturer and reader (UK); however, the title is not connected to any salaried position" (http://en.wikipedia.org/wiki/Privatdozent).
3. This data was compiled by Brazil's Ministry of Science and Technology.
4. According to *CSImago Journal and Country Rank.* http://www.scimagojr.com/countryrank.php.

References

Balbachevsky, Elizabeth, and Simon Schwartzman. 2009. The academic profession in a diverse institutional environment: Converging or diverging values and beliefs? In *The changing academic profession over 1992–2007: International, comparative and quantitative perspectives,* ed. Research Institute for Higher Education, 145–164. Hiroshima: Research Institute for Higher Education, Hiroshima University Press.

———. 2010. The Graduate Foundations of Research in Brazil. *Higher Education Forum* (Research Institute for Higher Education, Hiroshima University) 7:85–100.

———. forthcoming. Job satisfaction in a diverse institutional enviroment: The Brazilian experience. In *The changing academic profession in international comparative perspective,* ed. L. Geodegebuure. Hiroshima: Research Institution for Higher Education, Hiroshima University Press.

Balbachevsky, Elizabeth, Simon Schwartzman, Nathalia Novaes Alves, Dante Filipe Felgueiras dos Santos, and Tiago Silva Birkholz Duarte. 2008. Brazilian academic profession: Some recent trends. *The changing academic profession in international comparative and quantitative Perspectives, RIHE International Seminar Reports* 12:327–344.

Becker, Gary Stanley. 1964. *Human capital.* New York: Columbia Univ. Press.

Bourdieu, Pierre, and Jean Claude Passeron. 1990. *Reproduction in education, society, and culture.* London: Sage.

Brown, Phillip. 2003. The opportunity trap: Education and employment in a global economy. In *Working Paper Series 32.* Cardiff, NY: School of Social Sciences, Cardiff University.

Coelho, Edmundo Campos. 1999. *As Profissões imperiais: Advocacia, medicina e engenharia no Rio de Janeiro, 1822–1930.* Rio de Janeiro: Editora Record.

Collins, Randall. 1979. *The credential society.* New York: Academic Press.

Confederação Nacional da Indústria. 2011. Falta de trabalhador qualificado na Indústria. *Sondagem Especial*: 2.

Glänzel, Wolfgang, Jacqueline Leta, and Bart Thijs. 2006. Science in Brazil. Part 1: A macro-level comparative study. *Scientometrics* 67:67–86.

Hirsch, Fred. 1977. *The social limits to growth.* London: Routledge.

Instituto Brasileiro de Geografia e Estatística. 1993. *Anuário Estatístico do Brasil 1993.* Rio de Janeiro: Instituto Brasileiro de Geografia e Estatística.

Leta, Jacqueline, Wolfgang Glänzel, and Bart Thijs. 2006. Science in Brazil. Part 2: Sectoral and institutional research profiles. *Scientometrics* 67:87–105.

Nunes, Edson, and Marcia Marques Carvalho. 2007. Ensino universitário, corpo-ração e profissão: Paradoxos e dilemas brasileiros. *Sociologias* 9:190–215.

Organization for Economic Cooperation and Development. 2009. *PISA 2009 results: What students know and can do: Student performance in reading, mathe-matics and science.* Paris: OECD.

Schultz, T. Paul. 1994. Human capital and economic development. In *Discussion paper.* Yale University Economic Growth Center.

Schwartzman, Simon. 1991. *A space for science the development of the scientific community in Brazil.* University Park, PA: Pennsylvania State University Press.

———. 2007. Brazil's leading university: Between intelligentsia, world standards and social inclusion. In *World class worldwide: Transforming research universities in Asia and Latin America,* ed. P. G. Altbach and J. Balán, 143–172. Baltimore, MD: Johns Hopkins University Press.

———. 2008. *University and development in Latin America: Successful experiences of research centres.* Rotterdam: Sense.

———. 2011. O viés acadêmico na educação brasileira. In *Brasil: A nova agenda social,* ed. E. Bacha and S. Schwartzman. Rio de Janeiro, Brazil: Editora LTC.

Schwartzman, Simon, and Elizabeth Balbachevsky. 1996. The academic pro-fession in Brazil. In *The international academic profession: Portraits of fourteen countries,* ed. P. G. Altbach, 231–280. Princeton, NJ: Carnegie Foundation for the Advancement of Teaching.

Steiner, João E. 2005. Qualidade e diversidade institucional na pós-graduação brasileira. *Estudos Avançados* 19:341–365.

Stepan, Erica Nancy. 1971. *Scientific institution-building in a developing country: The Oswaldo Cruz Institute of Brazil.* Los Angeles, CA: University of California.

3

Changing Realities: Russian Higher Education and the Academic Profession

Gregory Androushchak, Yaroslav Kuzminov, and Maria Yudkevich

Three perspectives dominate modern debates about higher education in Russia and the prospects of national universities. Some observers believe that the Russian higher education system is one of the best in the world, referring to the success of Russian specialists internationally. Others say that the former point of view is harmful because the quality of the country's education is a myth and the universities have undergone fundamentally negative changes during recent decades, which cannot be abolished. Finally, the third group of people prefer to talk about the current challenges the Russian education system faces and the goals that need to be addressed in order to build an effective system of professional education to suit the modern labor market and to produce fundamental research and application studies, based on international standards in the global academic market.

In many countries, discussions have recently been under way about building universities that reflect international standards. This goal—as well as the task of developing an efficient national higher education system—cannot be achieved without coordinating the best specialists in higher education and creating conditions conducive to productive research and teaching. Faculty are at the core of institutional quality and the most valuable asset for any university; therefore, decent remuneration is key to success. An academic profession is a specific career path, with its unique incentives, inner motivation, and payoff. Thus, narrowing the characteristics of faculty's remuneration down to the financial element would only be ignoring the nature of the university itself. Therefore, providing adequate remuneration does not simply constitute offering a decent level of payment but also signifies ensuring academic freedom, a top-level academic environment, and ample opportunities for further professional development. In other words, institutional frameworks that provide such conditions and incentives are essential for the functioning of universities, and these elements together comprise what are called academic contracts.

This chapter will show how changing academic market conditions and the recent developments in the Russian economy, as a whole, have influenced the way academic contracts, incentives, and faculty's opportunities are organized and what the consequences of these changes involve.

What is so interesting about analyzing academic contracts and remuneration in the Russian higher education system? First of all, the issue is academic contracts, per se. Second, it is the consequences of sharp shocks experienced by the Russian higher education system, when the Soviet economy collapsed. Examining the academic profession in Russia over the past 30 years gives striking examples of how a certain institutional equilibrium disintegrates, while new forces emerge (and turn out to be less efficient). Third, features of the current academic contract system have to be taken into account when moving toward the integration of the Russian system with the global one.

The current systematic underfunding of higher education results in salaries that are insufficient for professors' primary employment. According to the survey of university administration, which took place in 2009 in the framework of Monitoring of Educational Markets and Organizations (2009),[1] in order for faculty to abandon additional sources of income and focus exclusively on teaching and research at the institution where they are employed, their salaries should be more than doubled (see Figure 3.1). Further estimations, based on the same survey, demonstrate that for the university to attract faculty with advanced academic skills who are able to teach and do research, to a high standard, it should be able to increase wages by four times—which is not really much, compared with current total incomes of university teachers.

As a result, the conditions and opportunities outside their primary contract shape employment patterns and priorities for university faculty. They include private tutoring, where one's status as a university teacher offers definite advantages, working in the business sector, and adopting an additional teaching load. Since all of these further responsibilities create separate (often strong) incentives for and expectations of faculty members, the supplemental activities should be considered as part of an academic contract, in the broader sense.

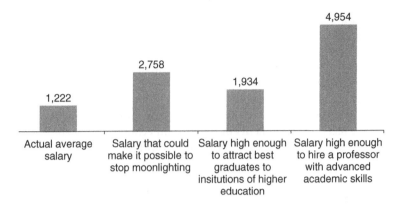

Figure 3.1 Average and "optimal" monthly salaries of faculty in institutions of higher education, 2009 (per month, PPP US$).
Source: Monitoring of Education Markets and Organizations (2009).

Institutional legacy

Currently (in 2012) the Russian system of higher education includes 662 public and 474 private institutions and slightly more than 1,600 related regional branches; approximately two-thirds of which relate to public and one-third to private institutions. This chapter focuses on higher education institutions only and does not consider academic contracts and salaries at research institutions affiliated with the Russian Academy of Sciences—which is, based on a long-standing tradition, separated from the university sector in Russia.

There are three types of higher education institutions: universities, academies, and institutes. Universities offer a wide range of educational programs—including postgraduate programs (PhD and doctorate) and research—and coordinate research and methodological activities in their key areas of expertise. The Academy of Sciences and other academies differ from universities by offering a narrower range of programs, as well as narrower areas of research. Institutes are different from universities and academies and offer an even narrower range of ongoing educational programs and research activities—for a discussion on different types of higher education institutions in Russia, see Androushchak and Yudkevich (2012).

The largest number of institutions—just over half of all public higher education institutions—are affiliated with the Ministry of Education and Science. Twenty-two other ministries and agencies have higher education institutions under their jurisdictions. Among the largest operators are the Ministry of Agriculture, the Ministry of Health and Social Development, the Ministry of Culture, the Ministry of Transport, and the Ministry of Sport and Tourism.

There are 7.4 million students in the higher education system, with only 17 per cent of them enrolled in private universities. In the past, only 65 per cent of secondary school graduates enrolled in higher education institutions. In 2009, 89 per cent of all 17-year-old youths became first-year university students. Naturally, with such a low level of selectivity, the average portion of the entering population becomes a central problem.

While 45 per cent of the total number of students at Russian higher education institutions are enrolled as full-time students, 4 per cent of students are enrolled part-time, and the rest of students (over 45%) are enrolled in a type of distance-learning program. The quality of part-time and distance-learning programs differ drastically from full-time programs. Moreover, in most cases, the former programs basically mean acquiring a formal title, without any relevant competencies.

At the present time, the total number of faculty at public universities is estimated to be around 0.948 million people. See Figure 3.2 for the approximate distribution of positions.

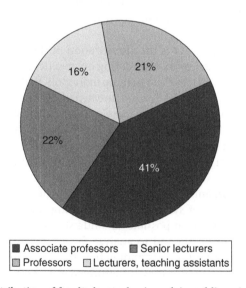

Figure 3.2 Distribution of faculty by academic rank in public universities.
Source: Federal State Statistics Service (Rosstat) (2009).

Some conditions and challenges face the higher education system now. First of all, there is an ongoing demographic decline, caused by the harsh recession and the degradation of living standards. In the early and mid-1990s Russian families faced much uncertainty and, thus, had fewer children. So, the birth cohort of those applying to universities is declining in comparison to previous years. This basically exaggerates the lack of selectivity at low-quality universities, which are worried about filling government-funded places.

Second, the public consensus is that higher education is a social imperative: even with the record-breaking numbers of secondary school graduates entering universities and an accompanying deterioration in overall quality, the percentage of people pursuing higher education (even though it is extremely high now) should not be decreased. Everyone needs at least some type of further education.

Third, the Unified State Exam results now determine who gets admitted to which university in Russia. The Unified State Exam replaced specific exams that were held by each university. It opened up more opportunities for students and has also begun providing additional information for the main actors in the education market—universities, households, schools, and the government. For example, comparisons of universities are provided through data on the quality of admitted students, and ultimately secondary schools will be evaluated (on the basis of the Unified State Exam results of their graduates and the universities they attend).

Finally, another impact is the globalization of the education market. More and more students are considering universities abroad at the bachelor's, master's, or PhD level, so that the monopoly that local universities in all regions once enjoyed is now threatened by foreign competition. This issue primarily affects the most academically talented and economically well-off students. This challenge, faced by universities, is also drawing the best graduates to PhD programs abroad. In both cases, the figures are low on a national scale, but they are growing and will grow even faster.

The current organization of the Russian higher education market results from a series of systemic changes during the past two decades. However, it would be impossible to understand how academic contracts function in Russia and to analyze faculty incentives within the present system without understanding how the Soviet higher education system was organized and how it performed. So, the next section will focus on the Soviet, post-Soviet, and modern stages of higher education development.

The legacy of the Soviet higher education system

The number of universities in the Russian Soviet Federative Socialist Republic remained virtually the same between 1940 and the beginning of perestroika (481 higher education institutions were functioning in 1940 versus 494 in 1980), yet the percentage of young people pursuing a university degree started to grow in the middle of the 1960s. In 1970, there were 474 universities, nearly a quarter of which were situated in Moscow and Leningrad (now Saint Petersburg)—76 and 41, respectively. A significant number of universities were situated in the research centers in Siberia, which were founded during the 1950s and 1960s (11 in Krasnoyarsk, 14 in Novosibirsk). At that time, there were 2.67 million students at the universities (1.3 million full-time, 0.39 million part-time, and 0.985 million at distance-learning programs). There were 204 students for every 10,000 people.

Higher education was free. Moreover, all full-time students with a good academic performance received a scholarship—enough support to live without financial aid from one's parents or a part-time job. Students coming from other regions were always provided with dormitory accommodation, usually for a nominal payment.

Also, the large distance-learning sector accounted for up to one-third of all students. At the time, studying in that sector usually meant that students had to actually come to the university twice a year, for exam sessions. Distance education enabled individuals employed full-time to earn a degree and was usually necessary to fulfill requirements related to the development of one's career. Multiple distinctive characteristics of the Soviet system are summarized next.

The planned economy and mandatory job assignments

In the framework of a planned economy, one main feature of the higher education system was the system of mandatory job assignment. Accordingly, each university graduate received a specific and unavoidable assignment. She or he could be assigned to remain within the university in an academic job, to stay in a big city or even in the capital, or to go to some production site in a faraway district of the country. The type of the assignment depended on various factors: academic performance, social activity, ideological loyalty, or relations with the decision makers involved in the process of distributing assignments. Receiving an assignment for postgraduate studies was considered a fortunate result—the first step toward a successful career.

To balance supply and demand of qualified specialists, each university was allocated a fixed number of places for new students and an amount of public funding, for each educational program. Today, the government assigns an enrollment plan to each public university that receives state financing; this determines the number of places for university entrants, secured with public funding. This vestige of the Soviet period only creates incentives to lower admissions requirements, to preserve the existing level of state financing and to receive even more.

Besides universities that were under the auspices of the Ministry for Education, there used to be a number of them under various industry-specific ministries. The existence of these ties was caused by a certain degree of vertical integration. Thus, the educational program was tailored to match the needs of the corresponding industry and needed to be flexible in adjusting to the new demands of the industry. In addition, the program meant that graduates would be provided with a job at one of the production sites subordinate to the ministry. Employers were quite interested in a broader division of the professions. It allowed them not only to get specialists who were perfectly suited to industrial needs but also to minimize the potential risks that employees would be drawn to other industries.

In other words, specialists were trained not for the labor market as a whole (which did not really exist) but for specified segments of the system. Each production site was a channel for the inflow of graduates from specific universities. The balance between the industry's needs and higher education was reached not only due to the formal mechanisms but also to informal connections between universities and organizations—through which university administrations secured job positions for their graduates. The Ministry of Defense, Ministry of Agriculture, Ministry of Health, as well as Ministries of Light Industry and Heavy Industries were among those that had the most subordinate universities. The orientation of student enrollment was biased toward engineering jobs: up to 40 per cent of students graduated in engineering.

Efficient contracts

To understand the contract between university and faculty during the Soviet period, it is essential to bear in mind the following trends of the system. First, from the formal status point of view, faculty did not differ much from the other types of civil servants. At the same time, the academic profession was prestigious. Furthermore, faculty members with the highest positions in academic hierarchy had access to additional benefits—such as food purchase orders, discounted holiday vouchers, and better medical services—and rarely suffered a shortfall.

Second, inter-university mobility was practically zero. So, one began an academic career as a teaching assistant and moved toward the position of a professor or head of chair, within the same university. The academic sector was a rather closed system; professional mobility between universities and other organizations was virtually nonexistent. Academic positions were highly attractive, which made the system quite selective. Individuals who enjoyed a high status in the non-academic sector (factory administrators, party administrators, etc.) needed to begin at a relatively low position, in order to join the academic profession. Wages depended on the position and, hence, employment history.

Finally, Soviet higher education included a smooth-running system of reassessment and skill improvement, for which each professor had to complete a retraining course, at least once every five years. This practice mostly guided the improvement of teaching methods.

Even though employment agreements were signed only for a limited period (i.e., several years), cases in which they were not renewed occurred extremely rarely. The academic system of control over faculty's research and teaching activities was closely related to the party-controlled system. So, each faculty member's commitment and desire to keep their place and progress in their career led to maximum compliance with the rules.

It is possible to talk of an efficient contract for university faculty during the Soviet period. First, there was heavy regulation of the production sphere and public administration in the Soviet Union. Without entrepreneurship in the country, universities, as well as research institutes affiliated with the Academy of Sciences, remained the only territory of even limited freedom. Of course, people who valued personal freedom gathered into the higher education system.

Second, academic work was well remunerated. A university professor's wage was about 300 per cent higher than the average wage, while a young teaching assistant—at the start of his or her career and without an advanced degree—received approximately 110–120 per cent more than the average wage. So, both pecuniary and non-pecuniary remuneration at Soviet universities were rather high. Despite ideological pressure, universities developed reasonably well-functioning mechanisms for academic control and quality control. That led to the famous phenomenon of Soviet education, which was valued all over the world during this period.

As already mentioned, an employee's salary was dependent on his or her position in the academic hierarchy. A teaching assistant without an advanced degree earned around US$120–150 per month, in today's dollars, a senior lecturer around US$200, while a full professor's monthly salary was about US$400–450. These wages were the same in all disciplines—only universities working for the arms industry had higher salaries. An average wage in the industrial sector, at the time, was about US$190 per month.

Having a candidate of sciences degree (only about 45% of faculty did) or even a doctor of sciences degree (5% of faculty) provided not only some extra pay but also certain social benefits. For example, a better standard of housing was provided to the holder of these degrees.

Beside the actual wage, faculty members also had access to additional ways of earning, through the so-called economic contract. This was basically research, commissioned by organizations, regional authorities, and other groups and carried out by university chairs and individual faculty members. Such commissions were initiated by heads of chairs and deputy heads of departments. On average, professors could earn up to half of their wage through such contracts. At the same time, even though many people had an opportunity to earn such income, standing out too much was not encouraged, so the faculty did not let colleagues neglect their main contract.

Postgraduate studies and the replacement of specialists

Recruiting new faculty from the university's own graduates (inbreeding) was common. The source was normally postgraduate programs. Even though being admitted into a postgraduate program was quite hard in itself (additional work experience was usually required), it was even more difficult and more prestigious to get a job assignment, and to remain with the department. Many graduates regarded the opportunity to stay at the university as a teaching assistant to be one of the most attractive career paths. A postgraduate scholarship allowed the student to focus on research, while flexible working hours provided the conditions expected by research institute staff. The replacement of specialists caused the formation of certain schools of thought with all their strengths and weaknesses.

Institutional shock: factors and external disintegration

The transformation of economic institutions affected higher education; comparing the working conditions and the remuneration system of university faculty in the last years of the Soviet Union with the current faculty contracts makes this evident.

When the Soviet Union collapsed, educational budgets decreased by three or four times, as did the budgets in all sectors of the economy. However, while the rest could just disappear or dramatically diminish in size (like the arms industry, for example), the educational system did not decline but continued to grow. It grew both in the number of universities (which more than doubled after 1990) and the percentage of young people who continued their studies toward a university degree. Thus, the higher education system has doubled in size since 1991, to 520 students for every 10,000 people. This is approximately 15–20 per cent more than in the United States or Finland. Thus, these days higher education is considered as a social imperative; yet, financing was cut despite such a huge increase in demand for higher education.

In 1992 a new federal act—On Education in the Russian Federation— was passed, which created a legal framework for the establishment and functioning of new educational institutions; and those institutions began to grow in number, exponentially. The nongovernmental sector basically grew, from nothing (zero), in the past 15 years. Privately financed education is a relatively new phenomenon in the Russian higher education market.

Public and private institutions differ in their organizational and legal structures. Public universities receive public funding for training students who achieve high academic results in the entrance examinations—since 2009, the State Unified Exam—at high school graduation. Public institutions are provided with buildings and basic infrastructure. A limited number of public universities receive public support to finance their research activities. The share of public funding to higher education has increased over recent years and, according to the Federal State Statistics Service (Rosstat), currently constitutes approximately 60 per cent of the total funds available to universities, as compared to about 40 per cent at the beginning of 2000/2001.[2]

Private universities do not receive any government funding to support even the most talented students or to cover research costs. By late 2003, the Russian Ministry of Education and Science had started to develop mechanisms that would allow private institutions to receive government financing for students or research on a competitive basis.

Private universities usually teach economics and management and/or humanities. They usually admit less-prepared students or those who choose not to spend a lot of time and effort on education—for example, attending classes, doing homework, or writing essays or term papers.

Because of that, private higher education has, from the very start, been associated invariably with low-quality education.

Divergence from the productive sector: lost ties with industry

The privatization of government-owned production sites disrupted job placement channels for university graduates. Although in the government-owned sector demand for recent graduates remained stable—and even grew, due to the massive migration of competent senior specialists into the business sector—it was not financially attractive anymore. In the absence of mandatory job assignments and compulsory "binding" between graduates and employers, the inadequacy of the wages in the public sector led to few applicants. Many graduates, whose education, qualifications, and competences were tailored to match the needs of a specific industry (as in engineering, for example), just were not in demand anymore. The job assignment system ceased to be efficient. When it broke down, direct market control of the quality of education weakened significantly. The development of new control mechanisms was going to take some time.

The sharp external changes, which caused systemic internal transformations, unsettled the equilibrium in the former contract system. That led, in its turn, to the breakdown of efficient contract equilibrium in Russian universities during the first decade of democratic development during the 1990s.

The gap between the wages of university faculty and people with the same educational level in other fields, grew so big that it was no longer compensated by the intrinsic nonmonetary rewards of an academic career. Moreover, the wages fell so low in absolute value that faculty could no longer live without additional income and were obliged to look for it either within academia or externally.

Many faculty who would have preferred to stay within universities decided to leave. The mass exodus of talented individuals from universities was not only caused by the fact that wages fell below subsistence level. Underfunding also affected equipment, expendable materials, and other expensive components, crucial for research, in many disciplines. No information was accessible about the latest international scientific achievements; subscriptions to scientific journals were cut down, and hardly any foreign books were purchased.

Only faculty who had nowhere else to go kept their positions—those who were not sought by the business sector, foreign universities, the public sector, or anywhere else. Up to 50 per cent of all faculty left. As well as the mass migration of former university teachers to the external labor market within Russia, the country also suffered a significant brain drain during the 1990s (Agamova and Allakhverdyan 2007). Attending conferences at universities abroad, Russian researchers often found that the conditions for research were incomparable with Russian ones, and many of them made a decision to emigrate as a result. It is estimated that no less than 7 per cent of all university employees moved abroad.

Those who stayed in the country tended to be less professionally talented and accomplished. In addition, standards of consumption and income in the business sector—primarily in industrial areas such as banking and finance, insurance, real estate, and a few others—grew dramatically. People employed in these spheres could earn US$2,000–4,000 monthly in the 1990s, while a university lecturer's wage was US$100 per month.

As most of the best professionals left, the system was replenished with younger scholars or people from other sectors, who were usually academically weak. The competence level of these scholars was low, as was their professional status, which did not match the standards in the business sector. These new entrants were initially willing to violate academic standards, for money. The 2005 survey of Russian university teachers of all ages, investigating incentives and behavior, included the following question: "In certain circumstances, would you agree to accept a material remuneration from a student in exchange for some study-related services provided to him?"—the softest form of admitting corruption. Only 10 per cent among the respondents over the age of 65 answered "yes," among those over 50 years the proportion was about 20 per cent; among those over 40 years, it was already 30 per cent; and it was more than 50 per cent among those aged 25–30 years.

Thus came about the failure of academic culture and the downfall of the established institutional equilibrium, with its long-standing academic norms and conventions. New people filled the profession, and the behavioral patterns and value system changed.

Contracts and salaries today

In the beginning of the 2000s, earnings in the academic sector were 25–50 per cent lower than the average in the economy. However, during the last five years the gap has been decreasing mostly due to a significant rise in public spending on higher education. By 2009,

Figure 3.3   Earnings of professional workers and university professors—average wage in the economy (%).
Sources: Monitoring of Educational Markets and Organizations (2008); Federal State Statistics Service (Rosstat) (2009).

the gap between earnings in academia and the rest of the economy averaged at about 10 per cent. However, faculty salaries are still noticeably lower than the earnings of specialists with higher education employed outside academia, let alone senior and mid-level managers (see Figure 3.3).

Today, in contrast to the Soviet period, considerable variations in wages exist between academic fields, which correspond to the demand for the relevant study programs. In any case, as in most countries, the remuneration of a university-employed specialist (e.g., an economist or lawyer) is much lower than that of the same specialist in the business sector. The most in-demand and therefore highly paid departments are economics and social sciences, while the least in-demand and therefore poorly paid are arts and natural sciences (see Figure 3.4).

The main determinants of academic salaries at universities are rank—which determines a budget category on the wage scale and, consequently, the size of the wage component of the budget—academic degree, teaching loads (extra loads are especially important), and administrative services (see Figure 3.5). Relevant payments constitute about 70 per cent of the earnings of a higher education institution teacher. The remaining 30 per cent is paid in the form of bonuses.

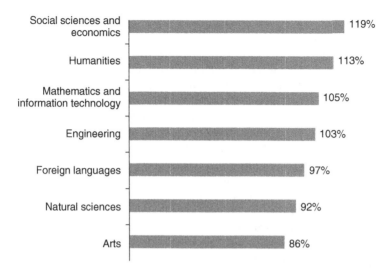

Figure 3.4 Ratio of average wages of faculty in various disciplines, based on average salary in the university sector (%).
Source: Monitoring of Educational Markets and Organizations (2009).

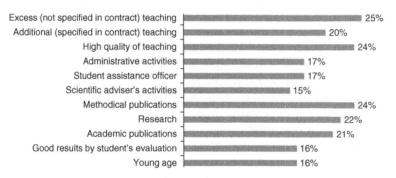

Figure 3.5 Percentage of teachers receiving various allowances.
Source: Monitoring of Educational Markets and Organizations (2008).

Overall, with regard to setting up faculty remuneration, university policy is based on several aspects of a prevailing model of university governance. First, according to federal regulations, the principal decision maker within a Russian university is the academic senate—the "soviet" of faculty. The rector, in turn, is just supposed to be the administrator. However, in reality, the hierarchical model of decision making prevails in Russian universities, with the rector as a major decision maker, and the academic senate just formally approving their decisions (Panova 2008).

Second, most of the universities receive just enough federal funding to cover the costs of teaching and property maintenance, as determined by the current allocation-per-student formula. Some universities receive additional public funds, to cover the costs of research; but that amount is significant at only 5 per cent of Russian universities, so public funding for research is negligible. Therefore, average faculty salary received for teaching activities from their primary employment contract does not differ significantly between various universities. No substantial differences occur between universities in Moscow and the regions, either between main campuses and their regional branches or by discipline. Probably the only exception is the north of Russia, where people receive the so-called northern allowance. However, living costs there are generally higher, and that may outweigh the allowance.

Third, the system of approved per-student spending, calculated for each university, was introduced as recently as 2011, based on historical patterns of per-student spending that previously depended primarily on the rectors' communications skills and connections in the ministries.

Fourth, given the extreme rigidity of federal prescriptions regarding spending of public funds, academic councils are pursuing policies aimed at attracting as much private funding as possible, which in Russia comes mainly from tuition. Those funds can be redistributed at the discretion of the universities—that is, academic councils and rectors. Obviously, no less than 70 per cent of private funding ends up in the payroll.

In academic contracts, the basic part of salaries is rather small and is usually secured with public funding. By cleverly allocating time between teaching and research and some forms of internal moonlighting, faculty may receive quite substantial additions to the basic teaching salaries; but the obvious downside is an overloaded faculty. Universities with a large share of funds coming from private sources use them to increase faculty salaries.

Pension schemes and health-care plans are legally guaranteed to all employees, including university faculty. There are few additional benefits beyond a two-month annual paid leave. In a small number of cases, a teacher may receive temporary housing at the university. This may even be the primary motivation for working for a university, but such cases are rather exceptional and not the rule.

It would, however, be incorrect to say that the long summer vacation is the only nonmonetary benefit. The main issue in this situation is that, despite relatively low salaries, for many faculty members the professorial status at a public university, in conjunction with a sufficiently large amount of free time, is of great value. This status can be monetized through private tuition, part-time teaching in other public or private universities, and in other ways.

Formal contracts and informal supplements

The academic contract system in Russian higher education not only represents the formal parts of the contract but also the existing system of expectations—between universities and individual faculty members—and the mechanisms that support such expectations. The way academic contracts are formally organized in Russia is largely a result of the internal organizational peculiarities of Russian universities. These are described below.

Chairs

Chairs (*kafedras*) are the smallest organizational units (subdepartments) and, at the same time, the center of decision making relating to the educational process (including faculty recruitment). Formally, a chair is defined as a narrow research area, developed by those employed by the chair. This position is a highly hierarchical structure ruled by the head of chair, which, basically, makes all the main decisions. Therefore, when new faculty are hired, they are employed by a specific chair, rather than a department. An average state university in Russia has approximately 15 chairs, while a private one has around ten chairs. A state university employs an average of 12 teachers in an average chair, while a private one has just 8. Departments, which may be called institutes in some universities (usually engineering ones), make up another hierarchical level in Russian universities. Departments effectively unite chairs that provide courses within one educational program. Unlike departments at US universities, chairs in Russia are characterized by a greater concentration of power, stronger hierarchical patterns, and the fact that a chair is a teaching unit in the first place.

Teaching load

The main tool for coordination, planning, and control of the educational process is determining an individual teaching load (at the chair level) and an aggregate load for the chair (at the department level). The teaching load is the amount of instruction a teacher (or chair) needs to provide, during an academic year. The annual load is calculated in hours; a teaching assistant's workload is 750 hours per year, versus

600 hours for professors. Such a workload means that a teacher has at least three full days of instruction a week, sometimes even four, which leaves minimum time for research.

Activities in individual workloads

Most of the teaching process takes place in lectures and seminars, which are not equivalent in value for calculating the workload; lecturing hours are recorded at double rate. Besides contact hours, the teaching load also takes into account the time spent on grading homework, test papers and exams, tutoring term papers and theses, and working with postgraduate students. There are no graders (students hired to review homework) in Russia; all work is done by the teachers themselves.

Hiring policies: theory and practice

To hire a new faculty member, a chair should have a relevant open position, available with a guaranteed teaching load. Formally, it is a competition-based recruitment: if there is a vacant position or if term contracts with some faculty members are about to expire, the university publishes advertisements as part of the hiring process—on the university's website, in mass media, or through employment services, including private ones. Finding new faculty on the "open market" usually takes place when a university is opening new educational programs. In all other cases, there is no open competition (or any, at all). While information about new positions is distributed, no one regards it as a real opportunity for anyone outside the university. In fact, the head of the chair—with his or her connections (including informal ones)—decides on the extension of existing contracts and new recruits for associate professor positions and higher ones. Teaching assistants and teacher positions are usually filled by young graduates or postgraduate students of the same chair (for reasons mentioned above).

Only in exceptional circumstances is an existing contract not extended. Yet, meeting formal requirements for faculty (such as published research and methodology papers or positive feedback from students) is significant. These are one of the parameters used to assess the chair's performance as a whole, for which the chair head is responsible. At the same time, the chair's publications—both research and didactic ones—are relevant at the university level, as well. The relevant ministry provides additional allowance for university administration, if faculty members are strong and manage their work effectively. As a result, there is an internal system of rewards for faculty members, based on productive work within universities.

Full-time faculty sign a standard employment contract for one, three, or five years. The first contract will usually be signed for one year, the next one for three years; and then the contract is extended every five years, if there are no complications or complaints on either side. The extension of a contract does not entail any major changes (regarding workload, wage, etc.). While tenure does not exist, due to the lack of any real competition for teaching positions and the fact that contracts are extended nearly automatically, faculty members treat their contracts as permanent. Thus, while there is no de jure tenure system, a de facto tenure system does exist. People's expectations and hence strategies are formed under the assumption that their job positions (not job conditions or remuneration) are secure. However, the decreasing number of students will, probably, lead to a cutback in teaching positions at universities, until about 2016, and will cause more internal competition. The main things defined in the contract are basic salary and teaching load. A lecturer's contract determines the teaching load for their position, while the individual curriculum is determined yearly.

A chair's aggregate load is defined by the courses assigned to it in the program's syllabus. This creates strong incentives for chairs to increase their number of courses in the academic curriculum. The chair's load is distributed among its faculty, by the head of the chair, before the beginning of each academic year. Therefore, the decision of the chair head determines the real teaching load of each employee.

Contract expectations

Faculty's main function is teaching, which is heavily regulated by the teaching-load calculation procedure. Yet, lecturers are supposed to do research, as well; so, they work under the looming imperative that "one has to do research in order to be a good teacher."

However, the labor contract defines neither the amount of research to be produced nor the expected results. Any attempts to formalize the time split between teaching and research are unlikely to succeed, given that most faculty members do not even hold their own workplaces and only come to the chair offices in between classes.

In any case, the university contract is a rather incomplete framework, regarding mutual responsibilities, and reflects conditions in a general form (not specific to each individual). Many faculty members have just a vague idea about the contents of their contract, which is a well-established, semi-formal convention. The results of a faculty survey demonstrate that only 55 per cent of respondents mention that the total teaching workload is mentioned in the contract, while in reality it always is (Monitoring of Educational Markets and Organizations 2008). Only slightly more than half of the respondents know that it is formally stated in their contracts that they are required to produce research. So, faculty never consider their contracts as working guidelines—relying mainly either on academic norms that exist in the department or in direct agreement with the department chair, who is viewed as a direct employer in most cases.

Basically teachers cannot negotiate their contract conditions, due to the highly hierarchical nature of faculty–administration relations. However, they face an increase in real workload, given the vast paperwork now required for formal reporting on teaching and research (Panova 2008) and the high level of hierarchic control in Russian universities.

The heavy teaching load in their primary job and additional employment (to be discussed further) means that, for most teachers, research output either diminishes to a mere formality or is not done at all. According to the Monitoring of Educational Markets and Organizations, only about 20 per cent of all university faculty engage in paid research. On average, research is allocated around 8 hours per week (compared to the 18 contact hours and 11 hours of preparatory work).

Also, research performance does not serve as a significant factor when it comes to extending academic contracts. University chairs and departments are, on the whole, interested in the impressive research results of their faculty, which are required for external reports. Thus, they create opportunities for the improvement of such criteria, through publishing internal paper digests, internal conference proceedings, and other options.

Without a single faculty assessment system, there is no review of performance results; instead "inputs" such as teaching load, compulsory teaching materials stored at the chair, and detailed syllabi of the courses taught are monitored.

Calculating wages

The wage that is specified in the contract includes several parts: a state-budget component—a legally fixed minimum wage that does not exceed one-fourth of the average salary in the country; and allowances—that is, non-budget means. The minimum guaranteed wage is provided from the budget. Faculty may receive allowances for research at the chair head's discretion. On average, though, budget-funded salaries in state universities are about 65–70 per cent of the average salary level in the country. The allowances, including budget-funded ones, are determined mainly by the heads of chairs.

In principle, universities with a significant private-funding component are more or less autonomous, since they can individualize faculty salaries and compete for the best by providing higher salaries, additional grants, and other incentives. The only thing that universities cannot do is decrease the teaching load, because it is fixed for each position and wage level. Likewise, universities do not really engage in competition for professors, even though in theory that would be allowed. The causes for this absence of autonomy include lack of financial resources, the non-existence of a research market, and high social-tension risks in the higher education system.

Therefore, new faculty members are often attracted with incentives other than financial reward. One is the manipulation of workload—that is, giving the person responsibilities that would match the required formal criteria in working hours but cause the member the lowest cost in real time. For example, a day spent in the State Examination Board can be equal in hours to a several-month-long course. Actually, this tactic is also used, in reverse, to dismiss "unwanted" teachers. The second tool is appointing teachers to administrative positions. Establishing a new chair "to suit a professor" is also a common practice if a department is interested in hiring a particular individual.

The way chairs and incentive systems are organized encourages conservation of current practice—in opposition to the modernization of education programs or even any changes in the education process. Being more interested in preserving and increasing their existing workload (and resource allocation), chairs often oppose more flexible curricula, where students might be free to choose their educational directions.

Employment patterns and sources of remuneration

Teachers have options for increasing their salaries, and the most common are described in the following sections.

Research

Participation in paid research has grown significantly in recent years. In 2006, only about 14 per cent of all faculty participated in research projects; by 2008 their share reached 20 per cent (see Table 3.1). Still, these indicators remain very low.

Table 3.1   Faculty engaged in different aspects of research, 2007–2008

Forms of research	Faculty (%)
Writing academic papers and monographs without additional funding	54.1
Participation in research projects financed by the university	37.9
Permanent position at a research department of a higher education institution	12.5
Grants for research-teams by research-grant providers	9.9
Research projects finances by governmental agencies	8.9
Research projects in other higher education institutions	8.5
Permanent position at a research institution or a research department in another higher education institution	6.2
Grants for individual researchers by research-grant providers	5.7
Permanent research or consultancy position at a commercial enterprise	2.5
Working on innovations and patenting activities without additional funding	1.8

Source: Monitoring of Educational Markets and Organizations (2008).

Research performance indicators listed in Table 3.2—based on a representative survey of university faculty—are also low. Performance is generally measured by publications in journals, produced within the same university; or by new teaching materials, developed for one's own courses. Sharing one's research results is unpopular, too. Faculty members usually give presentations at conferences and seminars, organized within their own university.

Many lecturers say that the main reasons why they cannot do research are lack of time and the fact that research is poorly funded, if at all (see Table 3.3). However, those who do participate in research earn up to one-third of their income from it. In 2008, teachers' average monthly income was around US$880, while research might represent an additional US$250; for reference, according to the Federal State Statistics Service, the average salary in Russia in 2008 was slightly less than US$600.

Yet, faculty participation in paid research is an exception rather than the rule. On average, only 6–8 per cent of the universities' aggregate income comes as payments for research or engineering development, and 80 per cent of all money spent on research comes from the state budget. Around 30 or 40 leading Russian universities receive a budget for research.

Table 3.2 Publications, conference attendance, and other activities related to teaching and research, 2008

Teaching and research activity	Proportion of academic staff engaged in the activity (%)	Average number of publications/ projects per faculty member per year
Publications in Russian academic journals	33.1	3.0
Publications in journals edited by the faculty member's higher education institution	40.9	2.2
Publications in academic journals edited by other higher education institutions	23.0	2.0
Working papers for the faculty member's higher education institution	8.9	2.3
Working papers for other higher education institutions	5.4	2.0
Chapters in books or monographs	9.8	1.8
Books or monographs	8.5	1.6
Textbooks	22.5	1.8
Other publications related to methods of teaching	36.8	2.7
Presentations at conferences held by the faculty member's higher education institution	40.6	2.0
Presentations at other conferences	30.9	2.3
Presentations at seminars held by the faculty member's higher education institution	21.0	2.0
Presentations at other seminars	11.9	2.1
Formal reports based on the results of completed research	15.3	1.7
Formal reports related to methods of teaching	5.9	2.0
Patents	1.9	2.0

Source: Monitoring of Educational Markets and Organizations (2008).

Table 3.3   Factors that impede faculty from carrying out research

Factors	Faculty[a] (%)
Lack of time	34.5
No economic rewards	31.5
No funding provision for conference attendance	25.7
Insufficient funding for research activities (data collection, expendables, etc.) or inadequate equipment	19.5
Results of research are not in demand overall	7.8
No relevant literature or academic periodicals	4.5
Personal expertise not relevant for research	3.7
No opportunities for publications	3.5
No interest in research	2.7
Poor health or lack of stamina	2.6

Note: [a] Faculty who mentioned the corresponding factors.
Source: Monitoring of Educational Markets and Organizations (2008).

Administrative responsibilities

Administrative work is an important source of income for university teachers. According to faculty surveys, up to one-third of them are, in one way or another, involved in administrative processes. Administrative responsibilities include coordination, control, and micromanagement in chairs—as well as responsibility for writing various reports for central university administration and external agencies. The time spent on that work compares to the average number of contact hours per teacher and amounts to 18 hours per week. The income of those who do administrative work, besides teaching, is about 50 per cent higher, compared to those who only do teaching.

Additional employment

For many teachers, working in several universities at the same time is a way to increase their income, substantially. According to the 2007 Monitoring of Educational Markets and Organizations, about 22 per cent of teachers worked in more than one university.

A lecturer with a higher workload within the chair (occupying more than one position) can also have positions at other chairs, within the same university. Such a practice means that a teacher signs several contracts, approved by all the heads of chairs involved; it is because of the lack of opportunity for a full workload within one chair or the desire to earn a little more.

In addition to their primary work, a faculty member may also teach at a "for-profit" educational program within the same university, something that is relatively widespread. This might be a master of business administration program or a vocational training program. This practice involves teaching only and is funded based on a separate labor contract or, more often, an ordinary contractor agreement, depending on the number of hours required. Hourly rates at such programs are usually much higher, and the opportunity to teach there is usually regarded as compensation for an underpaid primary job.

Statistically, faculty at private universities are more likely to teach at several universities. This is mainly because most faculty in the private sector are employed part time. No legal restrictions prevent faculty from working at several universities. While multiple commitments are not really encouraged, administrators do wish to keep good faculty. Yet, it is known that salaries are not high enough to prevent teachers from seeking additional income. Moreover, professors who receive low salaries at good public universities do leverage their status and reputation by giving private lessons to prospective students and/or teaching at private universities and gaining more earnings there.

Furthermore, multiple employment has a negative effect on interchair and interdepartmental cooperation. The time per day teachers spend at university boils down to contact hours, because the rest of the time is spent between several universities.

Tutoring

Until recently, tutoring prospective students (giving private lessons) was a substantial source of income for a large number of university faculty. Chiefly, this process was encouraged by the system of separate entrance exams, which existed at universities until 2007. Formally, such exams could not test students in areas outside the secondary school curriculum. However, some of the universities violated those rules—especially, in math, natural sciences, and economics—and used sets of problems in exams that could be solved by an insight or a sophisticated technique that was not supposed to be taught at schools. These questions in the exams usually required specific training and "insider information." This resulted in a high demand for private tutoring and, in 2006, up to 45 per cent of all teachers did such work (see Table 3.4).

Many households regarded tutoring as essential to prepare for university admission, and this attitude has proved to be extremely stable. Yet, with the countrywide introduction of Unified State Exam, which blocked informal ways of getting into universities, tutoring ceased to

Table 3.4 Teachers engaged in activities outside the home institution 2008 (%)

Activities	Social sciences (%)	Humanities and education science (%)	Natural sciences and mathematics (%)	Engineering (%)
Teaching at other government-funded institutions	29	22	20	9
Teaching at other private institutions	21	11	6	5
Teaching at special training courses for applicants to higher education or vocational secondary education institutions	4	6	6	2
Teaching at other educational programs (further education, etc.)	16	16	7	13
Work at research centers and institutes, etc.	6	3	7	7
Individual research projects, grant-funded research	5	5	6	4
Group research projects, grant-funded research	12	10	14	17
Writing books or articles, editing, reviewing, translating, etc., for a fee	16	12	8	8
Non-academic work in the public sector	3	2	1	2
Non-academic work in the private sector	8	3	3	6
Entrepreneurship or non-academic jobs	3	2	1	2
Tutoring, private education, private preparation for higher education or vocational secondary education institutions, schools, etc.	9	15	13	3
Private non-teaching services	6	6	2	3

Note: The percentages are based on the overall number of faculty.
Source: Monitoring of Educational Markets and Organizations (2008).

be as effective a means of guaranteeing admission. However, many households with high school students applying to universities still actively seek tutors. Therefore, that position remains important to faculty income, though it may lose significance over time. The incidence of finding additional, non-academic sources of income (particularly in consulting) varies by discipline (see Table 3.4).

Corruption and informal payments received from students

Informal or semi-formal payments from students remain a substantial source of income for most teachers at weak universities. These payments can contribute to a good grade, reduced course assignments (such as course papers), tutoring for weak students (usually on the subject taught by the same lecturer or assistant), or even an opportunity to retake an exam for additional money.

Given the extremely low wages, such informal payments are becoming crucial to keep faculty at universities. The university administration indulges such practices: first, because they are unable to offer adequate remuneration for teaching; second, because of the need to accommodate self-funded students, who provide a substantial part of the university's income. Since self-funded students are usually weaker than those accepted to government-funded places, they generally cannot master the education program (on average, government-funded students score 75 out of 100 on the Unified State Exam; the average score for self-funded students is 60).

Such a phenomenon makes the whole education system vulnerable because it creates pseudo-education, where a system of mutual need between teachers and students upsets a healthier equilibrium. Students can expect good grades (and a university diploma, in the end), without truly acquiring substantial knowledge or putting in serious effort; while faculty, in turn, minimize their teaching output and increase their income.

Inefficient lock-in

Low salaries, the "exodus" of highly qualified professionals, the low prestige of the academic profession, and the lack of integration with the production sector, these changed conditions, create a new institutional equilibrium. This equilibrium took shape in the late 2000s, when new institutions paying low salaries emerged.

The defining characteristic of this new culture involves academic and research provincialism. Many faculty and researchers who write articles and dissertations neither read nor cite relevant international publications.

Another pattern that developed during the past seven to eight years is in reality an imitation of research. Academic promotion still depends on quantity indicators, such as the number of research papers and other indicators. However, related phenomena consist of purchasing papers or articles, written by other people, and passing them off as one's own; or compiling manuscripts that are not really research papers but take the shape of dissertations, articles, or monographs. While the rate at which people with PhD degrees are awarded stays the same (in comparison to the 1970s to 1980s), the number of doctors of sciences has grown 300 per cent in the past two decades since 1990.

Moreover, two other types of corruption have emerged in higher education: entrance corruption, when faculty members charge prospective students for getting government-funded (free) places; and corruption during the education process, when students and faculty members trade for grades. Many young and middle-aged teachers are involved into such activity.

Yet, the safest and most socially acceptable practice for faculty to increase their wages is to acquire external employment (e.g., consulting and entrepreneurial activities). Honest teachers receive their main income outside academia, while dishonest ones obtain more cash inside universities, through corruption.

Qualifications and promotion

Most faculty at Russian higher education institutions achieved a higher education degree—a diploma or higher. About 64 per cent of teachers have PhD degree. To start an academic career at a university, a faculty member would mainly need a diploma (bachelor's level and above) to conduct seminars and tutorials. However, in order to provide lectures, faculty need (with few exceptions) a PhD-equivalent degree.

In the 1930s, the Soviets adopted the German academic system of two levels of postgraduate degree. The first level, candidate of sciences, is equivalent to the German *Doktor* degree and is required for an associate professor position; the second, doctor of sciences, corresponds with the German habilitation, is necessary for a full-professor position and various administrative posts in academia—such as heads of chairs, deans, vice rectors, and rectors (see Table 3.5).

Table 3.5 Highest degree of most professors

	Master's degree	% of higher education institutions	% of faculty in higher education institutions	% of candidates of sciences in full-time faculty	% of doctors of sciences in full-time faculty
Federal universities	Provided	2.3	7.2	49.1	14.2
National research universities		7.0	13.8	50.7	14.2
Leading technical and profiled technological universities		28.2	26.4	51.4	12.3
Socio economic, humanities and pedagogical universities		28.2	31.6	52.8	11.4
Bachelor universities and colleges	Not provided	34.3	21.1	51.7	9.3
Total/average		100.0	100.0	51.6	11.8

Source: Monitoring of Educational Markets and Organizations (2008).

Most faculty at public Russian higher education institutions are associate professors (about 40%), and 20 per cent are professors, including chair heads and heads of departments. In Russia, universities' higher administration (presidents, rectors, and vice rectors) are traditionally counted as faculty, too. On the whole, these administrators amount to nearly 2 per cent of all faculty. Senior lecturers and assistants constitute 21 per cent and 15 per cent of the faculty body, respectively.

Promotions at lower academic levels (e.g., from senior lecturer to assistant professor) are subject to obtaining a degree, and certificates to confirm the formal qualification. As for higher positions (e.g., professor), these important roles (contingent on a doctoral degree) are assigned, based on work experience at the same institution. Internal assignments to senior positions reflect low academic mobility between universities and the lack of competitive mechanisms for allocating positions.

Inbreeding

Inbreeding, which means recruiting one's own graduates as faculty and staff, is a common practice at Russian universities. Even though research shows the negative effect of inbreeding on academic performance at the individual, departmental, and national level, it happens at many Russian higher education institutions (Dutton 1980; Eisenberg and Wells 2000; Horta, Veloso, and Grediaga 2010; and Marwell 1974).

The 2007 survey of economics departments at Saint Petersburg universities, conducted by the Laboratory of Institutional Analysis at the Higher School of Economics (Sivak and Yudkevich 2009), shows that chair heads regard their own graduates as the target group for filling positions. Clearly, the low salaries make full-time university employment inconceivable for young people who have already entered the labor market and enjoy better salaries, but would not (for a rather long time) receive comparable money at a university. Thus, universities keep students and postgraduates who are inclined to do teaching and research. Inbreeding does, however, cause an additional negative result: graduates who remain at their universities—not usually the brightest ones—have little external work experience, do not belong to wider academic networks, and lack academic connections outside their own university or even the department. These graduates more or less pass on their own knowledge, received at the same university, to the next generations of students. Their academic supervisors and heads of chairs remain indisputable academic authorities for the graduates.

Of course, faculty members at universities where they graduated show stronger inbreeding-oriented recruitment strategies. Faculty who graduated from other universities are more likely to support externally oriented recruitment policy and welcome "new blood." Yet, as usually very few such colleagues exist, they provide little opportunity to influence the policy (Sivak and Yudkevich 2009).

Inbreeding affects many aspects of a university's academic life. Teachers without any outside experience rarely publish in external journals (since their writing is mostly focused on departmental or university publications) or participate in external conferences. They participate in narrower academic networks, usually only linked to their own colleagues within their chair or their department, and chained to their own academic supervisor or head of chair. Inbred faculty are much more inclined to teach rather than to do research (Gouldner 1957, 1958; Tuma and Grimes 1981). This preference seems rather logical because teaching includes certain university-related investments at the particular university—unlike research.

As a result, this exclusiveness affects the norms that regulate research in at least three ways. First, certain local rules and standards on research and publications emerge, and the alienation from the external peer environment negatively impacts research quality. Second, some local disciplines and fields appear, traditionally developed within only one university. Finally, developing or supporting a certain research field is defined not by external factors (such as marketability) but rather by the private interests of individuals.

Often, inbreeding enables a system of informal contracts (a system of mutual responsibilities and expectations) between older and younger, and senior and junior members of faculty. So, inbreeding encourages paternalism (guarding and promoting one's disciples) and a kind of clan system, as well as the tight informal connections.

The high level of specific investments and long hours spent at the university lead to faculty being oriented toward internal networks. In contrast, people aspiring to a mobile career want to remain competitive in the market. Therefore, they make fewer investments in teaching and administrative work and put more effort into research to achieve results that are viewed and valued in the external academic market. Thus, if the latter faculty share rather cosmopolitan values, the former prefer local values and show fidelity to their own university.

In an autonomous system, internal organizational rules dominate over external professional influences. In particular, external expertise is eclipsed by the internal expertise, which is not immune to the informal influence of internal networks. As a result, situations exist where promotion is based not on transparent academic achievements but on internal status and prestige. Moreover, inbreeding-oriented traditions make research performance less relevant compared to affiliation with a certain institution, school, or political group. All of that affects research performance and its competitive potential in the global academic market.

Differentiation on the academic landscape

Concerning academic contracts, faculty remuneration, and research performance, it would be misleading to describe the situation using averages. Indeed, the levels and structure of faculty remuneration, as well as participation in research, are not at all homogenous. However, the heterogeneity is quite difficult to measure by indicators alone; the system of reporting to the Ministry of Education and Science favors imitation and institutional "isomorphism."

At the same time, there are substantial differences. The division of universities by funding for research per lecturer and funding for teaching per student is quite indicative. Most of the 400 Russian universities are inadequately funded for teaching and produce little research. Only 25 to 30 of all universities receive better funding, have better research performance, and are in higher demand. Practically all were selected by the Russian government, in 2009, as members of the national research universities.[3]

Research practices

Examining the practices and views of the faculty in the economics department at one of the leading Russian universities,[4] helps in understanding research practices in the fields that suffered most during the transition period or whose tradition only began in post-Soviet Russia.

The majority of the teachers named their academic supervisor and head of chair as the person whose opinion on their research mattered most—rarely mentioning their colleagues or specialists from other universities. Most of the teachers are chained to the inner circle of the chair or department in their routine practices, values, and attitudes. External connections are mainly used only for external reporting requirements. Only 20 per cent of the respondents mentioned "the importance of the academic environment" as a necessary condition for effective research;

and fewer than 40 per cent claimed the need to have access to academic databases.

For most of the teachers, Russian-language books and articles are the main sources of information; less than half of them use foreign books or articles in their work. Most of their publications feature articles from conference proceedings (usually held at their own university), manuals and teaching notes (usually published by their own university), and articles in journals (again, usually at the university level). Many respondents also mentioned grant reports as the results of their research activities (the most frequent answer).

Paying journals and digests to publish articles is also widespread (even in good universities). Thus, 56 per cent of the respondents within this university admitted having paid to have their articles published.

Attempts at reform in contemporary Russia

What are the possible dynamics of both wages and academic contracts, within Russian higher education? What challenges face the academic profession, and what can universities and the state do to address them? To address these issues, it is useful to consider the conditions, opportunities, and limitations that Russian universities face.

Competition-based (differentiated) support mechanisms

A differentiated approach is needed to support universities in the Russian higher education system today, as the system involves so many universities. Indeed, the distribution of funding between the research universities and the rest of the institutions would lead to insufficient support of strong research teams, on the one hand, and an inefficient conservation of weak academic groups, on the other hand.

The government's first step to support higher education was targeted at a limited number of the best universities, selected on a competitive basis. The first competition (the Innovative Education Program) took place in 2006 and 2007. As a result, approximately 50 universities received substantial additional funding for two years. Significantly, this program mostly supported teaching practices—development of education programs, development of new courses and manuals, teachers' skill improvement, and new training equipment. Yet, at the end of the program, additional funding ended; then, universities that used the money to start some systemic changes faced serious problems.

In 2009, a new competition—again to identify the best universities—was announced and awarded 14 universities the status of national research university. These universities were selected on the basis of their level of research and on the quality of strategic development programs that they offered. Basically, both the present and future potential of these universities were judged.

Other criteria were discussed—such as the average level of income a professor received within the university. Another indicator is whether the university is involved in international projects with global academic networks, and international teaching and research standards. The level of links with global networks and the ability to embrace international expertise and standards of quality may be appropriate selection criteria for the government to determine the allocations of funds to universities.

The Russian government selected 25–30 universities to participate in the research universities experiment and to receive better financing, expecting them to show better research results. However, they represent 3–4 per cent of all universities, and this percentage is, of course, not high enough to influence practices and culture in the whole system.

Furthermore, systemic changes require not only supporting the best universities, but also working with average universities and developing policy measures aimed at eliminating weak universities. So, the government and the academy face another challenge. They need to not only to define strategies for national research universities but also to think seriously about how to change the majority of universities. Otherwise, the impact of the national research universities will not lead to a change of situation for the whole country.

Reorganizing the university system

With the decreased numbers of high school graduates, higher education institutions face more competition for students. Weak universities try to fill tuition-funded places and to preserve the number of places for university entrants secured with public funding at the current level; this means admitting even weaker students. Since these students are often only interested in higher education for the sake of credentials, they tend to apply to programs not in high demand. At Russian universities, these programs include engineering. So, such universities enroll students without the preparation or talent for the degree program, judging by their United State Exam results. In some cases, teachers accept money for good grades in exams or for additional classes, a practice which (as already stated) is further reinforced by low wages. This model does not receive any criticism from the university administration, since payments from students retain faculty—which their contract wages cannot do. Also, universities do not expel current students, given the budget implications.

To rationalize this system, the number of places funded with public funding, for certain specializations, could be decreased. Some steps in this direction have already been carried out. For example, in 2011, government-funded places in economics were significantly reduced at certain universities. Cutting budget-funded places means that universities will admit fewer students, who, in their turn, will be better ones. Moreover, this change in funding prevents the admission of really weak students.

In addition, since people view higher education as a social requirement, weak students should have the opportunity to study and to gain higher education diplomas, as well. One method would be to increase the variety of educational paths by forming so-called vocational bachelor's degree programs. These vocational programs would be aimed not at mastering a broad scientific grounding but rather at receiving a minimum amount of theory and the maximum relevant skills for work.

The Russian Ministry for Education and Science is discussing encouraging collaboration between certain weak universities and strong universities. Even though such a step creates some benefits, it brings a lot of risks. The first issue faces the negative effect for the academic staff of strong universities, if joined with faculty at weak universities. Of course, faculty at weak universities usually have a different academic culture: they are more tolerant of informal payments, cheating and plagiarism among students, paid publications, and so on. Moreover, administrators of a strong university will need to provide the same salaries to new employees. Thus, university administrations face the problem of introducing a real review system for teachers and ending contracts with those who are not up to standard. Even though that policy is a good one, such harsh measures do go against common Russian academic norms and practices.

The challenges and opportunities of internationalization

An important objective in supporting the best universities and creating healthier conditions at average universities is integrating the institutions with global academic networks. The integration requires efforts not only from the universities and researchers but also from the government, which must provide a supportive environment—in the role of long-term commitment by the state in building world-class universities, see Khovanskaya, Sonin, and Yudkevich (2009). One aspect of internationalization is recruiting teachers and researchers who studied in leading universities around the world and received internationally recognized PhD degrees. These individuals have, among other qualities, experience of working in a "healthy" academic environment (with the academic norms and routines of a world-class university) and are themselves bearers of the appropriate academic norms.

However, Russian universities, with few exceptions, do not maintain any specific international recruitment policy. First, Russian universities are limited in what they can offer, compared to the salaries at American and western European universities. Even if universities find sufficient funds, they face the problem of long-term guarantees and assurances of their obligations. Moreover, such a policy can create social tension among the faculty, which is bound to occur with differences between relatively low-paid long-employed professors and attractive contracts for younger, recent graduates. Finally, one can foresee a conflict between local and foreign academic norms. The foreign systems are more transparent in terms of recruitment and promotion, and are based on individual research achievements. The local norms are more communal, more informal, and reward age, experience, and time within the university.

The government is making some attempts to create conditions to encourage international cooperation, aimed forming prominent university research centers and labs for potential "breakthrough" research. Thus, the government first launched a competition, aimed at attracting foreign professors, in 2009. In 2010, as a result of the first stage of the competition, several laboratories were created at Russian universities under the supervision of leading academics from abroad, who receive substantial remuneration in exchange for agreeing to spend at least several months a year in Russia. However, this program requires high transaction costs for both parties, particularly due to the academic and bureaucratic differences between Russia and other countries. Complex formal reporting requirements, restrictions on spending state money on equipment, databases, and empirical studies, and other issues have a negative impact on the efficiency of these research groups. At the same time, even though the program's impact has not yet been judged, its positive effect is already clear.

Besides the financial issues, certain legal issues regarding academic employment of foreign nationals are still unsolved. Currently, this type of contract requires universities to apply for quotas and work permits for foreigners and then renew the contracts periodically. In such a situation, it is quite problematic to create a tenure and tenure-track system that would be supported not only by the university's informal structure but also by legal institutions.

In terms of planning the internationalization of national universities, the Chinese experience of recruiting graduates from the best research universities across the world and supporting world-class research centers could be a useful reference. In any case, Russian universities have to overcome the lack of a critical mass of internationally recruited specialists, which could make an impact on the Russian academic environment and address the challenges presented by high-transaction costs caused by bureaucracy and culture.

Notes

1. This yearly Monitoring of Education Markets and Organizations study consists of representative surveys of students and their families, teachers (at schools), faculty from colleges and universities, heads of colleges and universities, and employers. It is designed and administered by the Higher School of Economics, with financial support from the Ministry of Education and Science of the Russian Federation (http://memo.hse.ru/en/about).
2. The data on sources of income, except for public funding, for higher education institutions became available in 2006. By using the official chain price indexes for tuition, and time series for the number of "commercial" students who either paid tuition themselves or for whom the tuition was paid by their employer in 2000–2006, we obtained estimates for the private funding of universities and compared it to public funding. Surveys by the Higher School of Economics show that the proportion of private funding of research activities at universities was negligible during 2000–2008. See Shuvalova (2009).
3. In 2009, the Ministry of Education and Science introduced a new (to the Russian education sector) competitive mechanism for the provision of public funding—aimed at catalyzing research activities, academic collaboration, and renovation. Overall, the status of National Research Universities, and the funding, was granted to 14 universities in 2009 and to 15 universities in 2010.
4. In this section, we use the results of the 2007 survey of teachers and heads of chairs at the economics department of a Russian university, conducted by the Laboratory of Institutional Analysis at the Higher School of Economics.

References

Agamova, N., and A. Allakhverdyan. 2007. Russian brain-drain: Reasons and scope. *Russian Chemistry Journal* (in Russian) 51 (3): 108–115.

Androushchak, G., and M. Yudkevich. 2012. Russian higher education: Salaries and contracts. In *Paying the professoriate: A global comparison of compensation and contracts*, ed. P. G. Altbach, L. Reisberg, M. Yudkevich, G. Androushchak, and I. F. Pacheco, 265–278. New York and London: Routledge.

Dutton, J. E. 1980. The impact of inbreeding and immobility on the professional role and scholarly performance of academic scientists. Paper presented at the annual meeting of the American Educational Research Association, Boston, MA.

Eisenberg, T., and M. T. Wells. 2000. Inbreeding in law school hiring: Assessing the performance of faculty hired from within. *Journal of Legal Studies* 29 (1): 369–388.

Federal State Statistics Service (Rosstat). 2009. http://www.gks.ru/wps/wcm/connect/rossat/rosstatsite/main/population/wages/# (accessed December 30, 2011).

Gouldner, A. 1957. Cosmopolitans and locals: Toward an analysis of latent social roles I. *Administrative Science Quarterly* 2 (3), December: 281–303.

———. 1958. Cosmopolitans and locals: Toward an analysis of latent social roles II. *Administrative Science Quarterly* 2 (4), March: 444–467.

Horta, H., F. Veloso, and R. Grediaga. 2010. Navel gazing: Academic inbreeding and scientific productivity. *Management Science* 56, March: 414–429.

Khovanskaya, I., K. Sonin, and M. Yudkevich. 2009. A dynamic model of the research university, October. Social Science Research Network. http://ssrn.com/abstract=1103291.

Marwell, G. 1974. Comment on "An Examination of Recent Hypotheses about Institutional Inbreeding" by Hargens and Farr. *American Journal of Sociology* 79 (5): 1319–1320.

Monitoring of Education Markets and Organizations. 2008. http://memo.hse.ru/published_ib (accessed December 30, 2011).

———. 2009. http://memo.hse.ru/published_ib (accessed December 30, 2011).

Panova, A. 2008. Governance structures and decision making in Russian higher education. *Russian Social Science Review* 49 (5): 76–93.

Shuvalova O. 2009. Institutions of professional education: Human resources, economics and strategies. [In Russian.] *Information Bulletin of Monitoring of Economics of Education* 1 (36): 20–80.

Sivak, L., and M. Yudkevich. 2009. Academic inbreeding: Pro and contra. [In Russian.] *Voprosy Obrazovania* (1): 170–187.

Tuma, N. B., and A. J. Grimes. 1981. Comparison of models of role orientations of professionals in a research-oriented university. *Administrative Science Quarterly* 26 (2), June.

4
India: Streamlining the Academic Profession for a Knowledge Economy

N. Jayaram

In the land of the guru, the position of the teacher has for a long time been regarded with ambivalence. Traditionally, teachers were accorded the highest esteem and even venerated as a demigod (*deva*), but their economic status was low and they were poor. This was also reflected in the dissonance between the high education qualifications expected of teachers in higher education institutions and the low remuneration. However, as a result of the competing demands for talent in the knowledge economy, occasioned by globalization and the best talent turning away from the academic profession, the salaries of teachers have now been upwardly revised—to an extent that was unthinkable a decade back (Jayaram 2003). The professoriate is now comfortably placed; and the academic profession, it is hoped, will again become attractive in the employment market.

This hope, surely, is not totally misplaced, as improvements in pay packets and service conditions are necessary for rejuvenating the academic profession. They are, however, not sufficient to groom and orient the academic profession, and to realize the promise of higher education in the coming decades. The travails of higher education in India—"a quiet crisis... that runs deep," as the National Knowledge Commission (NKC 2007, 1) describes it—assume contextual significance here. How soon and how effectively India addresses these travails will determine whether this country, among the BRIC (Brazil, Russia, India, and China) countries, can reap the benefits of the demographic window for the next two decades (Altbach and Jayaram 2010; Jayaram 2009).

As Pawan Agarwal observes, "India's large size, long history and diverse culture and the complicated nature of Indian polity and policy process make Indian higher education a very complex enterprise"

(Agarwal 2009). This complexity is compounded by several issues. As a system, higher education has grown in fits and starts; its expansion—far from adequate, given the demand—has been hindered by accessibility and equity issues (Jayaram 2010); and its quality has been varied, with islands of excellence in the ocean of mediocrity. Monitoring and regulating quality has been resisted and ritualized. The language issue in higher education has remained unresolved, decades after independence (Jayaram 1993). There has been no consistent long-term higher education policy for the country as a whole: both federal and state governments make policies; and policymaking is, largely, in the nature of ad hoc response to contingent situations (Tilak 2004).

The system is set to function in the larger socioeconomic and political context. In the quasi-federal polity that India represents, regionalism and parochialism impinge on higher education, promoting inbreeding and impeding mobility. The multiplicity of regulatory mechanisms has bred corruption and nepotism in the system; reports on scandals in institutions of higher education are perennial in the media. In India, "the distinction between the public and private sector is somewhat blurred" with reference to higher education (Agarwal 2009, 67), resulting in blatant privatization of public resources. Even as the federal government dithers about a policy for the private sector in higher education, the faith reposed in this sector for enlarging access to and improving quality of higher education has turned out to be unfounded. Finally, there is the imminent prospect of opening higher education to foreign investment, with its attendant consequences.

Thus, one can hardly be sanguine about the prospects for the academic profession being rejuvenated in the short term or playing a significant role in realizing the promise of higher education in a globalized world. In this context, this chapter discusses the salient features, notable variations, and key issues in the recruitment and remuneration of the professoriate in India. The chapter is divided into 11 thematic sections, analyzing the typology of institutions, varieties of teaching positions, qualifications for the professoriate, the policy of protective discrimination, recruitment procedures, terms of appointment, career advancement, salaries, non-salary benefits, supplementary employment, and international faculty.

Typology of higher education institutions

There has been a rapid expansion of higher education since independence: from 20 universities and 496 colleges in 1947 to 399 universities and university-level (degree-awarding) institutions and 29,951 colleges by the end of 2009. These institutions employ about 488,000 teaching staff and cater to about 11 million students. India, thus, has the third-largest system of higher education in the world, behind China and the United States. This massive system is also diverse: the institutions vary in terms of degree-granting authority, legislative origin, and funding. Broadly, five types of educational institution can be delineated, forming an informal hierarchy:

- institutions of national importance;
- central universities;
- state universities;
- grant-in-aid colleges that are part of, or affiliated to, a university;
- unaided (purely private) universities/colleges.

The differences across institutions are reflected in their recruitment and remuneration systems.

Institutions of national importance include the 16 Indian Institutes of Technology (IITs), three institutions specializing in medical sciences, one specializing in statistical techniques and another the Hindi language.[1] These university-level institutions enjoy special status, accorded them by the Indian Parliament, and they are all funded directly by the Indian government's Ministry of Human Resources Development. They are empowered to award degrees that, according to the 1956 University Grants Commission (UGC) Act, can be granted only by a university. The IITs have carved a niche for themselves as institutions of repute for teaching and research in engineering and technology (Jayaram 2011). While the institutions of national importance are academically and administratively autonomous, they are governed by the rules and regulations of the central government. These institutions are all-India in their orientation, lay greater emphasis on research in addition to teaching, spend more per student, and offer better remuneration and working conditions, when compared to all other universities.

The 40 central universities were established by an act of parliament and are financed by the Ministry of Human Resources Development, through the UGC. They are multidisciplinary in their spread, combining postgraduate teaching (primarily) with research. They do not have colleges affiliated to them—the notable exception being the University of Delhi, which has constituent colleges. Besides these, the central government has recognized 130 institutions as "deemed-to-be universities" under the UGC Act, and some of these institutions are also funded by the Indian government. While these central universities and centrally funded, deemed-to-be universities are academically and administratively autonomous, they are governed by the rules and regulations of the central government. They, like the institutions of national importance, are all-India in their orientation, have better academic reputations, greater research orientation, better remuneration and working conditions, and spend more per student as compared to state universities.

The 239 state universities are established through legislation by the 28 states constituting the Indian federation. As public universities, they receive financial assistance (up to 85%) for five years for all development initiatives (including teaching positions) from the UGC; thereafter, they need to be funded by the respective state governments. They have a central campus housing schools and departments of study that offer instruction largely at the postgraduate (graduate) level and undertake research. Most state universities have colleges affiliated to them, whose academic work they regulate and oversee. While these state universities are academically and administratively autonomous, they are governed by the rules and regulations of the state governments. Some states have a common legislative framework for all their universities.

Grant-in-aid colleges are funded to the tune of 85–90 per cent by the state governments—a practice going back to colonial times. Some of these colleges were established with private resources and came to be financially supported by the state governments. They generally offer first-degree-level education and are affiliated to state universities. The academic standards of these colleges are determined and overseen by the university to which they are affiliated, which also conducts centralized examinations for the enrolled students. These colleges may be dispersed geographically but they are under the jurisdiction of a university, as determined by law. These colleges may be run either by the government, through its department of higher education or by private management bodies.

Unaided (purely private) universities and colleges are privately run institutions; they do not receive any financial support from the government. They rely almost entirely on funding from tuition fees and donations—often given as a consideration for enrollment at the institution. As universities, they are either deemed-to-be universities under the UGC Act or established by an act of the State Legislative Assembly.[2] As compared to the central and state universities, the private universities enjoy greater administrative freedom and autonomy. They are, nevertheless, governed by a broader framework of government rules and regulations. As colleges, they are established and managed by private trusts. While trust laws govern their administration and finance, their academic programs are determined and overseen by the university to which they are affiliated. Since they raise their own funds, the purely private universities and colleges mostly offer programs—like computer science, biotechnology, management studies, and so on—which are in high demand and are financially lucrative.

The bulk of the expanding student enrollments in higher education has taken place in colleges affiliated to state universities, and in first-degree courses (about 84%) leading to bachelor's degrees in arts (46%), science (20%), and commerce (18%) (Agarwal 2009, 10; Kaur 2003, 366). These institutions also employ most of the teachers, and their work almost exclusively entails teaching and examining candidates at the undergraduate level. Among degree-awarding higher education institutions, research is a priority only in the institutions of national importance, central universities, and select departments in state universities. That is, the university system has largely concentrated on retailing knowledge, rather than creating and refining knowledge—a function assigned to specialist institutes and laboratories outside the university system. This peculiar disjunction between universities and research institutes explains the paradox of why the large and experienced system of higher education in India is little known for its excellence in research (Jayaram 2007).

Be that as it may, despite the massive growth in higher education, the gross enrollment ratio has been very low—between the conservative estimate of 7 per cent (NKC 2007, 48) and the liberal estimate of 11 per cent (Agarwal 2009, 10)—compared to other BRIC countries, let alone the advanced industrial countries. Thus, there have been both inadequacies and distortions in higher education expansion in India. Obviously, more of the same policy would be passé, and new thinking to catch up with the rest of the world is called for. Among other things, the problem of faculty shortage—about 54 per cent, according to the Ministry of Human Resources Development's task force report (Times News Network 2011b)—warrants urgent action, as any hope of a well-balanced and sustainable expansion of higher education depends on qualified and capable teachers.

Two points need reiteration here. One is that, in India, the professoriate is devoted to undergraduate teaching in colleges. These colleges feed the state and central universities, where the emphasis is on postgraduate education and research. The second point is that the distinction between public and private sectors in higher education in

India is fuzzy. Many privately established colleges and some deemed-to-be universities gain financial support from the government. With the government having almost stopped financing newly established private institutions, the number of purely private institutions is increasing, especially in the fields of engineering and technology, medicine, and management.

Varieties of teaching positions

In India, the professoriate is not a homogenous category; the different types of teaching positions are characterized by their duration of employment and privileges. The most coveted is the permanent (tenured) teaching position in a public-funded university or college. Appointees to these positions are placed on probation for a period of two years. Probation provides an opportunity for the university/college to evaluate the appointee's strengths and weaknesses as teacher, colleague, and employee—just as it provides an opportunity for the teacher to ascertain the prospect of a suitable academic career. During probation, the institution can terminate the appointment of a teacher by giving one month's notice (or, instantly, by giving a month's salary), without giving any reason for termination. Similarly, a teacher on probation can resign by giving a month's notice (or by paying back a month's salary). In most universities and colleges, probation is viewed as a formality, and teachers on probation rarely have their positions terminated.

The appointees who successfully complete the period of probation are confirmed in the post. Once confirmed, it is rare for a teacher's services to be terminated, unless the individual is found guilty of moral turpitude. The procedure for termination is long and cumbersome, and courts often favor the teacher over the institution. The teacher, however, can resign from her/his post by giving three months' notice or three months' salary, in lieu of the notice period. Teachers in permanent positions wishing to move to another institution, for the same or a higher position, generally do so by tendering technical resignation—in order to retain, in their new job, the service and other benefits linked to a permanent position. This is done because teachers in public-funded higher education institutions (including grant-in-aid private colleges) are treated on par with civil servants, and under civil service regulations no person can hold two permanent positions concurrently.

The age of superannuation ranges from 65 years of age (as in central universities and centrally funded institutions) to 60–62 years of age in state universities and grant-in-aid colleges. Teachers holding a permanent position can voluntarily retire from their post with the benefit of a full pension, after completing 20 years of uninterrupted service. They can also be compulsorily retired (as a penalty), or prematurely retired (in the public interest), or retired on medical grounds (after 50 years of age or 30 years of service). All retirements (other than superannuation) can be effected by giving three months' notice. There are no gender differences regarding the superannuation of teachers.

In centrally funded institutions, superannuated teachers may be re-employed for one year at a time—for up to five years. Such a practice is subject to evaluation of the teacher and the teaching requirements of the institution. Re-employment is entirely at the discretion of the institution, and it cannot be claimed as a matter of right. Re-employed teachers continue to receive all the benefits that they had before superannuating.

Permanent positions are nonexistent in purely private universities and colleges. Appointment to teaching positions in such institutions is contractual in nature. The duration of the contract ranges from about five months (one semester) to five years. The terms of the contract may vary from case to case, and they are specifically spelled out in each case—unlike the terms of appointment to permanent positions, which are uniform and stipulated in the statutes and ordinances governing public-funded institutions. Given the shortage of well-qualified and experienced teachers, retired teachers often find opportunities for contractual appointments in purely private institutions. Since contractual appointments offer greater flexibility in human-resource management and involve limited long-run financial commitments, even public-funded institutions are now turning to such appointments.

Both permanent and contractual teaching positions involve full-time engagement in teaching and research in the institution. This is different from the part-time teaching position. In India, the concept of part-time teachers (who serve a specified number of teaching hours per week) and guest faculty (who help the college/department to complete portions of the syllabus) originated as a result of the unmet demand for teachers in particular disciplines. For some positions, full-time teachers were either not available (in narrow fields of specializations) or could not be appointed to a full-time position (as they would not have sufficient workload—defined as the number of classroom teaching hours). Typically, part-time teachers and guest faculty are paid a consolidated sum, as remuneration for the hours of teaching work in their assignment. Their monthly remuneration is nowhere near what a permanent teacher receives. Furthermore, they are not entitled to any statutory employment benefits—leave, medical insurance, a pension, gratuities, etc. Obviously, they are looked down upon within the system, as daily wage workers. Guest lecturers, if they are professionals (medical doctors, lawyers, chartered accountants, etc.), carry better status than those who are underemployed master's degree holders.

A modality of the appointment of teachers has gradually become an interim solution to a practical problem in academic administration, especially in private colleges that do not receive governmental support.[3] State universities also depend on part-time teachers, while central universities rarely do so. From the college or university's point of view, it is obviously more economical to employ part-time teachers instead of permanent teachers. There is greater flexibility in the hiring and firing of part-time teachers, particularly considering the large number of unemployed or underemployed master's degree holders.

From the prospective candidates' perspective, part-time teaching offers some employment opportunity and the possibility of gaining experience, which may be useful as (and when) opportunities arise for more stable or full-time permanent/contractual employment. Periodically, part-time teachers, with ten or more years of service, have brought political pressure to bear on the state governments to regularize their appointments on humanitarian grounds. Courts of law have also been sympathetic to this cause. To overcome the administrative and financial problems, which result from such backdoor entry into the academic profession as encouraged by grant-in-aid private colleges, some governments have abolished the post of part-time teachers and suggested the reappointment of retired teachers on a contract or hourly basis (Jayaram 2003).

For the optimal utilization of staff, several states have introduced a provision for the transfer of teachers between the colleges funded by them. Similarly, states with a common legal framework for universities have introduced a provision for the transfer of university teachers between states for administrative convenience. Such transfers often become contentious regarding claims of seniority and other issues. While some teachers use influence or bribes to get transferred to places or institutions of their choice, the educational bureaucracy uses transfer as a weapon for dealing with recalcitrant or vexatious teachers.

Thus, teachers in Indian higher education are heterogeneous in terms of the positions they hold in the system. While revising the salary and service conditions of teachers in higher education in 2006, the UGC has attempted the difficult task of standardizing the qualifications of various categories of teachers, the procedures for recruiting them, the requirements and process of their career advancement, and the salaries and non-salary benefits to which they are entitled. The following sections present this standardization, in various aspects of the academic profession.

Qualifications for the professoriate

Since January 2006, a three-tier academic hierarchy—namely, professor, associate professor, and assistant professor—has been standardized in publicly funded higher education institutions across the country. In most cases, entry into the academic profession is at the assistant professor's level, both in university departments and colleges.[4] To maintain the quality of higher education, the UGC has prescribed the minimum qualifications for appointment to teaching and other academic positions (such as college principals and various cadres of librarians, directors of physical education, etc.) in the universities and colleges (UGC 2010). Table 4.1 summarizes the minimum qualifications at each level of the professoriate.

Table 4.1 Summary of qualifications for professoriate

Designation	Level	Minimum educational qualification	Qualifying test	Work experience	Additional qualification
Assistant professor	Entry	Good academic record; master's degree in the subject with 5.5 points on a 10-point scale	NET/SLET[a]	Not necessary, but preference given to candidate with work experience	Not prescribed; but preference given to candidates with publications
Associate professor	Midcareer	PhD (plus the above)	None	Eight years	API Score[b]
Professor	Top-end	PhD and eminence as a scholar	None	Ten years	API score[b]

Notes: [a]NET = National Eligibility Test; SLET = State Level Eligibility Test.
[b]API score = Academic Performance Indicator Score.
Source: Adapted from UGC (2010).

For appointment to the post of an assistant professor—in arts, humanities, sciences, social sciences, commerce, education, languages, law, journalism, and mass communication—in a college, university or university-level institution, a candidate must have obtained a score of 5.5, on a 10-point scale, at the master's level examination in the relevant subject.[5] Furthermore, the candidates must have passed the National Eligibility Test or an accredited test (State Level Eligibility Test).[6] Candidates with a PhD degree are, however, exempt from the requirement of a National Eligibility Test qualification. Similar exemption exists for applicants with master's degrees in disciplines for which this test is not conducted.

For appointment to the post of associate professor through direct recruitment—besides a score of 5.5, as above—a PhD in the concerned/allied/relevant discipline is a mandatory qualification. In addition, candidates must have put in a minimum of eight years of teaching and/or research in an academic/research position equivalent to that of assistant professor in a university, college, or accredited research institution. They must:

- show evidence of being engaged in research and have a minimum of five publications as books and/or research/policy papers to their credit;
- have contributed to educational innovation, designing of new curricula and courses, and technology-mediated, teaching-learning processes;
- have successfully guided doctoral candidates.

Finally, they must have secured a minimum score as stipulated in the Academic Performance Indicator based on the Performance Based Appraisal System (UGC 2010, appendix III). The indicators covered for appraisal include:

- teaching, learning, and evaluation-related activities;
- co-curricular, extension, and professional-development-related activities;
- research and academic contributions—including publications , participation in seminars and conferences, research guidance, and organization of training programs.

For appointment or promotion to the post of (full) professor, the candidate must be an eminent scholar with a PhD in the concerned/allied/relevant discipline. Candidates for professorship must have ten years of teaching experience in university/college and/or experience in research at university- or national-level institutions/industries—including experience of guiding research candidates at doctoral level. They must have, for their credit, at least ten publications as books and/or research/policy papers; the guidelines are vague as to the quality of these publications. Other qualifications prescribed for an associate professorship are also applicable to professorship. Alternatively, however, scholars or professionals who are reputed in their discipline and who have made significant contributions to knowledge in the discipline may also be considered for appointment as a professor (UGC 2010, 6). It is left to the selection committee to verify and endorse the credentials of such scholars or professionals.

Almost all professors and associate professors in universities now possess doctorates. A majority of assistant professors in universities also possess doctorates. In colleges, the percentage of assistant professors with doctorates is low; those with a doctorate seek upward mobility as an associate professor (or even as an assistant professor) in a university. As a rule of thumb, if not as a formal guideline, a doctorate from an internationally renowned university is more valued, compared to a doctorate from a state or unknown foreign university. Incidentally, in publicly funded institutions, the regulations governing minimum qualifications can hardly be flouted. There are far too many applicants vis-à-vis the number of posts available. The slightest suggestion that an appointment was made by flouting a regulation is challenged in a court of law, and such appointments are struck down by the courts. The institutions have also become more careful after the enactment of the Right to Information Act, whose provisions will invariably be invoked by unselected applicants.

The purely private universities and colleges have greater flexibility in the matter of teachers' qualifications. However, they would also like to ensure the minimum as regards the academic qualifications of the faculty—such as the grade in the master's level and the doctorate. As for unaided private colleges, the university to which they are affiliated acts as the watchdog.

Protective discrimination in recruitment to professoriate

Meritocracy is of cardinal significance for excellence in higher education. While merit is emphasized in direct recruitment to academic positions in public-funded higher education institutions, these institutions are also required to reserve a certain percentage of such positions for candidates hailing from indigent sections of the population. As per the constitutional mandate, 49.5 per cent of the posts are reserved under the policy of protective discrimination (affirmative action): 15 per cent for the scheduled castes, 7.5 per cent for the scheduled tribes, and 27 per cent for the other backward classes.[7] Selection for reserved positions is also based on the merit of the candidates from among these castes, tribes, and classes. Besides this so-called "vertical reservation," there is "horizontal reservation" to the extent of 3 per cent (across categories) for people with disabilities, 1 per cent each for candidates with auditory, visual, and orthopedic disabilities.

The reservation of positions in public-funded institutions, called protective discrimination, is a form of affirmative action that is peculiar to India. This provision is mandated by the Constitution of India, in conformity with its avowed principles of equality and social justice. It is intended to rectify centuries-old inequities, resulting from the Hindu caste system, and ameliorate poverty, illiteracy, and other problems of the population. The constitution has identified three categories of the population for protective discrimination: the scheduled castes and scheduled tribes (so-called because of the schedules in which these castes and tribes are listed) and other backward classes. This provision has since been extended to people with disabilities.

Although initially intended for a period of ten years, the provision of reservation has been extended every ten years, through an act of parliament; and it is now widely regarded as a permanent part of state policy. In public parlance, it is a sensitive issue; and it has been frequently challenged in courts of law, including the Supreme Court of India. Generally, the legal position has been in its favor. However, opinion on its application in the sphere of higher education is divided: some observers view it as debilitating the quality of education, while others uphold it as an instrument of social justice and dub its critics as retrograde and elitist. For many reserved positions, no doubt, it is difficult to find suitable candidates. There is no provision of reservation in purely private universities and unaided colleges; the demand for reservation in the private sector has not yet gained political momentum.

Recruitment procedures

All vacancies in public-funded higher education institutions need to be advertised in the government's weekly *Employment News* (brought out in both English and Hindi) and at least in one national newspaper (also in a vernacular newspaper, in the case of a state university).

Vacancy advertisements are also posted on institution websites and in the *University News*, a monthly magazine of the Association of Indian Universities. The advertisement should specify the posts that are reserved for specific categories of candidates. While purely private institutions are not obliged to advertise their vacancies, they do so in leading newspapers and magazines.

All appointments in public-funded institutions are made on the recommendations of properly constituted selection committees. The composition of such committees for various posts is prescribed by the UGC (UGC 2010, 32–36) and incorporated into the statutes and ordinances of the universities and institutes. The UGC has also given guidelines for making the selection methodology transparent, objective, and credible. The scoring system—developed by the UGC, based on the Academic Performance Indicator—gives a quantitative dimension to the selection procedure (UGC 2010, tables I–IX of appendix III).

Since the number of applicants far exceeds the number of vacancies, some universities and institutes set up a screening committee to shortlist the candidates to be called for interview. To avoid applicants stalling the selection process—in state universities, by invoking legal intervention on the grounds that they have not been called for interview—all applicants fulfilling the minimum qualifications for the post are called for such a consultation. The process in such universities goes on for several days, and most often it is carried out as a ritual to satisfy the judicial requirements. Some universities and institutes examine candidates—by telephone or via teleconference.

To make the system more credible and efficient, some central universities and institutes, and all institutions of national importance, assess the candidates' teaching ability and/or research aptitude through a seminar or classroom lecture. Institutions vary widely in the procedures adopted, but such test seminars/lectures are held outside the purview of the selection committee. The faculty may give their feedback to the selection committee, on the suitability of the candidates, and rank them based on their performance. So as not to bias the selection committee, such a feedback is provided only after the interviews are concluded.

Appointments to the posts of assistant professor and associate professor are invariably made through interviews. While appointment to a professor's post is generally made through interviews, in exceptional cases a scholar may be invited to the position. However, such invitees must already hold a professorship in another institution, and the decision to invite somebody as a professor will have to be made by a duly constituted selection committee. Scouting for talent is a rare occurrence in higher education institutions in India and is confined to some institutions of national importance.

While the elaborate guidelines—suggested by the UGC—underline the importance of transparency and credibility in recruiting to teaching positions, in actual practice rules are bent and appointments are often manipulated and fixed. Not infrequently, complaints of favoritism, nepotism, and corruption are raised, even as most institutions go through the process of recruitment with a veneer of legality and fairness. In any direct recruitment to professor's or associate professor's posts, those already working in the institution have an advantage. Often, the drama of recruitment is enacted only to legitimize the appointment of internal candidates to higher positions. Unsuspecting applicants from outside the institution fall prey to such legitimization exercises. Similarly, in many institutions there are opportunities for backdoor entry into the academic profession for candidates who may only be marginally qualified. Such candidates are first appointed as ad hoc assistant professors and given an opportunity to gain experience. At the interview, the chairperson of the selection committee (the vice-chancellor, director, or the president of the governing body) pleads the person's case, and generally the external experts are obliging. Selecting candidates on extraneous considerations or through dubious methods often results in charges of nepotism and corruption in public-funded institutions.

By law, appointment to teaching positions in public-funded institutions is open to all citizens of the country. However, in most state universities and colleges, candidates from the state are preferred since they are familiar with local realities and the regional language. This system has had the inadvertent consequences of limiting mobility among teachers and deleterious inbreeding within the institutions. With the career-advancement scheme now in place (see below), teachers no longer have an incentive to move from one institution to another, let alone from one place to another. Thus, most academics in India retire from the university or college in which they began their career.

Some institutions of national importance—like the IITs and the Indian Institutes of Management—follow a pool system for recruitment. The qualifications for various teaching positions are posted on the institute's website, and the candidates can submit their applications all through the year. If the institute needs faculty for some departments, it will scrutinize the applications and interview the candidates. Thus, the institute can wait for suitable candidates to apply for the post, instead of mechanically going through the process of selection and appointing the best among the least suitable candidates.

The above system seems to be working well for the top Indian Institutes of Management, notwithstanding the general shortage of well-qualified teachers in the country. The best among them (i.e., those in Ahmedabad, Bangalore, and Kolkata) have been able not only to recruit the best among the available talent but also to retain them. The same cannot be said of the ten Indian Institutes of Management established in recent years; they face the same problem as central universities in finding well-qualified candidates for faculty positions.

The story is different in IITs. Even the best among them have been facing difficulty in recruiting well-qualified faculty, and more than half of the faculty positions in these recently established institutes have remained unfilled. This is because core engineering jobs in industry are preferred by graduates rather than academic appointments. For instance, in 2010, only 37 (3.82%) of the 969 IIT–Bombay graduates, including several with doctorates, opted for teaching jobs, down from 50 in 2009 (Times News Network 2011a, 4). This is because "the average MTech and PhD salary is lower than the average BTech salary in India"—an irony highlighted by Rangan Banerjee and Vinayak Muley in their 2005/2006 report on technology and engineering education in the country (cited in Chhapla 2011, 5).

The private universities and unaided private colleges are not bound by any formal guidelines for recruitment to teaching positions. They are not obliged to advertise their vacancies, and their advertisements are frugal on details. Their recruitment procedures are not transparent. Since they are de facto (though not de jure) for-profit institutions, the financial part of the institution interest outweighs quality considerations. Even so, some of the private universities—like the Amity University, Azim Premji University, and Symbiosis University—have proclaimed their commitment to quality in higher education. Given the type of resources that some of the private universities have been able to mobilize, they seem to have greater elbow room in the matter of scouting for talent and selection of high-quality teaching faculty. Incidentally, as private enterprises, they are not encumbered by the policy of protective discrimination.

Terms of appointment

In public-funded institutions, once the recommendation of the selection committee is approved by the executive body of the university/

institute, a letter offering the appointment and terms thereof is sent to the selected candidate. The person needs to communicate (in writing), within 30 days of receiving the letter, her/his willingness to accept the appointment and indicate the probable date of reporting for duty. Under special conditions and on request, this date can be extended at the discretion of the institution. In case the selected candidate does not accept the offer or does not report for duty within the stipulated period, the offer is treated as withdrawn, and the next candidate in the waiting list is offered the post. The list of selected candidates is valid for six months, after which the post again needs to be advertised.

In some state universities, the recommendations of the selection committee—as approved by the executive body—must be ratified by the chancellor, who is the governor of the state. The appointments at grant-in-aid private colleges need to be approved by the state government's department of education. Appointments to teaching positions in the government-run colleges are made by a statutory authority, called the state public-service commission.

The terms of appointment are specified in the appointment order, and they are enforceable in a court of law. Among other things, the order specifies the payment in the pay band (on the salary scale) relating to the post, and other allowances and benefits, as allowed by the rules of the government, which are adopted by the institution. Generally, in the universities, there is no negotiation on salary or other benefits. But, during the interview, the candidate can make a case for a higher starting income. If convinced, the selection committee may recommend a maximum 15 per cent increase. By and large, the appointment orders are uniform for different positions, excepting the item on payment.

In private universities, theoretically, the terms of appointment are negotiable. In reality, however, such negotiations take place only for faculty of high caliber or faculty in narrow fields of specialization. Thus, private institutions have the autonomy to compete for faculty and can use better salaries, fringe benefits, reduced teaching obligations, research subsidies, and further factors to make a more attractive offer than one by other similar or public-funded institutions. Some of them do have the financial resources for this. As a result, public-funded institutions are occasionally at a disadvantage. However, private institutions can hardly match the employment security, career advancement, and graduated increase in salary, or other statutory benefits, on offer in public-funded institutions. Not surprisingly, public-funded institutions, especially those funded directly by the Ministry of Human Resources Development/UGC are the best bet for aspirants to an academic profession.

While announcing the revised salary scales in 2008, the UGC (UGC 2010, 60) prescribed a workload of 40 hours a week during 30 working weeks (180 teaching days) in an academic year for teachers with full-time appointments. Moreover, teachers are required to be available in the university department/center or college, as the case may be, for at least five hours daily. The number of contact (teaching-learning process) hours for an assistant professor is 16 and for associate professor and professor, 14. Professors who are actively involved in extension activities and administration gain a concession of 2 hours.

Since the grant-in-aid colleges are dependent on government funds, they enforce workload norms strictly; and teachers with inadequate workload are required to teach in another college to complete it. If in any subject the workload falls well below the prescribed 16 hours, it is farmed out to part-time teachers. Due to paucity of financial resources, especially since the introduction of new pay scales, many state governments across the country have imposed an embargo on recruitment to teaching positions in universities. The state universities are permitted to recruit teachers only if they justify the need in terms of the necessity for more teaching. Central universities, centrally funded deemed-to-be universities, and institutions of national importance, however, do not observe the UGC prescriptions. There is no standardized workload in private universities, and the workload in private colleges is exploitatively higher than in grant-in-aid colleges.

The main responsibility of college teachers is to teach the prescribed curriculum to the students and prepare them for examinations conducted by the university. Besides teaching, university teachers are also required to be engaged in research. Only in a few university departments/centers and institutions of national importance is the primary emphasis on research. Thus, publication as an academic activity is more characteristic of university teachers than college teachers; and a college teacher being engaged in research and publication is commendable. Often this enables the teacher to move to a university, pursue her/his research interests, and improve her/his career prospects. In private universities, the emphasis is almost exclusively on teaching. In all universities and colleges, teachers are expected to assist the university/college in such administrative activities as processing applications for admission, counseling students, assisting the conduct of examinations (supervision, invigilation, and evaluation), and participating in extension, co-curricular and extracurricular activities. Some teachers perform nonteaching work as a matter of duty; most teachers avoid it, if they can.

Career advancement

For several decades, the job performance of teachers in higher education institutions remained unevaluated, and any attempt at evaluation was either resisted or done perfunctorily. Only in government-run colleges were confidential reports of teachers written by their principals and filed in their service registers. In universities and institutes, teachers on probation were confirmed, generally, on the basis of confidential reports by the head/chairperson of the department; or the dean, if the teacher was the head/chairperson of the department. However, as part of the package of pay revision and increases, performance evaluation of teachers in all public-funded universities and colleges has been introduced.

It is now mandatory that, in public-funded universities, institutes, and colleges, a service agreement has to be executed between the institution and the teacher at the time of recruitment. The self-appraisal and performance-based-appraisal methodology is included in this agreement. Henceforth, the appointment or promotion to associate professor's and professor's positions will be based on a minimum score, as stipulated in the Academic Performance Indicator.

The UGC (2010, 103–107) has listed three categories of teachers' contributions for appraisal:

- teaching-, learning-, and evaluation-related activities;
- curricular-, extension-, and professional-development-related activities;
- research and academic contributions.

For each category, indicators and weights are specified. The institutions may adopt the template provided by the UGC, or they may devise their own self-assessment, performance-appraisal forms for teachers in compliance with the Academic Performance Indicator, prescribed by the UGC. Purely private institutions do not have a mandatory or standardized self-appraisal system. Since this performance-appraisal system has just been introduced in the university system, it is too early to judge on its efficacy. But past experience with the UGC's mandatory measures (see Jayaram 2003), does not permit optimism, since the UGC, being a small organization, lacks staff and machinery to oversee hundreds of universities and thousands of colleges.

Career advancement scheme

The Indian professoriate is pyramidal in structure: there are fewer positions of professor than of associate professor, and fewer positions

Table 4.2 Career advancement scheme for professoriate

Designation (level)	Stage	Duration of service	Academic pay grade (Rs)
Assistant professor (bottom)	1	Entry level (direct recruitment)	6,000
	2	After four years in stage 1 with PhD After five years in stage 1 with master of philosophy After six years in stage 1 with master's	7,000
	3	After five years in stage 2	8,000
Associate professor (middle)	4	After three years in stage 3 or entry level (direct recruitment)	9,000
Professor (top)	5	After three years in stage 4 or entry level (direct recruitment)	10,000
	6	After ten years in stage 5	12,000

Note: All promotions under the CAS are subject to the candidate obtaining a minimum score as stipulated in the Academic Performance Indicator. US$1.00 = Rs 50.00.
Source: Adapted from UGC (2010).

of associate professor than of assistant professor. Not all members entering the academic profession at the associate professor's level can hope to become a professor. To improve the opportunities for teachers to move up the career ladder, and as an incentive to performance, the Career Advancement Scheme has been introduced. The scheme envisages six stages in a teacher's career, spread across three levels: an entry-level assistant professor (stage 1) can move up through two successive stages (stages 2 and 3); an associate professor (stage 4) can move up to stage 5; and a professor (stage 5) can move up to stage 6 (see Table 4.2). It is not possible for a teacher to jump stages under the Career Advancement Scheme.

To be eligible for promotion under the Career Advancement Scheme, a minimum score, as stipulated in the Academic Performance Indicator, has to be obtained. How soon an entry-level assistant professor can move to stage two depends on whether she/he possesses a PhD degree (four years of service), a master of philosophy degree (five years of service), or only a master's degree in the subject (six years of service). An assistant professor who has completed five years of service at stage two is eligible to move to stage three. After completing three years of service in stage three, she/he will be eligible to move to stage four and be designated as associate professor.

An associate professor, completing three years of service in stage four and possessing a PhD degree in the relevant discipline, is eligible to be appointed and designated as professor and be placed in stage five. A professor with ten years of teaching and research experience in that position will be eligible for promotion to stage six, without any change in the designation. Promotion from stage five to six is applicable only to professors in university departments, and it is restricted to 10 per cent of the positions of professor in a university.

Under the Career Advancement Scheme, promotions from stage one to two and two to three are conducted by a screening-cum-evaluation committee. However, promotions from stage three to four (i.e., from assistant professor to associate professor), from stage four to five (i.e., from associate professor to professor), and from stage five to six (i.e., at the professor level) are made by a duly constituted selection committee, whose composition is the same as the selection committee for direct recruitment to associate professor and professor positions.

The process of promotion should be initiated by the teacher through an application and duly completed Performance Based Appraisal System form as per the Academic Performance Indicator, in response to the notification issued (twice a year) by the university. The process needs to be completed within six months, from the date of application. Candidates who fail the selection process can be reassessed only after one year. The promotion will be effective after a minimum period of eligibility (see Table 4.2), in case of candidates being successful in the first attempt and from the date on which a teacher is successfully reassessed, in case of others. Promotion under the Career Advancement Scheme being personal to the incumbent teacher, the substantive sanctioned post will be restored on that teacher's superannuation.

The newly introduced Career Advancement Scheme is well-defined and more rigorous than the erstwhile Merit Promotion Scheme, which had almost been reduced to a time-bound promotion scheme—under which teachers were indiscriminately promoted to higher levels, based only on the number of years of service they performed. But India is a land of great rituals; only time will tell if the Career Advancement Scheme will live up to its expectations or will also be as diluted as its predecessor, the Merit Promotion Scheme (Jayaram 2003). Incidentally, seldom does one come across the case of a teacher, in a public-funded higher education institution, who has been dismissed from service as a result of poor performance. Thus, the university system in India is a haven for mediocrity.

Incidentally, student feedback is not taken into consideration in performance appraisals of teachers for the Career Advancement Scheme (nor was it under the Merit Promotion Scheme). Some centrally funded deemed-to-be universities and institutions of national importance obtain student feedback on curriculum and teaching, but such feedback is not a formal part of the performance appraisal of teachers. Given that private universities are fairly new institutions in India, little is known about their performance-appraisal practices. However, student feedback apparently influences the renewal of teachers' contracts in those universities.

Generally, in higher education institutions in India, incumbent teachers have no voice or influence in the recruitment or promotion of teachers. It is rare for a vice-chancellor or dean to seek the informal opinion of teachers on matters of appointment. In institutions where candidates for selection give a lecture or present a seminar, the feedback of teachers is provided to the selection committee; such feedback, however, is not binding on the selection committee, and it does not carry much weight, either.

Salaries: constituent components

Salaries and service conditions for teachers in universities and colleges are fixed by the UGC, as approved by the Ministry of Human Resources Development. Central universities and centrally funded institutes adopt these salaries and service conditions in totality, with effect from the stipulated date. The state governments, however, adopt them with modifications regarding the age of superannuation (retirement) and allowances, the date of implementation of the new salaries, and the payment of arrears, which may accrue due to the delay in implementation. The ministry fixes the salaries and service conditions of teachers in institutions of national importance—the Indian Institute of Science, Bangalore; IITs; Indian Institutes of Management; and others.

The gross monthly salary of a teacher consists of five components:

- the amount in the salary range: assistant professor, Rs 15,600–39,100 (US$312–782); associate professor, Rs 37,400–67,000 ($748–1,340); professor Rs 37,400–67,000 (US$748–1,340)[8];
- academic grade pay;
- transport allowance;
- dearness allowance (cost of living)[9];
- house rental allowance.

Table 4.3 Salaries of university faculty, as on August 1, 2010

Pay details	Rank		
	Professor	Associate professor	Assistant professor
Top of salary band			
Payment	67,000	67,000	39,100
Grade payment	10,000	9,000	6,000
Transport allowance	3,200	3,200	3,200
Dearness allowance	28,070	27,720	16,905
House rental allowance	23,100	22,800	11,910
Gross salary	131,370	129,720	77,115
Middle of salary band			
Payment	55,000	52,200	27,350
Grade payment	10,000	9,000	6,000
Transport allowance	3,200	3,200	3,200
Dearness allowance	23,870	22,540	12,793
House rental allowance	19,500	18,360	10,005
Gross salary	111,570	102,420	59,348
Bottom of salary band			
Payment	43,000	37,400	15,600
Pay grade	10,000	9,000	6,000
Transport allowance	3,200	3,200	3,200
Dearness allowance	19,670	17,360	8,680
House rental allowance	15,900	13,920	6,480
Gross salary	91,770	80,880	39,960

Note: All figures in Indian rupees; approximately, US$1.00 = Rs 50.00.
Source: Adapted from UGC (2010).

The gross salary drawn by different cadres of teachers at the top, middle, and bottom levels of the income scale are shown in Table 4.3. Being in the higher ranges of income, all teachers in higher education institutions now pay graduated income tax (10%, 20%, or 30%), depending on the band in which their gross income falls after taking advantage of tax concessions and incentives for saving. In public-funded institutions, payment of income tax can hardly be evaded, as it is the employer's responsibility to deduct income tax from the employees' salaries.

In public-funded institutions, irrespective of the academic field, all professors are paid similarly. However, in private institutions, teachers are paid differentially, depending upon the demand for and supply of teachers in particular disciplines. Teachers in institutions of national importance (like the IITs and the Indian Institutes of Management) are paid marginally better salaries. Even among public-funded institutions, teachers in centrally funded institutions gain relatively higher gross salaries than those in state-funded institutions. In many states, transport allowance is not paid; and the house rental allowance is fixed as per state government rates, which are invariably lower than the central government rates.

Over decades, the gap in salaries between academic and other professions has narrowed considerably. Nevertheless, professionals in the management, information and communications technology, and biotechnology sector, well-established advocates, chartered accountants/financial consultants; and medical practitioners/surgeons earn considerably more than teachers. However, in India, regarding teachers' salaries, the general comparison is with that of the bureaucrats; and the salaries of these two are now more or less comparable, though the bureaucrats receive better perquisites.

There is a minimum salary for each level of the professoriate, irrespective of the department of study—though the minimum gross salary may vary between central government–funded institutions and state-funded institutions, and between universities in general and institutions of national importance. In fact, the UGC has fixed the remuneration even for part-time teachers and guest faculty. To ensure transparency and avoid cheating by grant-in-aid private institutions, the salary of teachers is credited to their bank accounts. In contrast, there is no minimum income in purely private universities and colleges. Their salary scales and allowances are not advertised. Most of these institutions are evasive on salary matters; many of them pay their teachers in cash.

In all public-funded institutions, teachers are entitled to gain an annual increase of 3 per cent on their basic salary. Stoppage or deferment of increments is viewed as a punishment, and it must be justified through appropriate disciplinary procedures. Apart from this, teachers get a bigger hike in salary if they are promoted under the Career Advancement Scheme. There is, however, no negotiation on salary size or service conditions. In purely private institutions, renegotiation is possible; most often, such negotiations are to the advantage of the management.

On average, the professoriate's salaries and service conditions are revised once in ten years, and it generally takes place along with those of the central government employees. Parallel to the commission appointed by the central government to recommend payment revision for its employees, the Ministry of Human Resources Development appoints a committee to recommend pay revision for teachers in public-funded institutions. The committee holds wide-ranging consultations, with various stakeholders—teachers' unions, educational administrators, management, experts on higher education, and so on—before arriving at its recommendations. The committee's recommendations are examined by the government (the Ministry of Human Resources Development and the Ministry of Finance), before they are approved by the cabinet of ministers. On approval, the Ministry of Human Resources Development advises the UGC to go ahead with the implementation of the revision.

Once the UGC issues the notification, the revisions are instantly implemented by the centrally funded institutions. The implementation of the revisions by the state governments is not uniform; sometimes, the basic structure is accepted but specific allowances are truncated. As a consequence, there are variations in the gross emoluments of teachers in different parts of the country, as well as the same teaching position across the different types of institutions, in a given city. In some states, the recommendations—even in their truncated form—are implemented only after prolonged agitation by teachers.

Overall, academics in public-funded universities and colleges now lead a comfortable middle-class lifestyle, based on the salaries they are paid. Housing and travel allowances are additional components of the salary. Inflation in the economy—that is, the rise in cost of living—is also addressed through biannual revision of the dearness allowance, as noted earlier. Also, no difference exists in salary scales among academics in different faculties: those teaching English or mathematics get paid the same as their counterparts teaching Urdu or history. Since the pay scales are now uniform across the country, though with minor interstate differences, the quality of life of academics living in small towns has also improved. For teachers in purely private universities and colleges, the story is different; market conditions rule here, and there are large salary differentials—in terms of the disciplines and the qualifications of the teachers. In some private institutions, the salaries are exploitative. In all institutions, part-time teachers are invariably worse off.

Non-salary and service-related benefits

For the Indian professoriate, salary is the most important component of income. It constitutes the key element in attracting faculty. Location of the university/college, reputation of the institution, availability of facilities for research, and other factors could also be influential for the few who have a choice. The non-salary benefits that teachers obtain are all as per government provisions, and they have no bearing on the choice of teaching as a career or of a particular institution.

For those who were appointed to permanent positions before January 2004, the government superannuation pension scheme (for life and with survival benefit to the spouse)[10] was an attraction. In fact, many teachers, who had in the 1970s subscribed to a contributory provident fund scheme, switched over to the pension scheme when the option was given for the last time in the mid-1980s. Those appointed to permanent positions since January 2004 must contribute 10 per cent of their basic income to the pension fund, and the government makes a matching contribution.

Teachers in public-funded institutions are also eligible for a gratuity— a British colonial legacy, under which a sum of money is paid to an employee at the end of a period of employment. A retirement gratuity is due to all employees who retire after completion of at least five years of service—at the rate of one-fourth of the payment for each completed six-month period of qualifying service, to a maximum of 16.5 times or one million rupees (US$200,000). Theoretically, someone retiring after 20 years can collect this gratuity and accept a job in the private sector. Practically, however, teachers would not leave a permanent job that carries so many supplementary benefits (see below), unless the private sector offered a substantially attractive package or on health grounds. Death gratuities are payable to the teacher's nominee, in cases where the teacher dies while in service; its rate varies, depending upon the service put in by the teacher. However, it cannot exceed one million rupees (US$200,000). The nominee will also get a one-off payment at the time of death, amounting to two months pay.

Teachers are eligible for a variety of paid leave, but none of them can be taken as a matter of right. There are also restrictions on the combination of different types of leaves. Every academic year, a teacher can take eight days of casual leave (to meet exigencies), and this leave cannot be accumulated. She/he can have one day of earned/privilege leave for 11 days of work, and this leave can be accumulated to a maximum of 300 days. Part of this leave can be exchanged for additional payment—once in two years or fully at the time of superannuation/retirement. The most attractive aspect of the academic profession is the fully paid vacation leave of eight weeks per year.

Female teachers get a maximum of one year's fully paid maternity leave during their career, and their spouses get a maximum of 15 days fully paid paternity leave for each child born (for not more than two children). Besides maternity leave, female teachers are entitled to two years' fully paid childcare leave, provided they have exhausted all other leaves to their credit. This leave can be taken at any time, until the child reaches 18 years of age; it can be split between two children.

Teachers can benefit from travel concessions (return fare for self and dependents)—once in two years—by using their vacation or applying for leave to go on a holiday in India. In lieu of this, teachers hailing from outside the vicinity of their workplace can receive home travel concessions to visit their home town (as declared at the start of the job). The amount paid by the university or college toward such travel is taxable.

Teachers are eligible for medical leave and medical assistance, for themselves and their dependents. They are entitled to the use of central- or state-government health-service facilities. In lieu of this, some institutions have extended medical insurance coverage to teachers, or they reimburse medical expenses up to a particular amount. To check misuse of this facility (by the hospitals, insurance companies, and teachers), there are elaborate norms governing medical assistance.

As part of their salary, teachers are given a percentage of the basic amount as house rental allowance, depending on the location of the university/college. According to the Indian government's classification, those in category A cities (e.g., Bangalore, Chennai, Delhi, Hyderabad, Mumbai, and Kolkata) receive 30 per cent; those in category B cities (e.g., Ahmedabad, Chandigarh, Jaipur, Lucknow, and Patna), 20 per cent; and the rest, 10 per cent. In cases where the university provides housing (no college does), teachers do not obtain house-rental allowance; they have to pay a small sum as license fees and maintenance charges, and the electricity and water charges are payable at the rate of consumption.

Housing provided by the university is in great demand, as it provides residential security and obviates the need to commute. However, some teachers prefer to stay away from campus, especially if they can get cheaper accommodation, as they can save some money from their house-rental allowance. Furthermore, with income-tax rebates given to those who build houses or buy apartments it is doubly advantageous to stay out of campus. This choice is exercised particularly by teachers who have decided to settle down in the city where they work. Besides house-rental allowance, there are special categories of allowances such as tribal area allowance, hardship area allowance, island special payment, and others; but these are applicable in a limited number of institutions. Before the liberalization of lending by banks, until the mid-1990s, universities had surplus funds and advanced loans at concessional rates to teachers for buying or building houses and buying cars.

As an incentive for promoting smaller families, male teachers undergoing vasectomy or female teachers undergoing hysterectomy are given one increment in payment, on production of a certificate from a medical authority. Such teachers must have one surviving child and not more than two children. To be eligible for this incentive, the male teacher must not be over 50 years of age, and his wife must be between 20 and 45 years of age. Similarly, the female teacher must not be over 45 years of age, and her husband must not be over 50 years of age.

The foregoing non-salary and service benefits are statutory entitlements in public-funded institutions. That is why, once in a permanent job, generally no teacher would voluntarily retire. These benefits are, however, a matter of contractual agreement in purely private educational institutions; in rare cases they will offer a more attractive package than public-funded educational institutions.

Supplementary employment

A teacher occupying a permanent position in a public-funded university or college cannot take up supplementary employment. However, with the permission of the institution, a teacher can undertake a teaching assignment in another university/college, as a visiting/guest faculty for a brief period (by using the 30 days of duty leave to which they are entitled in a year). The remuneration received for this work is called an honorarium (not salary) and is liable to tax. Generally, teachers collect the honorarium in cash and do not disclose this in tax returns. Teachers can undertake long-term teaching assignments in another university/college by using extraordinary leave, during which period they are not entitled to any salary or increment benefits. Teachers can use any earned/privilege leave they may have to their credit (which, however, cannot exceed 300 days) to cover this period.

The restriction proscribing working in more than one institution does not apply to part-time teachers. In purely private institutions, this restriction may be part of the contract. Of late, some universities and institutes have introduced the concept of adjunct faculty, whereby a teacher anchored in one department/center concurrently holds a position in another department/center. These universities/institutes state this provision explicitly in the letter offering the appointment. Such appointments are a matter of administrative convenience (e.g., to balance workload), and they do not carry any benefits in pay or allowances. Universities and institutes running a self-financing diploma or certificate programs pay a separate honorarium to teachers, if the teaching is done outside the normal working hours.

The percentage of university teachers doing consultancy work is negligible, and consultancy is largely unknown in colleges. Professors in science, technology, and management departments in universities and teachers in institutions of national importance do consultancy work. Teachers in social sciences and humanities departments seldom obtain consultancy work. Where consultancy is permitted, there are clear guidelines governing the duration of the teacher's engagement, and the sharing of fees accruing from it.

One source of additional income for some college teachers (rarely for university teachers) is private tuition. Since they are formally employed in full-time permanent positions, this raises the question of professional ethics (Jayaram 2003). Private tuition—especially for science and mathematics courses and in the English language—has now become such a profitable enterprise that some reputed college teachers have taken voluntary retirement or resigned from their college jobs to devote themselves to it full-time.

Moonlighting (holding a second job) by university and college teachers is not totally unknown. Some teachers undertake consultancy, run insurance or transport agencies, or even become involved in retail trade. To circumvent institutional regulations, these activities are mostly done in their spouse's name. Another source of supplementary income for a few college teachers is writing guidebooks (in a question-answer format) on behalf of students appearing for university examinations.

International faculty

By law, universities in India can only appoint Indian citizens to teaching positions. Non-citizens can, however, work in Indian universities as visiting professors, under specific exchange programs. Given the pressure for expansion of higher education institutions and acute shortage of well-qualified faculty, especially in institutions of national importance, the appointment of foreign nationals to teaching positions has now become inevitable. To start with, the IITs have been permitted to appoint foreign nationals (including non-resident Indians who have changed their nationality) on a contract basis for up to five years. A proposal to open up teaching positions to foreign nationals is now under the consideration of the government. If approved, the citizenship act will have to be amended.

Conclusion

India has one of the largest and most diverse systems of higher education in the world. Not surprisingly, the diversities in this country's higher education institutions are reflected in the varying systems and practices of recruitment of the professoriate and its remuneration packages. The institutions of national importance (like the Indian Institutes of Science, IITs, and Indian Institutes of Management) have developed the most effective systems and best practices of recruitment, even as they work under the broad regulations of the central government. They also pay higher gross salaries and offer better service conditions. Closely following them are the well-established central universities and centrally funded university-level institutes, which come under the umbrella of the UGC.

But the vast majority of teaching positions are in state universities and their affiliated grant-in-aid colleges. For teachers working in these universities and colleges, salary and allied benefits could not be upgraded. As yet, it is unclear how much the quality of teachers in these institutions would improve in the light of the attractive pay packages now available and the rigorous conditions stipulated for their career advancement. However, previous experience with well-intentioned policy measures and programs of the UGC does not promote full optimism.

Regarding purely private universities and colleges, the vagaries of the higher education market will continue to mediate their recruitment practices and remuneration packages. Yet, if private universities hope to carve a niche for themselves in higher education, they will need to improve on the current offers from centrally funded institutions. Only then will they be able to attract the candidates with the best teaching and research talents. This is what some private institutions, backed by leading industrial houses and committed academic administrators, aim to achieve. But it will take some time before their efforts will bear fruit. They, too, can hardly ignore the general economic and political conditions in which the higher education system is set to function in the country.

The political dynamics in India, as they impact on higher education, warrant some observations. According to the federal constitution of India, higher education is in the concurrent list—that is, an area in which both the central Parliament and state legislative assemblies can enact legislation and initiate policies. The constraints under which central and state governments engage in higher education are different. While the central government has to address long-term, all-India, and international issues, regarding policy matters, state governments need to address short-term, region-specific, and populist issues. The two obviously do not gel. The central government is also beset by the constraints of coalition politics, in which the coalition partners on whom the main ruling party is dependent often hinder policymaking. Thus, successive governments, since the 1990s, have dithered on key policy issues in higher education.

Corruption is another big constraining factor affecting higher education in India. With a score of 3.3 out of 10, India (along with Albania, Jamaica, and Liberia) ranks 87 among 178 countries in the Corruption Perception Index (i.e., perceived levels of corruption in the public sector), computed by Transparency International (2011, 79–80). The general malaise of corruption, a big issue in the country today, has not left the sphere of higher education untouched. Stories of corruption in higher education abound; permission to start colleges (or universities in the state) and granting of affiliation, fixing of intake, and appointment of principals (or vice-chancellors in universities) and teachers—all aspects appear susceptible to corruption and nepotism.

Another dimension of corruption, related to higher education, is the fraudulent practices indulged by academics. In the rat race for advancement in an academic career, teachers have increasingly resorted to such practices. A study by T. A. Abinandanan of the Indian Institute of Science (Bangalore) has found that, in India, the rate of scientific misconduct has risen from 10 per 100,000 papers during 1991–2000 to 44 per 100,000 papers during 2001–2010 (Yousaf 2011).[11] Academics guilty of this misconduct "are not only from lower-tier institutions, but also from top institutions in India," including national-level laboratories, a central university, and an IIT (Yousaf 2011). That there has been a drop in the number of reported scientific misconduct cases since 2007 is, no doubt, good news.[12] However, a scary scenario among state universities, whose faculty mostly publish in Indian journals, is that these institutions have no formal monitoring systems yet.

Finally, given the rapid expansion of higher education institutions and the imminent entry of foreign educational establishments into the country, the competition for well-qualified and experienced faculty is sure to increase. Only institutions offering the best remuneration and service conditions can expect to gain the best teaching talent. Viewed in this light, the prospects for state universities and grant-in-aid colleges, which constitute the largest segment of the higher education system in the country, do not appear to be bright.

Thus, for observers who have been inspecting the higher education scenario, the prospects appear to be mixed. Like the proverbial elephant, higher education in India will trudge on, with incremental improvements here and tinkering of the system there. But, hopes of any significant change in the next decade or so will remain sanguine. The changes introduced in 2006—for recruitment of teachers, their pay scales and service conditions, their performance appraisal and career advancement, and further trends—are bold and forward looking. What impact these changes will have on the academic profession, in particular, and higher education, in general, remains a question.

Notes

1. The Indian Institutes of Management (13 in all), which have established a niche for themselves in graduate business education and assist industry through research and consultancy, are not granted the status of institutions of national importance. These institutes are not authorized to award degrees as universities do; they award diplomas and fellowships that are considered equal to degrees and doctorates awarded by the universities. A recommendation for enacting legislation to allow the Indian Institutes of Management to award degrees without any erosion of their existing autonomy, made by a committee headed by Professor Madhava N. Menon, has been placed before the Ministry of Human Resources Development (Seshagiri 2011).
2. The Indian Parliament is yet to legislate on private universities. Meanwhile, invoking the existing legal provisions (e.g., the UGC Act), several private institutions of higher education have been given deemed-to-be-university status. The controversy resulting from this is now before the Supreme Court of India. Also, considering that higher education is a concurrent subject under the constitution, some states have enacted legislation for establishing private universities.
3. Reliable data on part-time teachers are hard to come by. As early as in 1983, the National Commission on Teachers (NCT 1985) found that only 70.7 per cent of university teachers and 68.5 per cent of college teachers had permanent employment with all statutory benefits. Given the restricted appointments to teaching positions on a permanent basis in most states, since the introduction of a structural readjustment program in the 1990s, the percentage of part-time teachers has increased considerably.
4. In institutions of national importance—such as the Indian Institute of Science (Bangalore) and the IITs—a fourth level, namely, assistant professor (to be recruited on contractual basis)—was introduced in September 2009. This assistant professor position is not part of the regular faculty cadres in these institutes, and appointment to this position is made on contractual basis to enable bright, young doctorate-degree holders to teach and earn experience in premier institutions. It is stipulated that at least 10 per cent of the total faculty strength should be recruited at this level.
5. In academic fields—such as engineering and technology, medicine and pharmacy, management/business administration, occupational therapy and physiotherapy, physical education, music and performing arts, and others—special qualifications are prescribed for different levels of teaching staff (UGC 2010, 4–36).

6. The National Eligibility Test, jointly conducted by the UGC and the Council for Scientific and Industrial Research at about 90 centers in the country, is held twice a year. Many state governments have been permitted by the UGC to conduct a State Level Eligibility Test, which is treated as equivalent to the National Eligibility Test. In some states, to cope with various demands, the standard of the State Level Eligibility Test has been so appallingly diluted and the norms so brazenly flouted that the UGC has had to withdraw permission for the state to conduct it (Jayaram 2003).

7. This odd percentage is explained by the fact that the Supreme Court of India has ruled that reservation shall not exceed 50 per cent of the total posts. In states like Karnataka and Tamil Nadu, populist politics has pushed reservations beyond this limit, and the matter is now before the Supreme Court.

8. Although the pay band is the same for associate professors and professors, the former start at the bottom of the pay band (i.e., Rs 37,400 or US$748) and the latter start at a higher level in the pay band (i.e., Rs 43,000 or US$860).

9. The dearness (expensiveness, in British English) allowance is intended to compensate for inflation; and it is revised twice a year (in January and July, respectively), based on the price index (100 points as on January 1, 2006). As on July 1, 2011, it was 51 per cent of payment.

10. A superannuation pension is given to an employee of a public-funded institution after she/he has completed the required number of years of service—that is, on superannuation. This is different from a retiring pension, which is given to an employee who retires voluntarily or is prematurely retired (as a punitive action) and is proportionate to the service that she/he has put in, subject to a minimum. The maximum pension that a superannuating/retiring teacher can get is 50 per cent of the highest basic pay drawn. Dearness allowance is permissible on pension, but at a reduced rate.

11. According to Abinandanan, as many as 70 out of 103,434 papers published during 2001–2010 have been retracted, 45 of them for text, self- or data plagiarism. These 45 papers "had over 130 authors; and 12 authors had at least three (overlapping) retractions due to misconduct" (cited in Yousaf 2011, 1). Internationally, the rate of retraction is 17 for 100,000 papers: in comparison, China (48) and South Korea (44) have a higher rate of retraction; and Japan (16), United States (14), and United Kingdom (13) have a lower rate of retraction (Yousaf 2011).

12. Abinandanan surmises that this may be due to "the real reduction in the number of misconduct cases"; more plausibly, an increasing number of international journals have begun using plagiarism detection software to screen papers submitted for publication (cited in Yousaf 2011, 11).

References

Agarwal, P. 2009. *Indian higher education: Envisioning the future.* New Delhi: Sage.

Altbach, P. G., and N. Jayaram. 2010. Can India garner the demographic dividend? *Hindu,* December 1.

Chhapla, H. 2011. IITs' PhD jinx: BTechs command higher pay. *Times of India,* July 30.

Jayaram, N. 1993. The language question in higher education: Trends and issues. In *Higher education reform in India: Experience and perspectives*, eds. S. Chitnis and P. G. Altbach, 84–114. New Delhi: Sage.

———. 2003. The fall of the guru: The decline of the academic profession in India. In *The decline of the guru: The academic profession in developing and middle-income countries*, ed. P. G. Altbach, 119–230. New York: Palgrave Macmillan.

———. 2007. Beyond retailing knowledge: Prospects of research-oriented universities in India. In *World class worldwide: Transforming research universities in Asia and Latin America*, eds. P. G. Altbach and J. Balán, 70–94. Baltimore, MD: Johns Hopkins University Press.

———2009. Beyond demographic dividend: Some aspects of the sociology of youth in India. *Rajagiri Journal of Social Development* 1: 1–16.

———. 2010. Disparities in access to higher education in India: Persistent issues and changing context. In *Higher education and equality of opportunities: Cross-national perspectives*, ed. F. Lazin, M. Evans, and N. Jayaram, 161–181. Lanham, MD: Lexington Books.

———. 2011. Toward world-class status? The IIT system and IIT Bombay. In *The Road to academic excellence*, eds. P. G. Altbach and J. Salmi, 167–194. Washington, DC: World Bank.

Kaur, K. 2003. *Higher education in India (1781–2003)*. New Delhi: University Grants Commission.

National Commission on Teachers. 1985. *Report of the national commission on teachers, II, 1983–85*. New Delhi: Controller of Publications.

National Knowledge Commission. 2007. *Report to the nation–2006*. New Delhi: National Knowledge Commission, Government of India.

Seshagiri, Mathang. 2011. It's time IIMs give degree, not diploma: Panel. *Sunday Times of India*, May 1, http://articles.timesofindia.indiatimes.com/2011-05-01/india/29492823_1_iim-directors-iim-b-indian-institutes (accessed October 4, 2011).

Tilak, J. B. G. 2004. Absence of policy and perspective in higher education. *Economic and Political Weekly*, 39: 2159–2164.

Times News Network. 2011a. Core engineering jobs rule IIT–B placements this year. *Times of India*, July 29.

———. 2011b. Higher edu short of 54% teachers. *Times of India*, August 10.

Transparency International. 2011. *Annual report – 2010*. http://www.trans parency.org./publications/annual_report (accessed October 3, 2011).

University Grants Commission. 2010. *UGC regulations on minimum qualifications for appointment of teachers and other academic staff in universities and colleges and measures for the maintenance of standards in higher education*. New Delhi: UGC.

Yousaf, Shamsheer. 2011. India tops in academic fraud. *Deccan Herald*, August 14.

5
The Chinese Academic Profession: New Realities

Ma Wanhua and Wen Jianbo

The Chinese higher education system is the largest in the world, in terms of student enrollment and faculty numbers. In the coming decade, the system will continue to grow, especially within the public sector. While the public sector plays the dominating role, the private sector faces many challenges for survival and quality control. A national discussion has been initiated by the private sector regarding the problems of recruiting students and qualified professors.

The higher education system

After three decades of development, since the early 1980s, the Chinese higher education system has become the largest in the world. In 2009, the total number of students taking part in higher education nationally exceeded 28.26 million (National Bureau of Statistics of China 2010). In 2009, the gross enrollment rate was 24.3 per cent. In comparison with other developed countries, the enrollment rate is low, and there is still much room for growth. It is predicted that the number of students in higher education will be 33,500,000 by 2015 and 35,500,000 by 2020; the gross enrollment rate will be 36 per cent and 40 per cent, respectively (Ministry of Education 2010). It is easy to predict that in the coming decade, higher education in China will experience another leap forward.

Most of the increase in student enrollment took place after 1999. According to the Ministry of Education's data, in 1978 the total gross enrollment rate was only 1.59 per cent; and in 1998, it reached 10 per cent. In 1999, many provincial universities increased their number of students by 30 per cent. Since then, the scale of higher education in China has expanded notably. In 2002, the gross enrollment rate was up to 15 per cent (Ministry of Education 2009c). Since then, the number of graduates at all levels of higher education in China has approximately quadrupled.

Two important events helped the growth of higher education in China: first, the presidential call for building world-class universities at the centennial of Peking University in May 1998; and second, the mandated increase of enrollment by the Ministry of Education, in 1999. Then, it was estimated that by 2010 at least 20 per cent of high school students would be enrolled in some form of higher education institution. The second goal of increasing the gross enrollment to 20 per cent was realized before 2010. Now, according to the Outline for Mid- and Long-Term Higher Education Plan, the gross enrollment rate will reach 40 per cent in just another ten years (by 2020). Chinese higher education might make another leap forward, in the coming decade. In order to provide more access, the system of Chinese higher education has been diversified with different providers.

Now, Chinese higher education consists of "regular" higher education institutions, adult education institutions, *Minban* higher education institutions, independent colleges[1] and self-study programs by radio and TV universities. The radio and TV universities could be considered as the Chinese style of "open university" or continuing education, administrated by the Ministry of Education. Regular higher education institutions and adult education institutions are public and controlled by the ministry, provincial, and local governments. *Minban* higher education institutions and independent colleges are private. In 2012, in the public higher education sector, there are 1,090 four-year institutions and 1,215 three-year vocational or technical institutions. These 1,090 institutions include 112 institutions in the 211 Project, and these 112 universities have 49 universities in the 985 Project. The 211 Project is the Chinese government's endeavor, launched in 1992, aimed at strengthening about 100 higher education institutions and key disciplinary areas, as the national priority, for the 21st century. The 985 Project is another project to promote the Chinese higher education system, prompted by President Jiang Zemin's speech at the 100th anniversary of Peking University, on May 4, 1998. The goal of launching such a program is to have a few world-class universities, and to be globally competitive.

In China, students who study in three-year colleges cannot transfer to four-year universities. Thus, only those students in the 1,090 public four-year institutions have the opportunity to get bachelor's degrees, and the students in the 211- and 985-Project universities would have easier access to master's and PhD degree programs. The Academy of

Sciences and the Academy of Social Sciences should also be included as offering master's- and PhD-level education, because both academies have graduate programs. The total enrollment of graduates in China is 1,404,942—of which, in 2010, 246,319 students were in PhD programs and 1,158,623 were in master's degree programs.

In addition, there are about 1,470 private colleges and universities, of which 370 institutions are authorized to issue four-year education certificates, and 39 are authorized to issue bachelor's degrees. In total, there are about seven million students studying in private institutions. China also has a large self-study examination system, and participants can apply for diplomas or certification through the self-study programs administrated by the Ministry of Education. Those who pass all the required examinations could get a qualification equal to a four-year undergraduate education.

In 1981, China adopted the American style of academic degrees, which includes bachelor's, master's, and PhD degrees. Currently, there are different professional degrees—with an executive master of business administration, master of business administration, doctor of education, and others. In China, as mentioned above, a student usually takes three years for a technical education, four years for a bachelor's degree, two to three years for a master's degree; and for a PhD degree, it generally takes another three to four years after the master's degree. Yet, currently, only 796 higher education institutions are accredited by the Ministry of Education to offer graduate degrees.

In terms of finance and governance of Chinese higher education, a two-level provision is in place for public colleges and universities. The two-level provision system means the central government is responsible for policymaking, quality controls, and core funding—mainly research grants, infrastructure-building capital, basic faculty salary, and subsidies; and the local governments or provincial governments are responsible for managing admission, funding, and placement of graduates—in accordance with national policies and laws for local and provincial colleges and universities.

Currently, the central government provides core funding to the universities in the 211 and 985 Projects. Since 1998, when the 985 Project was established, the central government has appropriated additional funds for the country's nine leading research universities. Other universities are partially financed by the central government and by provincial and local governments.

While China continues to surge onto the global economic stage, it is undergoing one of the most ambitious higher education expansions in the world. However, given the absence of sufficient funds during this fast growth, many universities have borrowed heavily to pay for expansion. Many researchers have tried to estimate, but have not yet discovered, the scale of the debt. Only one 985 Project university in the northeast part of the country—carrying a debt of US$3 billion, after merging with several local colleges and universities—caught the national government's attention. The debt problem is not unique to that single university. It is estimated that the total debt of higher education in Huan province was US$2.25 billion (at an exchange rate of 6.50 RMB to US$1.00) (Jiang 2010).

Now, there are discussions on how to pay back the loans to the banks; many suggestions target an increase in national government support to higher education, and more autonomy for universities to tap different resources. As a result, in leading research universities, many special programs now charge higher tuition and fees than for regular programs. So, commercialization is reflected in many aspects of Chinese academic life. Faculty working with enterprises and establishing commercialized labs in university science parks and providing training programs by collecting fees are some of the fund-raising strategies.

Private higher education

Ownership, governance, and finance of private higher education are complicated. During the 1980s, Chinese higher education witnessed a series of reforms. In 1985, a document for higher education reform was published, noting the boom of private higher education institutions. In the 1990s, the central government attempted to achieve regional decentralization or the devolution of authority from central to local government. Local governments received opportunities to develop higher education institutions, according to local requirements. The introduction of market forces to China, throughout the 1990s, has resulted in tuition and fees, more research cooperation with private enterprises, and the growth of private colleges. The privatization of Chinese higher education may indicate two things: the appearance of private colleges and universities and the commercialized behavior of public higher education. Currently, public colleges and universities have more autonomy to generate their own revenue—by operating enterprises, providing commissioned training, and collecting tuition and fees for different academic programs. However, major financial support in public higher education is still provided by central and local governments. In Chinese higher education, the term "private" is used to encompass all private institutions. They are called private mainly because of their financial independence. They are self-financed, mainly through student tuition and fees, while the central government provides regulations, requirements, and policies for the development of private colleges and universities; and provincial governments provide quality controls.

It is worth noting that, in China, the "privatization" of higher education inherited from the socialist government is different from the prevailing notion in the Western world. In essence, in Chinese higher education, privatization is concerned with the transfer of responsibility, originally shouldered by central and provincial governments, to the private sector; or with a change in the nature of government involvement. China's experience certainly differs from much of the world because the strategies adopted by the Chinese leadership are highly "instrumental" in terms of creating more educational opportunities in response to the emerging market needs (Zha 2006).

The rapid expansion of private universities and colleges in China, at the end of the 20th century, sparked many debates about the nature and ownership of private higher education institutions. China's first national legislation on private education, the Act for Promoting Minban Education in the People's Republic of China, was finalized in 2002, after many years of deliberation. Since the promulgation of this education law, more emphasis or attention is given to quality control in private higher education institutions. Still, most of the private institutions acknowledge the immense difficulties in competing with their public counterparts, because public higher education plays a dominant role in the country.

Reform of the public higher education system

The demand for higher education is immense in China; and while the higher education system just cannot keep pace with this compelling need, a series of reforms have taken place. According to the Ministry of Education, five strategies have been implemented: the reform of education provision, university management, the financing of higher education institutions, recruitment and job placement, and finally internal academic management. Among the five reforms, the changes to the financing of higher education institutions, recruitment and job-placement, and internal management are of greatest importance, because they relate directly to hiring and salaries of faculty and staff. In China, faculty and staff in public higher education institutions used to be considered as government employees, so they all carried official titles. But administrative staff in universities enjoy more senior titles than academic professors. This means they also have priority over faculty in accessing the university's organizational support and administrative resources. In order to increase academic autonomy and faculty status, in 2004 Peking University first started personnel reform in the university in correspondence with other reforms in higher education.

The overall objective of the reform was to harmonize the external relationships of higher education institutions with government, society, and industry; and internal relationships between administrative staff, faculty, and students. The overall reforms helped to set up a new system, in which national government is responsible for the overall planning and macro-management, while the higher education institutions follow the laws and enjoy the autonomy of providing education according to the needs of society. The personnel reform at Peking University helped to create a supportive environment for faculty to conduct research, teaching, and other academic activities. Through Peking University's personnel reform, the tenure system was introduced to Chinese higher education. Of course, the Chinese personnel reform in higher education has resulted in a lot of difficulties, but at least the "iron bowl," which means lifelong employment for faculty and staff, was removed. After Peking University's personnel reform, only full professors are tenured, and all of the rest of the academic and administrative staff have contracts.

Academic contracts and faculty hiring

According to the most recent official statistics, in 2009, China had approximately 2,233,722 faculty and staff in higher education institutions, in total. Of these, 2,195,647 are in public higher education, and the rest are in private higher education. Faculty numbers in vocational colleges and private institutions account for approximately 13 per cent. There are 1,363,531 full-time faculty, of which 1,345,650 are in public higher education institutions, and 17,881 in private higher education institutions. The student–teacher ratio is 18.84 to 1. Among the 401,173 part-time faculty, the 329,528 that are in public higher education include 51,519 in adult higher education and 20,126 in private higher education (Ministry of Education 2009a and b).

Based on those numbers, several things need to be pointed out. First, most faculty work in the public higher education sector; and second, in public higher education the faculty to staff ratio is almost 1:1—this indicates that Chinese public universities comprise a large administrative body in university management; third, there are only 141,999 full-time and 68,019 part-time full professors in China's whole higher education system. Of the 141,999 full-time professors, 140,130 work in public institutions and 1,869 are in private higher education institutions (Ministry of Education 2009a and b). According to this set of data, full professors only make up a small proportion of the total faculty in higher education, and most of them are in the public sector.

Historical change of the employment system

From 1949, in China, all working units including institutions in higher education have been public; staff and faculty in higher education were considered as government employees, and all were considered to be in the same category as civil servants in terms of employment, salary, and benefits. In society at large, it was said that Chinese workers and civil servants (then, intellectuals were considered as the working class) were well protected with three iron bowls: "iron rice bowl" (*tiefanwan*), "iron wages," and "iron chair." The iron rice bowl means lifetime employment, the iron wages offer a fixed reward system, and the iron chair refers to inflexible positions. Another term includes *guanbenwei*, which means "official standard."

Based on the employment system and the official standards, there was a tradition of inheritance (*dingti*)—in which jobs could be passed from parents to children or other members of the family (Warner and Zhu 2000). Although academic positions could not pass to children, it was likely that faculty members' children could easily become regular employees of the institution. Later on, if the children worked hard enough or were smart enough to get a degree, they could be promoted to administrative positions in the universities. This phenomenon shows something about the problem of less social mobility across sectors in China at that time.

Prior to the transition from a centrally planned economy to a guided market economy in the late 1970s, the so-called three-iron-bowls system prevailed. Under that system, at higher education institutions, qualified employees and academic staff (including all levels of faculty) were guaranteed lifetime employment—with the "cradle to the grave" welfare, such as medical, educational, and retirement benefits, provided for workers in governmental enterprises. Wage levels were centrally controlled.

After economic reform and beginning with the open-door policy in 1978, the lifetime employment (*tiefanwan*) system has been gradually phased out. In the 1990s, with a new, open market economic system, in which competitiveness and efficiency were emphasized and many workers in the old industries were laid off in order to increase productivity, discussion about reforming the system in higher education institutions began. Of course, with the serious brain-drain problem in institutions, reforms could not occur, given the great demand for academic staff. In institutions, a performance-driven reward system could only be implemented gradually. Eventually, the employment market was differentiated through altering the metaphor of the three metal bowls to: "golden bowls," (high wages and positions); "silver bowls" (better salaries); and "iron bowls," (the lowest salary and social status). It was after the publication of *Decisions on Deepening the Reform of Personnel System of Higher Education* in 1999 by the Ministry of Education in China, that higher education institutions started to reform regulations relating to lifelong employment.

Then, a more Western-style, human-resource management system with contracts was adopted in higher education institutions. All faculty and staff were required to sign a contract with the university at the turn of the century, which thus established the contract system. However, it is still hard for a university to fire faculty members if they are not considered qualified. Now the contract system prevails in all higher education institutions, due to an important reform in Peking University.

In 2002, the first personnel reform was initiated at Peking University, which was followed by other leading Chinese public research universities. At Peking University there was a debate on the best way to reform its personnel system. It took two years to resolve the debate, and a new program was implemented in 2004. The debate focused on how to remove lifetime employment. The final decision was to only give tenure to full professors; and all other academic staff—associate professors, lecturers, and assistant professors—are contracted. Of course, there has been significant resistance to these changes.

Laws protecting faculty employment

In theory, many laws provide protection to faculty in higher education institutions. The general labor law and trade union law are two examples. In 1994, the Labor Law of People's Republic of China, 1994 was enacted. According to articles 7 and 8 of this labor law, workers have the right to join or organize trade unions, and the trade union should initiate its activities independently, in order to protect workers' legal rights. Workers are also entitled to participate in democratic management and to negotiate with business organizations to defend workers' legal rights through the workers' assembly. Also, article 33 of this labor law says:

> The staff and workers of an enterprise as one party may conclude a collective contract with the enterprise on matters relating to labor remuneration.... A collective contract shall be concluded by the trade union on behalf of the staff and workers with the enterprise.
>
> (Labor Law of the People's Republic of China)

These articles of the labor law actually laid down a foundation for collective bargaining. However in higher education, in reality, faculty or administrative staff never bargain with the university or college deans—concerning salaries and other benefits—because basic salaries of faculty and staff are still decided by the central government.

"Collective bargaining" in China is a new concept, since there was never such a concept at all in the later 20th century. Thus, it is unclear to what extent collective bargaining actually occurs, even in the private sector. It is true that in China, all faculty and staff in universities are unionized; but they seldom express their grievances to trade unions, because they believe that the trade union has little authority to solve their problems. Trade unions in China are very different from the ones in the Western world, because in China they are still seen as administratively subordinate to different levels of government.

Labor contracts have been discussed:

> Chinese workers are disadvantaged in comparison to employers in employment relations. They do not have bargaining power to negotiate with employers on the contents of the contract, which are largely formalized by government labor administrations.
>
> (Shen 2007, 126)

A new framework for an employment system centered on the legal and contractual regulation of labor relations has, only recently, been gradually passed through national legislation—such as, in 2007, the Labor Contract Law. It mainly addresses some urgent concerns—such as overtime pay, delayed payment of wages, and unsafe working conditions. In addition, the Law of Employment Contracts that became effective in January 2008 is another important law for protecting the benefits of all employees. This law has been formulated to improve the labor contract system, to make the rights and obligations of both parties of the labor contract explicit, and to protect the lawful rights and interests of workers, in order to ensure a harmonious and stable labor relationship. With the Law of Employment Contracts, employees may now sue their employers directly, without going through the Labor Department and governmental agencies to file for employment grievances. Yet, those laws do not refer specifically to faculty and staff in higher education institutions. When real disputes occur between faculty and staff and the university administrative orders are frequently applied—instead of implementing legal procedures. This means, even in higher education, administrative orders still play a dominant role in the relationship between management and workers in respect of decisions on salary, benefits, and other issues.

The "standardized" practice of faculty hiring

Generally, all universities are required to publish information about vacancies, in order to encourage all qualified and interested persons to apply for the positions. For equal employment, universities always advocate fairness and equality, which means that all employment-related decisions are based on principles of individual merit and achievement—including skills, knowledge, education background, and abilities relevant to the positions.

The primary criterion for academic appointment is, thus, academic and professional excellence; and no candidate can be recommended who does not meet the criteria for the appointment in question. The employment decision is usually made by the academic committee at the school or college, but it varies at the different institutions. The academic committee members usually consist of the dean, associate deans, department heads, and full professors. The full professors on the academic or recruiting committee are sometimes appointed by the dean. In current hiring practices in academic professions, males are usually preferred to females. If candidates do not differ in academic performance, younger candidates are also preferred. In many job descriptions, one may find that a PhD candidate of a certain age is encouraged to apply. Here, women and older applicants are at a disadvantage.

Though hiring faculty in Chinese universities is the responsibility of the dean or the chairperson of a department authorized by the personnel committee of the university, sometimes senior faculty can make recommendations, too. Occasionally professors can also be invited to participate in the decision-making process; and at times even students are invited to offer their opinions, if the applicants on the short list give public lectures. In schools and colleges, the dean and the academic committee are responsible for making the final decision or the recommendation to the university; the academic committee is responsible for ensuring that fair practice is followed throughout the hiring process. Criteria for faculty hiring vary by discipline. But in general, they should include knowledge of the subject matter, effective teaching, scholarly background, and potential academic and administrative contribution to the related schools.

Academic qualifications for faculty positions differ by institutions, too. In general, to enter into the academic profession, one at least needs to hold a master's degree. In leading research universities, one must have a PhD degree with two years of postdoctorate research experience. But in some technical colleges and private institutions, a baccalaureate degree may be sufficient for a teaching position, though universities always prefer those who have master's and PhD degrees.

A hiring process includes the following steps: first, the positions or vacancies are advertised through the internet, newspapers, or other media, with a description of the job requirements and the selection process. Applicants can then apply online. Or, if there is a vacancy, some senior professors could make recommendations. There is no standard application form, but a curriculum vitae with educational background and academic achievements, professional development interests, a list of PhD thesis and published papers are required. The recruiting committee, chaired by the department head or the dean, establishes the criteria for selection, organizes reviews, and determines which applicants will be interviewed—based on the preferred qualifications established for the position. As part of the interview process, the candidate may be required to give a lecture or a public speech, as designated by the academic committee.

The candidate may also be asked to meet professors and, sometimes, may be required to take a series of written tests—such as professional knowledge, computer skills, assessment, and English proficiency tests. The tests are developed by each institution separately and used to ascertain the candidates' basic qualification. However, educational background and academic achievements are valued most highly in the academic profession. If a candidate receives an offer, he/she is placed on the eligibility list and ratified by the dean and school academic committee; then, the decision is submitted to the university personnel office for approval. Once an appointment is approved, the newly hired candidate with a fresh PhD degree may obtain a three-year contract as an assistant professor or a lecturer. After two to three years, the faculty member is likely to be promoted to associate professor.

The faculty selection process in the top Chinese universities does not seem much different to hiring faculty in Western universities. However, faculty inbreeding linked with academic favoritism is still a problem, because academic favoritism can sometimes bypass the required faculty hiring procedures. The desire for well-qualified graduates to become junior faculty at their home institutions led to generations of academic inbreeding. Now, in order to stop faculty inbreeding, leading research universities have tried to recruit faculty members internationally. In 2004, Peking University announced that, in principle, it would not hire new faculty from the graduates of colleges, schools, and departments with a single academic lineage in the same year in an effort to stop academic inbreeding and to eliminate academic favoritism.

Regulations on faculty hiring

Regarding hiring faculty, there does not seem to be any national regulation. However, the Teachers Law of People's Republic of China, 1993 directly initiated the current faculty hiring system and provides guidance for faculty hiring and contracting in higher education institutions. According to this law, teachers at all levels of the education system with qualifications for taking up a position upon evaluation are employed by institutions in accordance with the responsibilities, conditions, and terms of office of the prescribed teachers' positions. Yet, this law does not seem to have much direct effect on specific hiring practices in universities, because it is too general. Chiefly, the regulation of hiring faculty is built into the governance structure. In each university, there is a department responsible for regulation, which is considered to be independent from the university administration but is under the leadership of the chairperson of the university council. This department is mainly in charge of selecting deans and directors for the university administration, and preventing any corruptive activity on campus. If there is a grievance regarding faculty hiring and promotion, it is also dealt with by this department.

Faculty positions and contracts

The Chinese faculty consists of assistant lecturer, lecturer, associate professor, and full professor. Within each category, there are different ranks and salary scales. "Full professor" is divided into four ranks, with the fourth being the entry level. "Associate professor" is divided into three ranks, while "assistant professor" and "assistant lecturer" may be divided into two ranks. Within higher education, a first-rank professor is considered at the top of the academic profession, and so gets the highest bonus relating to position. The basic salary, allocated by the central government, depends on the number of year of services and the rank held.

The tenure system was established in China, following the introduction of the employment-contract system. In 2002, when Peking University launched its personnel reform with the introduction of a tenure system, many other universities followed them in adopting this practice, though it generated hot debate inside the university and across the country. Now all 985 Project universities and most of the 211 Project universities can appoint full professors. However, in most other universities, the situation differs because they do not have the autonomy to confer full professorships.

According to personnel regulation at Peking University, associate professors in arts and sciences and lecturers in all subjects are contracted for three-year terms, for up to 12 years (four contracts). Theoretically, if faculty fail their promotion after academic assessment within the fourth contract period, they should leave voluntarily. Yet, in practice, an associate professor can voluntarily postpone the request for promotion, if they do not believe themselves ready for promotion; and they can stay in the same position until retirement. Not all universities adopted the Peking model of personnel management, but some use different hiring and promotion arrangements. However, all universities adopted the contract system.

Apart from teaching responsibilities, all faculty are required to publish, including those at non-research universities; the difference lies in the research quotas and teaching loads. In China, with the exception of leading universities like 211 and 985 Project universities, most universities classify themselves as teaching and research universities, which means they lay equal significance on teaching and research. However, regarding evaluation and promotion, research ability and publication carry more weight than teaching effectiveness. Thus, the "publish and perish" term is very popular at Chinese universities. While not many faculty really "perish," they may obtain less remuneration and take longer to be promoted. Thus, to get promoted, a faculty member needs to at least fulfill the university publication quotas.

Other elements concerning faculty hiring

In China, since most research universities and research institutions belong to the public sector—usually managed and supported by the central or provincial governments—faculty and staff enjoy good working conditions; and they are well protected by laws, in comparison with faculty in the private sector. Faculty in private colleges and universities are paid less and in general do not have fixed-term employment status. Many faculty in private higher education institutions have a minimum one-year contract, and there are no tenured positions. At the end of each contracted year, the contract can be easily terminated. In this chapter, many generalizations apply only to the public higher education sector but not to the private sector.

Only a few tenured positions are awarded to faculty in local public universities; so, there are not many full professors in local public universities. At local universities, though few faculty have tenure, there is still a presumption of lifetime employment for academics; and their contracts tend to be extended automatically by the university. Few contracts are terminated, even when the institution faces financial difficulties. Most tenured positions are in Peking University, Tsinghua University, and Zhejiang University. At those universities, appointments to full professor are carefully monitored and awarded by the appointment committee of the university, and competitively nominated at colleges and schools.

The contract or tenure a professor holds does not prescribe teaching hours, nor does it specify any requirement for research. The research and teaching requirements are set by individual departments and schools. All faculty are expected to perform research and teaching, simultaneously; but the teaching loads of professors, associate professors, lecturers, and teaching assistants are determined annually. Depending on the actual length of school terms, all faculty are required to teach at least 32–36 weeks per year and two to four courses per academic year. As there is some weighting of teaching time according to the instructional setting (seminar, lecture, practical, or field work), the weekly teaching load of a professor can be as low as four hours in leading research universities. At other universities, the teaching load for professors could be eight to ten hours per week. Hours taught in excess of this teaching load are paid as overtime at a flat rate, which has nothing to do with the basic salaries set up by the government.

The primary responsibility of faculty in 985 and 211 Project universities is research—thus, the teaching load is much less in comparison with local teaching universities. Individuals receiving employment contracts in 985 and 211 Project universities are often given quotas on the number of publications in designated journals that should be attained within a limited period of time. Job performance is evaluated mainly on research rather than teaching, especially on publications and the number of the research grants a professor receives.

In China, the ranking of a university is mostly based on research productivity. So, in order to attract the most talented faculty and to enhance scientific research, many universities have the autonomy to compete for top professors by offering better salaries, fringe benefits, reduced teaching loads, and other incentives.

Factors influencing academic salary and remuneration

Currently, information about faculty salaries in China is difficult to obtain, because of the complexity of faculty remuneration and the lack of national data. Historically, this was not a problem, since professors were paid according to the national common guidelines. The central government set up the regulations for payment, according to rank and official title; so then, everyone knew what and how everyone else was paid.

The academic salary has been improved greatly, though many faculty members consider themselves underpaid. Research shows that, in PhD programs, the proportion of male students with a rural family background is high. This may indicate that less young urban dynamic and talented male students are achieving PhD degrees, and more are entering into other professions—like business, finance, and better-paid industries. Also, more talented male students went abroad for PhD degrees. Thus, the academic profession has become less attractive for the younger generation in the field of humanities and social sciences, while in the sciences and engineering, and in professional fields such as management would be different. It has been pointed out that the remuneration of the academic profession is central to the success of higher education enterprises everywhere and is also critically important for individual academics around the world (Rumbley, Pacheco, and Altbach 2008). This is very true within China.

As discussed previously, the basic salaries of faculty and staff in public higher education institutions are set by the central, provincial, or local governments. So, the base salary and scale salary for faculty of the same rank are roughly the same nationwide. The tables in this chapter illustrate the general situation regarding salary in higher education institutions in China. In order to improve faculty and staff salaries in higher education, universities are now given more autonomy to tap different resources for institutional development. Under the central government's guidelines for faculty compensation, higher education institutions can use some of their self-generated resources to recompense faculty and staff. But some universities are doing better than others in tapping different resources—that is, there are variations in compensation levels at different institutions.

Even in the same university, the gap can be huge between schools and colleges, because some schools and colleges can generate more money than others. The well-known business schools of leading research universities can generate more money in many different ways, so faculty incomes in those business schools may be many times higher than in humanities and social sciences.

This situation is in accordance with Todd M. Johnson's study:

> Besides wages, work units in China typically provide a host of other monetary and non-monetary benefits to their employees. Because basic wages for government workers tend to be inflexible and fall within a rather narrow range, it is often the variations in fringe benefits that differentiate the rewards of various jobs.
>
> (Johnson 1991, 139)

This is very true in the university as a work unit. Faculty may receive additional money through the fluctuation of benefits that include medical care, housing, pension, and unemployment insurance, as well as others.

Factors that influence faculty incomes in public higher education institutions include the number of years worked, the academic field, the academic rank, teaching load, and research grants. Besides, in order to increase faculty income, many universities tacitly allow faculty to engage in a range of additional activities—such as consulting and night-class teaching. Many professors engage in consulting and cooperative research activities, especially at the leading research universities. Thus, faculty at these universities may earn more in comparison with academics at teaching colleges and universities. In addition, many professors in leading research universities can obtain research grants from different government research programs and industries; this is especially true for science and engineering in leading research universities. Though there are restrictions on the use of government research grants, a certain amount may be taken as research compensation. Since most of the government research and development money goes to sciences and engineering, faculty in humanities and social sciences have limited access to research grants. Even when they receive grants, the amount is not comparable to the grants in the areas of science and applied research.

Leading national research universities tend to be more successful in securing government funds than local universities:

> Generally speaking, national institutions have more budget than local ones for at least three reasons. Firstly, per capita fiscal allocation at national level is higher than local due to better fiscal condition; secondly, there are several dedicated projects supported by central budget, funding from which usually go to national institutions; thirdly, national institutions receive more research funding due to their mission and stronger capacity. There is less discrepancy among national institutions, but more among local institutions due to local economic and fiscal imbalance.
>
> (Yan 2009)

No doubt, most of the government research grants go to 211 and 985 Project universities, and this definitely will affect faculty income in those universities.

Education may not be a factor influencing individual faculty income, though it is considered usual for a doctoral degree holder to receive more pay than a master's degree holder. However, in China, one hardly notices a difference in salary between a master's degree and a PhD degree holder. The only variation is that a PhD holder gets promoted much faster than someone with a master's degree.

Additional compensation

As mentioned previously, faculty and staff used to be treated as part of the civil service and were paid according to government regulations. In the mid-1980s, based on anecdotal experience, some top professors were paid about 200 RMB (US$54.05) per month at the high end of the scale. Back then, the exchange rate was about US$1.00 to 3.70 RMB. Since the salary was so low for academic staff and scientists, it was said that "scientists who did research on the atom bomb were paid less than peddlers who sold 'tea eggs' on the street." It is only in the last two decades that there have been great increases in faculty salaries. In the last ten years, universities were given more autonomy to use institutional revenues to provide subsidies to faculty and staff. Faculty and staff in universities began to receive increases in salary, bonus, and subsidies, according to government regulations.

Usually faculty receive their school and university bonuses and subsidies on top of the government salary. This makes Chinese faculty salaries more complicated and difficult to analyze, because the benefits could be monetary or non-monetary. Some universities may provide more bonuses and subsidies than others, and schools' bonuses are ad hoc in nature. Generally, university bonuses, determined by faculty positions in public universities, ranged from 3,000 to 10,000 RMB (US$468–1,562), when the bonus was first initiated in 2000. A fourth-rank full professor's salary and remuneration from a well-known university with specializations in business and finance demonstrate the complexity (see Table 5.1). It is not our intention to generalize from this case because there are many variations among the universities

The fourth-rank professor's total income is 9,807 RMB (US$1,520) per month, before tax and after the deduction of the public reserve fund. In China, the public reserve fund is equivalent to the American faculty retirement plan. The fund is mandated by the government and directly deposited by the university into the faculty's reserve account. For this retirement account, the university is also mandated to dedicate matching funds provided by the government, for an additional retirement pension for faculty. After the public reserve fund and the tax deduction, this fourth-rank professor would take home around 8,000 RMB (US$1,240). If the optional living subsidy is removed, the net income should be about 7,000 RMB (US$1,085) monthly. The first two items of this fourth-rank professor's pay statement are 1,975 RMB (US$306) and 555 RMB (US$86) which is 2,530 RMB (US$392). This demonstrates that the bonuses and subsidies a faculty member receives can be three to four times higher than the basic salary.

Some bonuses are not reflected in the fourth-rank professor's pay statement, such as the payment received from the university and the department for teaching above the normal teaching loads, rewards for influential publications, and compensation for research projects. These payments could represent anything from a few thousand to more than one hundred thousand renminbi, or even more, annually, depending on the professor's teaching load, research grants, and publications. These rewards also differ greatly between disciplines and universities. For example, a faculty member from Peking University, who published a paper in *Science*, might earn 5,000 RMB (US$775) as a research bonus; if she/he were from another university, especially a provincial university, she/he might receive between 30,000 RMB (US$4,651) and 50,000

Table 5.1 Monthly salary of a fourth-rank full English professor in foreign language studies, 2010 (RMB)[a]

Base salary	Scale salary	Teaching subsidy	Duty subsidy	Food subsidy	Telephone	Laundry	Transportation	Magazine subscription
1,420	555	50	1,995	50	100	10	315	27
Housing subsidy	Living subsidy (optional)	Position subsidy	Unemployment insurance	One-child subsidy	Price subsidy	Public reserve fund	Other subsidies	Total
115	1,100	3,900	12	50	10	817	100	9,807

Notes: In this university, professors are divided into four ranks. The fourth rank refers to the entry level for a full professor. Information in this table may not be generalized to another university, because the category of subsidies may vary from university to university.
[a] US$1.00 = 6.50 RMB.

Source: The data is from the faculty member's pay statement.

RMB (US$7,752), because a provincial university might assume that as not many of its faculty members will publish in *Science*, it is better to use the reward as an instrument to increase the faculty's productivity. It is also possible that the professor might not receive anything at all if the provincial university does not have the same reward policy.

Again, the fourth-rank professor in our example is from a well-known university, specializing in business and finance, so the payment received is likely to be higher than a regular fourth-rank professor from other universities. Telephone and transportation subsidies shown in Table 5.1 are not required by the central government but are options offered at the discretion of each university. If the university has the money to provide those subsidies, it funds them; but if not, nobody can complain. Additionally, the position subsidy for this fourth-rank professor is 3,900 RMB (US$605); at other universities, normally this income would be between 2,500 RMB (US$388) and 3,000 RMB (US$465). In this case, the university is more self-sufficient in financial terms. Yet, this fourth-rank English-language or literature professor is not likely to be eligible for a publication bonus because, in that field, it is hard to publish papers in recognized international journals.

A first-rank professor would receive a much higher salary and bonus than this fourth-rank English-language or literature professor. But not many professors can reach the first rank, because there is always a quota for the number of first-rank professors in universities; this is especially the case for social science and humanities. Usually, the members of the Chinese Academy of Sciences, the Chinese Academy of Engineering, and top-level university administrators receive the first-rank professor's salary and bonus.

The Chinese Academy of Sciences, established in 1949, is the leading research institution in natural science, technological science, and high-tech innovation in China. As a research institute, it has its own scientists and researchers. But the organization also has the responsibility to select academics. A number of academics are regularly nominated from both research institutes and universities. In the China, being selected as an academic is not only considered an honor but also a promotion, with an increase of academic rank and salary. Currently, there are 704 academics selected by this academy; a number come from universities and some from the Academy of Sciences and the Academy of Social Sciences. The Chinese Academy of Engineering, established in 1994, is the comparable national academy for engineering; currently it has 747 academics. Faculty named as academics by these elite institutions automatically become first-rank professors.

Given the quotas, this leaves few opportunities for faculty in humanities and social sciences aspiring to first-rank professorship. However, based on the fourth-rank English-language or literature professor's salary and bonuses, we can estimate a first-rank English professor's salary and bonus, demonstrated in Table 5.2.

The first-rank English-language or literature professor enjoys many additional benefits—like special government subsidies, research grants, academic rewards, and university housing—compared to the fourth-rank professor. However, Table 5.2 only shows an estimated salary because the actual incomes are not disclosed. It is generally understood that some first-rank professors in science and engineering can receive millions in research grants annually, from national research and development and industry. Thus, one cannot begin to estimate those professors' actual income at all.

In contrast, professors in private universities are employees of a particular university, whose salary and fringe benefits come solely from the university or, more specifically, from student tuition and fees. Generally, faculty salaries in private colleges and universities range from 3,000 RMB to 6,000 RMB (US$465–930), per month. Besides, private colleges and universities do not seem to provide any benefits such as medical care insurance, pension plans, or others. So, their salaries or incomes are much lower in comparison with their counterparts in the public sector. However, a top-level administrator's salary in a private university could be very high. At a well known private university, in 2000, the university president's annual salary was reported to be 200,000 RMB (US$31,007), which is not unusual at private universities. At that time, this salary could have been three times higher than that of the president at a leading public research university.

Fringe benefits for junior professors

There are a number of direct subsidies included in the monthly payment to university administrators, similar to those shown in Table 5.2. But Table 5.3 shows the details of how junior faculty members are paid, and it also provides a comparison of the incomes for an associate professor, a lecturer, and a teaching assistant at the case-study university. In Table 5.4, one may find that a junior professors income is not high in comparison. In order to increase junior professors' income and productivity, Chinese government and universities have established various programs that are only available to junior professors. In 2000, the National Science Foundation established the Young Science Fund to

Table 5.2 Estimated monthly salary of a first-rank English professor in foreign language studies, 2010 (RMB)[a]

Base salary	Scale salary	Teaching subsidy	Duty subsidy thousand separator	Food subsidy	Telephone	Laundry	Transportation	Magazine subscription
2,020	1,610	50	2,995	50	100	10	315	27
Housing subsidy	Living subsidy (optional)	Position subsidy	Unemployment insurance	One-child subsidy	Price subsidy	Public reserve fund	Other subsidies	Total
185	n.a.	6,900	12	n.a.	10	1,335	100	15,719

Notes: The salary is based on the authors' estimation, since it is hard to get access to the actual information on a professor's income. From this estimation, we suppose that the first-rank English professor would get 15,719 RMB monthly.

n.a. = not applicable.

[a] US$1.00 = 6.50 RMB.

Source: The data is based on the authors' estimation.

Table 5.3   Possible monetary subsidies for junior faculty in, 2010 (RMB)[a]

Subsidies	Associate professor	Lecturer	Teaching assistant
Teaching	50	50	50
Duty	1,675	1,240	1,040
Food	50	50	50
Telephone	100	100	100
Laundry		10	10
Transportation	325	315	300
Book and magazine	27	27	27
Housing subsidy	95	80	70
Living[b]		1,100	900
Rent[c]			600
Internal	2,800	1,800	1,600
One child	10		
Price	10	10	10
Public reserve fund	743	505	488
Total (before taxes)	5,895	5,287	5,245

Notes: [a]US$1.00 = 6.50 RMB.
[b]Living subsidy is optional because if the faculty member already received the benefits of welfare-oriented distribution of public housing or the person was given a certain amount of money equal to the value of a house at one time, she/he cannot get living subsidy, and vice versa. As the table demonstrates, the associate professors already enjoyed the welfare.
[c]Rent subsidy is only paid in the faculty member's first contract period, which lasts three years.
Source: The data is estimated based on a case study in a university specializing in business and finance.

support 160 young scholars each year, with a grant of 0.8–1.0 million RMB (US$12,000–160,000) for four years. And in 2004, the Department of Education established the New Century Excellent Young Scholar Plan, to provide external help to those excellent junior professors. Of course, those programs are very selective, and they do not benefit all junior professors.

In Chinese faculty income, the largest monetary variations result from the university bonus allocated according to rank. Subsidies for each rank are determined by each university and the differences can be as much as between 50,000 RMB (US$7,752), at the highest level, and 3,000 RMB (US$465), at the lowest, annually. This represents a striking 17-fold difference (Chen 2002). The pay scale applies to faculty, staff, and administrators in the university system, but most likely no faculty are awarded the lowest-level subsidy; the lowest level is designed for lower-level staff. Junior faculty receive 10,000 RMB (around US$1,500). While not much difference exists in the fringe benefits among associate

Table 5.4 Data on full-time and part-time teachers in private higher education institutions

Teachers	Total	% of all
1. Full-time teachers	17,881	47.04
Female	8,691	22.86
Senior (professor)	1,869	4.92
Subsenior (associate professor)	3,984	10.48
Middle (lecturer)	6,123	16.11
Junior (teaching assistant)	3,287	8.64
No rank	2,618	6.88
2. Part-time teachers	20,126	52.96
Female	8,601	22.63
Senior (professor)	3,415	8.98
Subsenior (associate professor)	7,078	18.62
Middle (lecturer)	6,483	17.05
Junior (teaching assistant)	1,563	4.11
No rank	1,587	4.17
Foreign teachers among part-time teachers	371	0.97
Total	38,007	100.00

Source: Data on academic qualifications of full-time and part-time teachers in private higher education institutions (Ministry of Education 2009a).

professor, lecturer, and teaching assistant, there is a huge gap compared with professors—particularly the first-rank professors.

Other monetary bonuses

Bonuses are paid by departments or schools and sometimes by the university, from a special bonus fund, and are not included in the salary or fringe benefits listed above. The composition of these bonuses is even more complex and hard to calculate. Mainly, they consist of rewards for additional teaching, the number of graduate students a faculty member advised, and participation in activities to generate funds, and other factors.

Of course, a professor should teach classes. Generally, a professor is required to teach two to four courses in an academic year, as discussed previously. Thus, a professor needs to teach at least one course per semester—and will therefore receive additional bonuses at the end of the semester from the university, though this function is considered as the professor's duty. If teaching two courses, the professor would get more additional bonuses. A professor who teaches more than two courses would be entitled to receive an additional bonus on top of the university bonus. For the case-study university, the professor will get 50 RBM (US$7.70) for each class taught, from the university. The school in which the professor teaches will pay another 80 RMB (US$12.40), as a matching bonus. So, putting the two payments together, the total amount would be 130 RMB (US$20.60) for each class taught. This remuneration will not appear on the monthly pay statement but will be paid at the end of the semester as a reward. But again, it is hard to estimate the range of reward, because it varies so much.

The case-study university used for elaboration in this chapter is a well-known university in business and finance, and many schools in this university run different short-term or long-term training programs, for higher tuition and fees. The training programs could be transnational or local. These programs are very profitable. The cost of tuition ranges from 20,000 to 30,000 RMB (US$3,200–4,651); higher tuition would be charged for programs designed for executives or senior managers. While the university takes a percentage as an administrative overhead, the schools or departments that run the programs keep the majority of the income for the school's operational needs, and a certain amount can be used for faculty and staff bonuses.

At the end of an academic semester, each faculty member will also get some bonuses for the classes taught at the school; this is only one example of how schools can provide bonuses to faculty and staff. There is a great discrepancy in the size of the bonuses among departments and schools, even within the same university, due to differences between disciplines and fields of study.

Additional employment (moonlighting)

Professors without much bonus pay or with fewer research grants might choose to teach outside of the university—to earn extra money by teaching in private colleges and universities in the evenings or offering courses for self-study programs. Well-known professors are sometimes invited to give a regular course in another university, an opportunity for moonlighting for which they receive generous payments. Most professors who teach in other institutions, as well as their main place of employment, are in economics, business, and finance. While the percentage of professors who teach in more than one institution has not been calculated exactly, Table 5.4 offers data regarding full-time faculty moonlighting elsewhere. In the Chinese public higher education system, part-time faculty are seldom hired unless they are moonlighting.

Table 5.4 shows that more than 20 per cent of faculty members have a part-time contract at a private higher education institution. Among this 20 per cent, there might be professors who have full-time contracts at public universities, while moonlighting at private university for supplementary employment. Since private institutions have full management autonomy and responsibility for their own profits and losses, they may intentionally choose to hire professors from public universities as part-timers in order to reduce the human cost. In China, it is rare for professors to have more than one position but, in order to get more money, it is possible for them to moonlight in private higher education institutions in the evenings.

Moonlighting has been allowed, but not encouraged, because universities fear that additional employment will erode the quality of teaching and research. Still, academic staff do moonlight in accordance with their financial need, academic discipline, skills, and time. Because of the ad hoc nature of moonlighting, it is hard to determine how much money faculty can thus earn. Faculty could sometimes double their monthly income by moonlighting. This is in accordance with Philip G. Altbach's (2009) conclusion that it is difficult to measure non-salary income.

Universities have a few ways of tracking income sources, though individual faculty members—particularly those with creative ways of boosting their incomes—have little incentive to report extra income. So now, universities are always required to use a faculty member's personal identification number to transfer payment to an employee's bank account instead of paying by cash.

Qualifications for the academic profession

The educational qualifications for an academic professor, stated in the Higher Education Law (article 46), prescribe that higher education institutions incorporate a qualification system. The Teachers Law Provision 5 (article 11) also stipulates that, to obtain qualifications at a higher education institution, a teacher should have a postgraduate degree.

According to those laws, to enter into the academic profession at least a master's degree is required, but in most leading research universities a doctoral degree is required. In fact, several of the research institutes at China's leading research universities—such as the China Center for Economic Research in Peking University—have a minimum requirement of a foreign PhD. Exceptions to these requirements are made under very rare circumstances in leading research universities now.

At public higher education institutions, it is not surprising to find that more than one-third of professors only achieved undergraduate education. This is because China's doctoral education only has a 30-year history, and those old professors have never had an opportunity to obtain a PhD degree. Today, to be a professor in a leading research university, a PhD degree is a prerequisite. Table 5.5 shows that in public higher education institutions, 40 per cent of professors have doctoral degrees and 36.1 per cent have bachelor's degrees. In private higher education institutions, as shown in Table 5.6, 56.9 per cent of full-time professors just have bachelor's degrees. In order to raise quality standards, many of those institutions rely heavily on moonlighting professors from public universities as their teaching staff.

Most faculty members with PhD degrees are in leading research universities, such as Peking University, where more than 70 per cent of the academic staff hold PhD degrees, and more than 40 per cent have a foreign PhD. But in those universities, the relationship between education background and salary are undocumented and require further investigation. Determining monetary reward remains primarily based on teaching loads, research grants, publications, and the number of master's and PhD students advised.

Academic promotions and assessment

Universities are now establishing their own internal quality-assessment systems to maintain a sustainable evaluation of individual faculty performance. They have adopted a performance-based system of promotion or assessment. Promotion occurs on the basis of individual assessments. The criteria for faculty promotion focus mainly on research grants, and publications in core journals, and teaching is considered to be secondary. However, a certain number of years of services are also required, before further promotion. Faculty are graded annually or every two or three years, on their performance (as defined above). This is a move away from the previous seniority-based promotions. In theory, an assistant professor with a PhD degree would need seven years at leading research universities to be promoted to a full professor; but in practice, it would take longer. In local universities, it would take even longer. Privileges do exist for faculty who have made great contributions to the university or society or have distinguished themselves in research or teaching, as they may be promoted sooner. In regular practice, for junior faculty in local universities, it always takes more than ten years to be promoted to full

Table 5.5 Degrees held by professors in public higher education institutions

	Total	Doctoral degrees		Master's degrees		Bachelor's degree		Associate bachelor	
Full-time professor	138,161	55,263	40.0%	31,146	22.5%	49,895	36.1%	1,857	1.4%
Part-time professor	62,157	20,962	33.7%	18,501	29.7%	21,700	34.9%	994	1.7%

Source: Data on academic qualifications of full-time and part-time teachers in regular higher education institutions (Ministry of Education 2009b).

Table 5.6 Degrees held by professors in private higher education institutions

	Total	Doctoral degrees		Master's degrees		Bachelor's degree		Associate bachelor	
Full-time Professor	1,869	224	12.0%	518	27.7%	1,064	56.9%	63	3.4%
Part-time professor	3,415	713	20.8%	1,048	30.7%	1,598	46.8%	56	1.7%

Source: Data on academic qualifications of full-time and part-time teachers in private higher education institutions (Ministry of Education 2009a).

professor. In most cases, faculty are appointed at the level of lecturer 1 or as assistant professor and promoted to associate professor after two or three years if they fulfill the university's research requirement. A faculty member with a PhD degree from a well-known Western university—with some overseas work experience or with postdoc research experience at home or abroad—will normally be appointed to associate professor, and sometimes as a full professor in a provincial or local university.

Recruiting international scholars

Domestic faculty mobility has become more common, since China adopted the flexible personnel employment policy. Factors such as reputation, location, and better salaries encourage some individuals to move from one institution to another. But the mobility generally follows a unidirectional pattern—from local, provincial, and leading research universities—as revealed in the Chinese expression: "Man struggles upwards; water flows downwards."

To increase the country's capacity for technical innovation and creativity, a range of high-level and urgently needed overseas professionals are being brought back to the country through different projects or plans. The Changjiang Scholar Plan and the 111 Plan are two of the best known.

The Changjiang Scholar Plan is aimed at attracting experts from abroad to work in Chinese universities for a longer term; it was originally called the International Partnership Program for Creative Research Teams. The program is sponsored by the Chinese government, with donations from Hong Kong. This was the most prestigious government program, intending to recruit world-known professors to teach and carry out research on Chinese campuses, at the end of the 20th century.

At the earlier stages of the program, humanities and social sciences were excluded; so only 100 professors in sciences and engineering were selected. In 2004, with the idea of developing the country with science and technology and strengthening the country with talent, humanities and social sciences were included in the plan. Currently, there are about 100 Changjiang professors at Peking University. Again, most of them are in the science fields, with humanities and social sciences a small fraction.

The Changjiang professors can have a three-year appointment or a lifelong appointment—as a special-appointed professor or a chair professor. A special-appointed professor needs to work full-time on campus, while a chair professor does not need to serve a full-time position but should be on campus for at least three months, annually. A Changjiang science professor should not be older than 45 years; and in humanities and social sciences, the individual should be under 50 years, at the time of appointment. These appointed professors' annual award is 100,000 RMB (US$15,500) on the top of a basic salary and bonus, plus a 2,000,000 RMB (US$310,000) annual research grant. The chair professors' monthly salary is 15,000 RMB (US$2,325) on top of basic salaries and bonuses. In social sciences, 500,000 RMB (US$77,520) may be available in research grants, annually.

In 2006, another plan—the Expertise-Introduction Project for Disciplinary Innovation in Universities—was launched for top scientists to work at the top research universities in China. The plan is jointly organized by the Ministry of Education and the State Administration of Foreign Experts Affairs. It aims to upgrade scientific research and create peer competition in Chinese universities, by establishing innovation centers and gathering groups of first-class intellectuals from around the world. The plan intends to bring in about 1,000 top scholars from the top 100 universities and research institutes worldwide. These experts will be integrated into domestic research infrastructure; alongside the creation of 100 subject innovation centers, set up in universities. Only universities from the 985 Project (aimed at developing a number of world-class universities) and from the 211 Project (aimed at strengthening about 100 institutions of higher education in key disciplinary areas for the 21st century) are authorized to recruit overseas Chinese under the 111 Plan. The plan states that under one 111 Plan professor, at least ten overseas scholars should be employed to organize a team. In each of these teams, at least one scholar should be an overseas academic mentor, while the foreign representatives can only come from the top 100 universities and research institutes. Generally, the academic mentors should not be older than 70 years—except for Nobel Prize winners—with other representatives under 50 years. Subjects should include basic sciences, technology, and project management, among others.

Both universities and the central government jointly sponsor the plan. Under this plan, recruited scientists would have an annual salary package of one million RMB (about US$155,038) on the top of their basic government salary and departmental and university bonuses, plus five million RMB (US$775,193), annually, as a research grant.

The two plans discussed above show the national government's determination to attract the most talented faculty. The 111 Plan, especially, is very attractive, even to foreign experts. Comparing the one million RMB annual award with the fourth-rank English-language and literature professor's annual salary reveals the disparity, but there are many positive signs regarding the 111 Plan (Altbach and Ma 2011). It shows the acknowledgment of the importance of knowledge and the value of top scientists. This acknowledgment reflects great social progress in recent Chinese academic history.

Conclusion

Since 1978, Chinese higher education has changed dramatically—not only in size and provision but in the profile and remuneration of the academic profession, as well. Several laws have been put in place to provide general protection to the academic profession, and numerous reforms have been introduced regarding faculty hiring and employment. Chinese higher education is quite different from only three decades ago.

Chinese faculty and academic staff are unionized, once they join the profession, but the Chinese trade union mostly functions as the coordinator of the relationship between government and union numbers, which is quite different from the Western concept of trade unions. Recently have there been debates about strengthening the trade union's role in coordinating labor relationships, especially in helping workers to solve disputes over labor contracts, hiring practices, and salaries; but it may not be directly applicable to professors in higher education.

The transformation includes the hiring of faculty and employment. Most universities have sought to establish regulations in order to standardize hiring and employment procedures. In Chinese culture, intellectuals always enjoy a high social status, though their salary may not be high. Faculty salary or income has improved greatly from a historical and developmental perspective. As mentioned earlier, in the 1980s scientists were poorly paid but not now. The current concern is the gap between professors from different disciplines, even within the same university. These differences may not be healthy for a university in the long term.

Of course, a number of challenges are facing the academic profession in China. When compared with some of their international counterparts in other emerging nations and developed countries, Chinese faculty salaries may be low. They may also be low in comparison with other professions inside the country, which might make the profession less attractive. The Chinese government has been trying to improve the situation, and universities are also trying to make use of salary subsidies and other incentives to attract excellent young faculty members. However, the size and range of these incentives vary substantially from university to university and from discipline to discipline. Again, humanities and social sciences are suffering because most of the policies favor sciences and engineering.

Due to China's salary system, Chinese universities may not be attractive to top scholars in the international labor market. In a survey of academic salaries in 15 countries around the world, Canada ranked at the top, with an average monthly salary of $6,548 per month (in purchasing power parity dollars); and China came last with a monthly salary of $1,182 (Rumbley, Pacheco, and Altbach 2008). Low salaries may have contributed to the brain drain in the past two decades. More than one million Chinese students who studied abroad did not return. But recently, with the global financial crisis and special policies from the Chinese government, the situation has begun to change. Now more and more fresh foreign PhD holders look for opportunities in Chinese universities—a good sign for brain circulation.

Since the beginning of the 985 Project, the Chinese government has injected billions of lump sum grants into building world-class universities. Backed by government funding, many leading research universities have started to attract world-renowned academics through the Zhangjiang scholarship and the 111 Plan. These scholars are provided with well-equipped labs, surrounded with the brightest students, and given tremendous leeway. Based on these initiatives, many more special projects have been established to try to improve young faculty members' salary and income—efforts that provide great hopes for junior faculty and staff.

This discussion analyzes many issues concerning Chinese faculty salary and remuneration, hiring, and contracts. Further research is needed on themes such as: compensation in local universities and technical colleges; whether there should be regulations on universities, schools, or even faculty's engagement in commercial activities; and even how to reform the Chinese faculty salary and remunerations structure to simplify the system.

Notes

1. The independent colleges used to be affiliated to public universities, and served as the commercial arms of these universities. In 2003 they were required to be "independent" from the public parent universities and to be self-financing and were named as independent colleges.

References

Altbach, P. G. 2009. The intricacies of academic remuneration. *International Higher Education* 54 (Winter): 3–4.

Altbach, P. G., and W. Ma. 2011. Getting graduates to come home—Not so easy. *International Higher Education* 63 (Spring): 8–9.

Chen, X. 2002. The academic profession in China. In *The decline of the Guru: The academic profession in developing and middle-income countries*, ed. P. G. Altbach, 107–34. New York: Palgrave Macmillan.

Jiang, Z. 2010. *Some thought on the solving of the higher education debt.* [In Chinese.] http://www.jyb.cn/Theory/jygl/201001/t20100127_338163.html.

Johnson, T. 1991. Wages, benefits, and the promotion process for Chinese university faculty. *China Quarterly* 125.

Labor Law of the People's Republic of China. http://www.law-lib.com/law/law_view.asp?id=255.

Ministry of Education. 2009a. *Academic qualifications of full-time and part-time teachers in private higher education institutions.* [In Chinese.] http://www.moe.educn/publicfiles/business/htmlfiles/moe/s4960/201012/113522.html.

———. 2009b. *Academic qualifications of full-time and part-time Teachers in regular higher education institutions.* [In Chinese.] http://moe.edu.cn/publicfiles/business/htmlfiles/moe/s4960/201012/13525.html.

———. 2009c. *Gross enrollment rate of schools by level.* [In Chinese.] http://www.moe.edu.cn/publicfiles/business/htmlfiles/moe/s4959/201012/113470.html.

———. 2010. *The outline for mid- and long-term higher education development plan for China (2010–2020).* Beijing: People's Publishing House.

National Bureau of Statistics of China. 2010. *Statistical Yearbook of China.* Beijing: National Bureau of Statistics of China.

Rumbley, Laura E., Iván F. Pacheco, and Philip G. Altbach. 2008. *International comparison of academic salaries: An exploratory study.* Chesnut Hill, MA: Boston College, Center for International Higher Education.

Shen, J. 2007. Labor contracts in China: Do they protect workers' rights? *Journal of Organizational Transformation & Social Change* 4 (2): 126.

Warner, M., and Zhu Y. 2000. An emerging model of employment relations in China: A divergent path from the Japanese? *Working paper* 12/2000, Judge Institute of Management. http://www.gurn.info.

Yan, F. 2009. China's academic profession in the context of social transition: Institutional perspective. *Economics of Education Research* 7: 2.

Zha, Q. 2006. The resurgence and growth of private higher education in China. hep.oise.utoronto.ca. *Special Issue*, March: 54–68.

6
The Changing American Academic Profession

Martin J. Finkelstein and Kevin W. Iglesias

Today, the American research university is widely recognized as the global "gold standard" for cutting-edge research, innovation, and graduate education. With the exception of a few subspecialty areas—ceramic engineering; oceanography (Goodwin and Nacht 1991)—American scholars and researchers have led the world in refereed journal publications, citations, patents, and Nobel Prizes. As a result, many look to American research universities as a model for the identification, incubation, and support of academic talent. Indeed, for scholars across the globe, American universities still serve as a magnet in the increasingly global academic marketplace.

It is useful to remember, however, that the United States only rose to a dominant global position in the higher education industry (graduate education and research) after World War II. This is, thus, a relatively recent development. As an account for this rise of the United States to academic preeminence over the past half century, several explanations may be offered. The most frequent focus is on the high degree of decentralization in the US system and the resulting autonomy from government control. In effect, the argument here is that academic distinction follows institutional independence. American universities, public as well as private, are autonomous corporations chartered by state governments to pursue their educational missions, and governed by a board of lay trustees. While they may be subject to general government regulations, these universities are nonetheless independent actors—free to pursue their place in the academic sun and to enhance their competitive position in the market for the best faculty and students. Among other advantages, this allows considerable institutional flexibility in competing with business, industry, and the professions in recruiting the best talent. The great strength of the private sector in the United

160

States—more independent and insulated from government—promotes this hypothesis. The second most frequent explanation focuses on the pattern of sustained and large-scale government support. American research universities first rose to global prominence largely as a result of the infusion of research support from the federal government's war-related defense efforts in the mid-20th century. Until quite recently, that support has been sustained and even grown—fueled by the establishment of the National Science Foundation, in 1958, and the National Institute of Health, in 1887. It was supplemented, beginning in the 1960s, by state governments that invested heavily in the establishment of public university systems—building upon one or two major universities and a system of former teacher's colleges and normal schools.

A third explanation focuses on the "magnet-like" capacity of the US system to develop and draw in academic talent from across the globe. Historically, this capacity is illustrated by successive waves of emigrating scholars—from Nazi Germany, the former Soviet Union, and developing economies such as China and India—seeking opportunities for academic careers in a context supporting academic and individual freedom. The key concept here can be claimed as opportunity. Indeed, the opportunity structure became developed in the post World War II period, offering at once a highly structured and predictable career track—defined by the American Association of University Professors' 1940 Statement on Academic Freedom and Tenure—and a robust job market, providing increasingly competitive salaries allowing academics to enter the growing American middle class (Bowen and Schuster 1986). That magnetism, while to some extent a result of general political freedom (with some exceptions), was a function of:

- a robust academic marketplace, with the flexibility to recognize the market value of faculty in certain fields and with certain accomplishments;
- an established career track that promised a safe and secure road to a stable career, if not spectacularly well-paid employment—irrespective of the results of the next national election or political coup.

In the past few years, however, alarm bells have begun to sound in the United States about gathering threats to American academic hegemony—parallel to the concerns raised about gathering threats to America's global economic and political hegemony, with the rise of the BRICs (Brazil, Russia, India, and China) (Zakaria 2008). Indicators of emergent trouble abound: a documented decline in the proportionate number of referred scientific articles produced by American scholars, as well as a proportionate decline in American representation in global scientific citations indexes; a decline in the US federal government's expenditure on basic scientific research as a percentage of gross domestic product; and both amid a sharp proportionate increase elsewhere in research and development expenditure and scientific publications, especially in East Asia and western Europe (Clotfelter 2010; Cummings 2008). More ominously, the downturn of productivity seems rooted in declines in conditions that produced American preeminence. While sociological theories of accumulative advantage suggest that privileged groups, by virtue of their initial privilege, tend to enjoy a substantial advantage in maintaining their position—even as the playing field changes; nonetheless, the prospects for continued supremacy of the American academic professions—especially in the longer term—are anything but certain (Clotfelter 2010).

In this chapter, the challenges that the American system is now confronting to these three pillars of its historic strength are considered. The changing opportunity structure of academic careers in the United States, associated with these challenges, will be reviewed in some detail, based on a particular focus on academic employment contracts and compensation. The discussion will conclude with some implications for the continued preeminence of the US academic profession—a profession that may no longer be indisputably the most secure and best paid in the world. However, initially, the basic parameters of the current US system need to be established, in terms of size and scope.

A system bifurcated by mission and control

The higher education system in the United States is today a large and highly decentralized one, with some 4,000 autonomous actors (institutions) currently offering instruction at the postsecondary level to some 17 million students by about 1.1 million faculty members (600,000 of whom are full time). The overall system is bifurcated along two major axes. First, in terms of mission and degree level, approximately half the system (about 2,000 institutions and nine million students) is oriented to vocational or workforce preparation (and offers either two-year degrees or non-degree certificate options). The other half provides traditional baccalaureate and graduate-degree-level instruction, in four-year colleges and universities, to a primarily full-time student body (Gumport 2000). Academic staff in the vocational sector serve primarily on part-time appointments; while those in the traditional baccalaureate and graduate-degree, four-year sector serve primarily full-time (Leslie and Slaughter 1995). This chapter focuses on academic staff at the traditional four-year collegiate and university-level institutions (the non-vocational sector).

Within the traditional four-year college and university sector, a second axis of institutional differentiation is between publicly and privately funded institutions. Beyond the appointment method of their respective governing boards (political appointment or election in the public sector and self-perpetuating succession in the private sector), public and private institutions have historically differed principally in terms of their revenue streams. Public institutions typically receive substantial subventions for their instructional mission from state and local government, allowing them to offer relatively lower tuition prices than the private sector—yet, still high by the standards of most other nations. Private institutions typically rely on (relatively high) student tuition fees, other private support (from alumni, for-profit business corporations, and philanthropic foundations) and government and/or corporate research funding.

In 2009, the institutional landscape of the four-year collegiate and university sector appeared as examined in Table 6.1. Perhaps most strikingly, this table shows the relative small size of the university sector: only 273 institutions or not quite 40 per cent of the four-year sector and barely 10 per cent of the entire postsecondary enterprise. Beyond the 273 research and PhD-granting universities (two-thirds public; one-third private), the remaining 1,300 institutions are about evenly divided between master's and free-standing, baccalaureate granting institutions, and are disproportionately (two-thirds) private. While private institutions, then, outnumber public institutions, enrollment in the public sector, led by the research and PhD-granting universities, outpaces that in the private sector by 2:1. The public sector includes a smaller number of much larger institutions. This is especially evident among the research universities. The sole exception here is among the baccalaureate institutions, the home of the traditional American free-standing arts college, where the private sector continues to dominate both in terms of institutional numbers and in enrollments.

As for faculty, their numbers closely follow student enrollment. The plurality of full-time faculty is located in the research universities and primarily in the public sector. Part-time faculty, on the other hand, are located in larger proportion in the private sector. The baccalaureate institutions, once again, provide the exception: part-time academic staff

Table 6.1   The number of institutions, students, and faculty, 2009

Type of institution	Number of institutions	Enrollment	Full-time faculty	Part-time faculty
Research university				
Public	139	3,398,874	209,111	55,363
Private	60	787,282	79,661	25,591
Total	199	4,186,156	288,772	80,954
PhD university				
Public	27	381,309	16,371	4,328
Private	47	336,407	13,516	14,669
Total	74	717,716	29,887	18,997
Master's level				
Public	266	2,531,700	97,714	55,215
Private	346	1,353,981	49,433	51,705
Total	612	3,885,681	147,147	106,920
Baccalaureate				
Public	151	511,129	18,635	12,924
Private	528	864,546	46,434	23,684
Total	679	1,375,675	65,069	36,608

Source: US Department of Education (2009).

are even more likely to be located in the quite small public-sector, baccalaureate-conferring institutions than in the private sector.

Current challenges

Over the past decade or two, the highly decentralized American system has encountered many of the same challenges encountered by nations worldwide: increased demand for access and growing constraints in public revenues/appropriations (Marginson and Rhoades 2002; OECD 2010). Thus, these challenges have fueled several trends that have become typical globally: increasing focus on institutional performance and accountability measures; increasing privatization in the public sector; and increasing reliance on contingent academic staff (Black 2004). Enhanced accountability pressures are reflected in the adoption at the state level of performance budgeting standards, moving partially to allocation based on outcomes (e.g., number or percentage of graduates, number of articles published), rather than purely on enrollment demand; and more generally, in the ascendance of what is now called "responsibility-centered" management (i.e., individual academic units responsible for generating revenues in line with their expenditures).

The declining public baseline institutional support has meant that academic staff are under increasing pressure to generate revenue from instructional, research, and service activities. That pressure is reflected in the trend toward increasing privatization: such as outsourcing of non-essential services (e.g., dining, security, bookstore); the establishment and/or expansion of fund-raising units and mechanisms at most public institutions that support academic quality enhancements; faculty and administrative salary supplements; and the spin-off of technology transfer units at most major research universities (Slaughter and Rhoades 2004). Over the past several decades, as state allocations for higher education have declined, the percentage of the institutional budget at large public research universities that comes from state subventions has declined in some cases to 10 per cent or less—in effect, making the annual state allocation only a minor share in the budgets of public research universities. Indeed, real state-level expenditure per full-time equivalent student in 2008 was actually lower than nearly a quarter century earlier, in 1985 (Zumeta 2009). From a resource perspective, then, these ostensibly public institutions have largely become privatized.

In terms of the academic profession, these financial pressures have reshaped instructional staffing, leading most four-year institutions to resort to contingent staffing.[1] While the two-year, vocational sector has typically involved the use of part-time faculty who teach one course here, in the four-year college and university sector, there has been a mushrooming of full-time, limited-term appointments. It has been reported (Schuster and Finkelstein 2006) that these limited-term, full-time appointments have over the past two decades constituted the majority of all new appointments in American four-year colleges and universities—allowing the proportion of all full-time faculty who are tenured to dip below 50 per cent, for the first time since 1940.[2]

While these appointments differ from tenure-eligible appointments on the face of it in their duration and prospects of permanence—and, as will be seen, in their salaries—there is growing evidence that these new types of appointments reflect a new trend toward increasing specialization in academic work roles. Historically, the American system in the post World War II period adopted the German Humboldtian model of integrating teaching, research, and institutional and professional service into the ideal typical academic role. All faculty—whatever their field or institution affiliation—were assumed to integrate all major functions of their institution in their own individual work role. Even outside the university sector, some notion remained that even if teaching assumed primacy, there was still an expectation that all academic staff members at a baccalaureate-level institution at least remain current in the latest developments in their academic field (even if they themselves were not active in primary research and publication) and also contribute service to their institution as good academic citizens.

In a pioneering study of full-time, limited-term faculty appointments, it has been reported that academic staff on full-time, non-tenure-eligible appointments tended to play more highly circumscribed work roles: including teaching only, research only, and administration only (Baldwin and Chronister 2001). Teaching-only appointments were typically employed to staff lower-division undergraduate courses, with large enrollments in fields that provide broad service to undergraduate education: English, foreign languages, mathematics, introductory courses in the health professions, and business. Research-only appointees might be hired to staff federal and industrial research grants—a more attractive alternative to the postdoctoral appointment historically typical in the life and physical sciences. Administration-only appointees might be hired to launch and maintain new and especially non-traditional academic programs that are offered either off-campus or via non-traditional modalities (distance learning), as well as to teach a course in that new program.

These developments over the past two decades have been exacerbated by the great recession of 2008 and its aftermath, which are as of this chapter still roiling the world economy. Most obviously, the extant decline in state support for public higher education has been accelerating. In six states, budget revisions during the fiscal year of 2009 took back 8–24 per cent of state funds already allocated. In California, the three public college and university systems (the University of California, the California State University system, and the two-year community colleges) all suffered 20 per cent cuts in new state funding. Other states—including Washington, Hawaii, Arizona, and South Carolina—experienced similar decreases. Unfortunately, in the absence of federal stimulus funds, severe cuts are likely to continue. Most public universities have resorted to substantially increasing student tuition fees—causing many students to downgrade their educational aspirations and spending—and to placing limitations on enrollment and the scope of course offerings. Even the elite private universities, normally immune to fiscal crises, have suffered significant damage. With the precipitous plummeting of endowment values among the wealthiest institutions, including Harvard and Princeton University, even they have been forced to pull back from their academic commitments and reconsider expansion plans and financial aid policies. Some have announced permanent budget reductions, suspended plans for campus expansion (Harvard's new science campus), instituted hiring freezes (during the recession, Stanford did not fill 50 open faculty positions), and reduced student financial aid (Geiger 2010).

Academic compensation has largely been frozen over the past three to four years: although averaging 1 per cent increments in the aggregate (AAUP 2011), many universities in the public sector have had to resort to staff furloughs and other forms of de facto salary reduction to avoid layoffs; and many have also had layoffs.

Perhaps most notable among these developments has been the accelerating decline of academic tenure in the United States. The percentage of full-time faculty who are tenured is now about 47 per cent—down from about 62 per cent in 1970; the percentage of faculty headcount who are tenured is now in the neighborhood of 15–20 per cent. While, no doubt, responsive to economic conditions, the trend toward contingent staffing is being accelerated by the introduction of alternative competing staffing models in the growing for-profit private (proprietary) sector of American higher education. Nearly 10 per cent of all US postsecondary students are enrolled in such institutions, accounting for nearly one-third of all US federal financial-aid dollars. These institutions offer vocationally based programs at all levels—ranging from the non-degree certificate, through the baccalaureate, master's degree, and even doctoral and medical education. These programs are structured around the development of specific skills and competencies and are largely taught by part-time faculty from syllabi developed centrally by administrators. They are perceived as offering serious competition to traditional four-year colleges and universities in a range of academic areas—including business administration, education, allied health, and information technology—and are clearly competing with public institutions constrained by budget cuts and, as a result, limited in the number of aspiring entering students they can accommodate. Even graduate universities are feeling the competitive pressures and wondering how they will maintain their advantage in these areas, with the tremendous expense of fully credentialed, full-time faculty.

What these current challenges have taught observers is just how vulnerable the three pillars of US historic strength are to economic dislocation. The decline in research support, and state-level disinvestment in public higher education, come just as emerging BRIC competitors are increasing their investment in research and development, as a percentage of gross domestic product, and increasing their investment in the university sector. Moreover, vaunted corporate independence cuts both ways: while this process preserves autonomy from government, it allows enormous freedom of action to introduce radical staffing and budget reconfigurations, without regulation or public scrutiny.

All of these developments, of course, are playing out differentially within an incredibly diverse system of postsecondary education—defined not only by the type of institution but by the academic field and faculty demographics. Differences within the system are enormous; and aggregate generalizations are frequently difficult to make. Policies for private research universities may not apply to public research universities, let alone small denominational colleges or public master's degree-level institutions. The options for the high professions (law and business) may not relate to the lower professions (education and nursing), let alone to the traditional liberal arts fields. The elements facing new entrants to the faculty may not involve the most senior faculty; and what applies to academic men may not apply to the rapidly expanding cohort of academic women.

The remainder of this chapter is focused on a detailed examination of these changes in the conditions of academic employment and of trends in academic compensation. The ultimate goal is to provide an appropriately "nuanced" basis for assessing the status of these main pillars of strength supporting the rise to global prominence of the American research university and the American academic professions, and for speculating on the prospects for the American academic profession's future.

Academic contracts, hiring, and promotion processes

In the United States, the 4,000-plus corporately independent institutions are the "buyers" that drive the academic job market. Positions are created at the institutional level in response to replacement demand—the retirement of current incumbents or their mobility to other academic institutions or to positions outside academe; and by growth demand—that is, changes in student enrollment (Carter and Scott 1998). Historically, the departure of an incumbent from an academic department created a vacancy. Over the past decade or two it has become increasingly rare for an incumbent's departure to lead to automatic replacement. At most institutions in the United States, an academic staff member's departure results in that specific position being returned to the central university pool—either to be reassigned to another academic unit on a more promising growth trajectory, with more pressing academic needs in the eyes of the central administration, or to be reallocated outside of the academic personnel rolls to other more-pressing institutional needs. That is, the position may simply disappear. In those cases in which the unit in question is able to justify retaining a position, that position may be reclassified from a tenure-eligible to a limited-term appointment or carved up into multiple part-time appointments—with any savings returning to the university pool. Quite beyond a vacancy created by the departure of a current incumbent, it is not unusual for a new faculty position to be created—either to support a new academic program or some other institutional priority. So while the United States serves greater flexibility in generating position vacancies, there is also considerably less systemic (bureaucratic) stability now in the number and distribution of positions.

Once a position is created—either through a vacancy or through a new addition—the search process for full-time academic staff positions, whether in the public or private sector, is typically highly decentralized. Searches are conducted by individual academic units (departments and even programs), and recommendations are made from the unit to the academic dean supervising the unit in question and ultimately to the campus chief academic officer (Matler 1991). Two aspects of these searches are particularly important: their scope and the legal parameters within which they operate. Regarding scope, most full-time-faculty searches at four-year institutions are national in scope—i.e., they seek to identify and recruit the most-qualified candidates in the United States in a field or subfield. At major research universities, the scope of such searches is increasingly international (Bair 2003). In reality, searches at lesser institutions and searches for limited-term appointments (even at the research-oriented universities) may be conducted less systematically and may be largely regional or even local in scope.

Historically, faculty searches in the United States were conducted through what sociologists referred to as a sponsorship, in contradistinction to an open, transparent system (Burke 1988; Caplow and McGee 1958). That is, faculty in hiring departments contacted colleagues at those departments producing the most PhDs in the field and sought recommendations from mentors of their best doctoral students. The primary consideration was to recruit the most promising students from the most prestigious departments (and most prestigious mentors), on the assumption that prestige in venue would likely provide the best guarantee of candidate quality and maximize the prestige value of the new hire.

Beginning with the passage of landmark civil rights legislation in the United States, in the 1960s and 1970s, searches for academic staff were conducted within the parameters of US government anti-discrimination policies, reflected in federal legislation protecting against discrimination in employment on the basis of gender, race/ethnicity, age, sexual orientation, and other issues. Typically, institutional human-resource (personnel) office staff have prepared recruitment guidelines covering scope of advertising, strategies for identification of women and minority candidates, permissible questions to ask at interviews, as well as other options (Twombly 2005). For example, it is not permissible according to such guidelines to ask a prospective female academic staff member if she is pregnant or planning to have children. Non-discrimination legislation would also restrict any questions about an applicant's race or sexual orientation, in screening for interviews. While informal collegial sponsorship networks still operate, they do so within the parameters of affirmative action requirements, which include establishing availability pools of minority and women PhDs in the field, mandatory advertising in media designed to reach those non-traditional candidates, mandated reporting on the number of women and minorities included in interviews for a given position, justifications of why a non-woman or non-minority candidate is preferred over a woman or minority candidate, and other aspects (Goonen and Blechmen 1999).

In terms of procedure, a hiring academic unit would recommend several candidates to the academic dean supervising that unit (often in some kind of rank order). The dean would make the actual hiring decisions, including not only which candidate should be selected but also negotiating terms and conditions of employment, covering rank and salary, directly with the candidate (Twombly 2005). So, in this sense, while the actual conduct of search and screening processes for academic staff are highly decentralized (albeit quite standardized), actual hiring decisions and negotiations are typically conducted more centrally; and academic deans and chief academic officers, especially in the private sector, have considerable discretion within basic institutional budgetary constraints.

At the point of initial authorization for recruitment to an academic staff vacancy, the type of contract or appointment is usually clearly specified. Contracts for full-time academic staff differ principally in whether they offer eligibility for the award of tenure after a probationary period of typically six or seven years or whether they offer a limited-term contract that may or may not be renewable for one or more succeeding terms (Clark and Ma 2005). The contract letter would make this clear. Irrespective of the type of full-time appointment (tenure eligible or limited contract), the actual length of the initial employment contract may vary typically between one and three years. Some kind of annual review is usually mandated, although it may be somewhat perfunctory for limited-term appointees. For tenure-eligible appointments, a review typically takes the form of annual assessments of progress toward tenure (Twombly 2005). The major high-stakes review for tenure-eligible faculty comes one year before the end of the entire probationary period, at which time a decision is made as to whether to award tenure. That decision is based on an assessment of the performance of academic staff members in their teaching, research, and service responsibilities. At research universities, research performance as reflected in publications and grant awards is emphasized, while at four-year institutions with a predominantly teaching mission, teaching performance is likely to be a more central consideration (although some sort of research or scholarly performance is expected).

The tenure review typically involves a year-long process conducted in successive stages by faculty committees at the levels of the individual academic unit and the larger academic super unit in which the focal academic unit is embedded, and by senior administrators including the dean of the academic super unit and the chief academic officer and president of the institution (Twombly 2005). While the recommendations of the faculty bodies are typically dispositive, the final decision is ultimately taken by the president and board of trustees. Typically, about 70 per cent of all eligible academic staff who come up for tenure consideration are granted tenure, although that figure drops to about 50 per cent at the research universities (Dooris and Sandmeyer 2006). In the US system, a negative tenure decision is tantamount to a non-reappointment decision, although in special cases it may be possible to retain such a faculty member on a limited-term, off-track appointment. Academic staff who are denied tenure often seek and accept academic staff positions at less prestigious colleges and universities, which set different standards for promotion and tenure or accept full-time positions off the tenure track.[3] However, some staff, no doubt, take a negative tenure decision as the impetus to move out of academia altogether.

For limited-contract academic staff, major evaluations and reappointment decisions are made in the middle of the year, preceding the final year of the contract. These exercises typically involve review by lower-level faculty bodies and the deans of major academic units.

Beyond the duration of their appointments and their eligibility for the award of tenure, fixed-term faculty typically differ from tenure-eligible faculty based on both their academic credentials and the scope of their work responsibilities. In terms of credentials, roughly 90 per cent of all tenure-eligible appointees to the entry-level rank of assistant professor hold a PhD degree at four-year colleges and universities (Clark and Ma 2005). The analogous figure for fixed-term-contract faculty would be about 50 per cent. Indeed, a large portion of these non-PhD faculty might include master's degree-prepared individuals in health fields such as nursing, or PhD candidates in English, foreign languages, or mathematics who are hired on a full-time basis to teach lower-division, introductory, clinical, or remedial courses. In terms of work responsibilities, tenure-eligible academic staff are typically expected to perform all three basic academic functions of teaching, research, and service—the latter including administration and institutional and/or external professional service to their academic field or the larger community. Indeed, they likely would have been hired, in no small part, on the basis of their potential for developing a productive research career—at least at research universities (Matler 1991).

Fixed-contract faculty typically have a much more specialized function and are hired to perform one principal function, more often teaching (especially for lower-division or introductory-undergraduate courses). However, sometimes, other functions involve research (on an external government or private foundation grant) or administration (typically, as director of an academic program that may be based off the main campus or digital/distance). Unless faculty are specifically hired on external funds to conduct research, such term appointments typically are not involved in research activity (Bair 2003). Beyond specialization among the trinity of teaching, research, and administration/service, full-time academic staff on limited-term contracts are frequently excluded from participation in faculty governance structures (Baldwin and Chronister 2001) and in certain kinds of professional development—including sabbatical leaves and internal institutional research grants. While institutional policy appears non-standardized, there is some evidence, at least in the humanities, that involvement in departmental governance is becoming more common. More than two-thirds of department chairs in English language and literature departments reported that non-tenure track, full-time faculty were authorized to cast votes in certain departmental matters (Modern Language Association 2008). Not surprisingly, they would be more likely than tenure-eligible faculty to be hired based on criteria other than research promise or past research record—for example, teaching experience, ability, or administrative experience.[4]

While fixed-contract appointments are present throughout the universe of institutional types (including free-standing liberal arts colleges, as well as research universities, both public and private), they tend to be concentrated in a handful of fields—especially in the humanities and in the professions—in which there are major lower-division teaching responsibilities (courses supplied for students in other major fields). These include English language, foreign languages, mathematics, business, nursing, and other health-related professions.

Except in a few fields in the humanities, especially English or foreign languages (see, e.g., Ehrenberg 2010[5]), it appears relatively rare for academic staff to move from a fixed contract to a tenure-eligible position and vice versa: about 30 per cent of fixed-term-contract faculty ultimately move into tenure-eligible position; and only about 10–15 per cent of tenure-eligible faculty move into fixed-contract positions (Schuster and Finkelstein 2006). When such mobility between appointments occurs, it almost always requires a change in the employing institution. This suggests that fixed-term positions are less a new rank within the traditional career ladder and are more an alternative career option or track, within a multi-track academic-staff career.[6]

Before proceeding to a discussion of full-time academic staff salaries, it is worth viewing the significant trends in numbers of part-time faculty appointments—in contradistinction to limited term, full-time appointments. In 1970, US colleges and universities employed 104,000 part-time faculty—about 25 per cent of the workforce of 474,000 full-time faculty. By 1975, the proportion of part-timers had increased by 81 per cent, to 188,000, while full-time academic staff had increased about 19 per cent, to 440,000. In the ensuing quarter century, the number of part-time academic staff swelled to 543,000—an increase of 289 per cent, compared to a 43 per cent increase in full-time academic staff to 630,000. While the largest increases have been in the public two-year vocational sector (the community colleges[7]), the university sector has hardly been immune. In Fall 2005, 61 per cent of the faculty at public research universities in the United States were full-time (41% tenured or tenure eligible, 20% fixed term), 20 per cent were part-time, and 19 per cent were graduate-student teaching assistants (JBL Associates 2008). Thus, for all practical purposes, about two in five faculty on the rolls of our public research universities are part-time.[8]

Academic salaries

Historically, salaries of academic staff in the United States were abysmally low through the first half of the 20th century (Ruml and Tickton 1955). Undergirding their low pay were the twin assumptions that academic life was a calling—much like the ministry from whence it came—and that academics traded off modest salaries for their unusual job security. Beginning in the 1950s and throughout the 1960s, faculty compensation registered a slow, steady ascent of 3.6 per cent annually, which largely paralleled the ascent of the American research university to global prominence. These gains were eroded by inflation in the 1970s: professors lost about 15 per cent of their purchasing power in the 1970s—the worst performance of any occupational group in the United States, outside agriculture (Schuster and Finkelstein 2006). Not until the mid-1990s did faculty salaries, in constant dollars, recover from the erosion in the 1970s. Indeed, it was not until 1997/1998—a full quarter century—that faculty salaries on average drew even with the real level they had attained in 1970/1971, although they had certainly appeared to rise almost fourfold in current dollars. In the last decade, salaries have increased modestly in constant dollars (about 6% over the decade).[9]

Notwithstanding their checkered internal history, academic salaries in the United States today are among the highest in the world. In a recent study by the Center for International Higher Education at Boston College (Rumbley, Pacheco, and Altbach 2009), the United States ranked third in overall average monthly salary (after Saudi Arabia and Canada), among 15 countries.[10] Together with the relatively high availability of positions of one sort or another (vis-à-vis, for example, Germany), such relatively high salaries in the United States serve as something of a magnet for academics in Europe (especially those in the United Kingdom, escaping the Thatcher reforms) and Asia (especially China and India, where many recruits to US doctoral education in the sciences and engineering stay to pursue academic careers) (Bhandari and Laughlin 2009).

While comparatively high overall, the available data suggest that academic salaries in the United States vary substantially by type of appointment: overall, they are generally higher for tenure-eligible, full-time faculty than for fixed-contract faculty. Yet, in some professional schools, fixed-contract appointments actually receive a salary supplement as a type of reward for forsaking tenure eligibility (Chait and Trower 1997). Moreover, salaries are substantially higher for full-time faculty than for those on part-time appointments. Indeed, the vast majority of part-time faculty are employed on a course basis, rather than as a proportion of a full-time appointment[11]; and they are paid that way. Many are employed by more than one institution. While there is a dearth of credible and/or useful salary data on part-timers, triangulating several sources produces a few reasonable generalizations. First, 91 per cent of part-time faculty earn annual salaries of less than US$25,000 from their employing institutions (64% earn less than US$10,000), although 27 per cent of part-timers at public research universities and 18 per cent at private research universities earn more than US$25,000 annually[12] (US Department of Education 2008). The available evidence on course salaries suggest that, on average, in the majority of fields, part-timers earn somewhere in the neighborhood of US$2,600 at public comprehensives and about US$4,200 per course at public research universities (JBL Associates 2008). Those figures vary somewhat by academic field and are higher in certain professions (e.g., law and architecture), but probably lower in certain fields in the humanities. If one were to compare the per course salary rate of part-time faculty to the per course salary received by full-time tenure-stream faculty, the full-time tenure-stream advantage would be in the order of 4:1 (JBL 2008).[13] Interestingly enough, in this same analysis of the public sector, full-time and term-limited faculty were reported to receive about 70 per cent of the salaries of full-time tenure-stream faculty, while in other analyses, the percentage has been 74 per cent (Curtis and Jacobe 2006).

Given that the evidence is not definitive and, furthermore, the focus of this study is on faculty in career-ladder appointments, the following discussion focuses on salaries of full-time faculty in tenure-eligible appointments.[14]

In the United States, although the salaries of full-time, tenure-eligible academic staff are, on average, substantially higher than for those academic staff holding non-tenure-eligible or part-time appointments, there is nonetheless substantial internal variation among tenure-eligible academic staff. That internal variation is accounted for largely by two factors: the type of institution/employer and the academic field.

Variation across institutional types

In terms of institutional type, the higher the level of degree offered by an institution (BA, MA, PhD/MD), the higher the salary it pays its academic staff.[15] That premium tends to increase with academic rank—that is, it is less discernable at entry level and much larger at the senior ranks. At the entry level, research-university faculty earn about 20 per cent more than entry-level faculty at baccalaureate colleges (US$60,000 vs. US$50,000); and at the full professor rank, they may earn as much as 50 per cent more on average (US$120,000 vs. US$80,000).

Beyond mission and degree level, in the United States over the past decade an increasing disparity has emerged between public and private institutions. This public–private disparity actually represents a significant new development in American higher education. Until 1990, public institutions in the United States actually enjoyed a salary premium over private institutions of close to 10 per cent. Since 1990, largely as a function of declining state appropriations for higher education, salaries in the public sector have atrophied. They are now consistently both lower and less flexible than at private institutions. Salaries are on average about 10–20 per cent higher at private institutions. That disparity, again, tends to grow larger at the senior ranks (Adams 2010), compromising the competitive position of many public research universities in the recruitment of senior scholars. Among private institutions, church-related colleges tend to offer, on average, lower salaries than those of non-religiously affiliated private institutions.

Variation by academic field

Unlike most other nations, the United States supports wide disparities in salaries by academic field, reflective of the market value of a particular field outside the university in the broader economy. For academic institutions to compete with business and industry (and even government) in recruiting academic talent in fields such as law, medicine, engineering, business, chemistry, microbiology, and others, they must offer higher salaries than for fields, such as English, philosophy, sociology, and others, with fewer lucrative opportunities outside the university. The distribution of fields by their outside market value roughly parallels the proportion of PhD recipients nationally who are employed outside academe. A newly appointed assistant professor of accounting, for example, would at a typical non-research university earn as much as a senior full professor of English literature or history (both in the mid US$90,000 range).

Table 6.2 shows the differences in average salary for university academic staff in several professional and liberal arts fields. The data suggest several observations. First, if the average salaries of the various professional fields are computed as a proportion of the average salary in English language and literature (one of the three liberal arts fields displayed in Table 6.2), the salary premium for the professions is found to range from just above one-quarter in business (27.4% in the public sector, 25.9% in the private), to about two-thirds in law (69.1% in the public sector, 60.7% in the private sector), with engineering at about 40 per cent (38% in the public sector, 50.7% in the private sector), and health professions at over 50 per cent in the public sector and nearly equaling law (above 60%) in the private sector. These are substantial differences: faculty in law and the health professions are earning about 1.5 times more than their liberal arts colleagues in

Table 6.2 Average salaries in selected fields and the average salaries in English language and literature, 2009

Discipline	University faculty			
	Public		Private	
	Average salary (US$)	Difference from English (%)	Average salary (US$)	Difference from English (%)
Business	82,970	+27.4	84,940	+25.9
Computer science	75,670	+16.1	76,260	+13.0
Engineering	89,920	+38.0	101,690	+50.7
English language and literature	65,150	0	67,460	0
Chemistry	77,230	+18.5	77,580	+15.0
Psychology	72,500	+11.3	71,570	+6.1
Health specialties	99,750	+53.1	107,380	+59.2
Law teachers	110,160	+69.1	108,440	+60.4

Source: US Department of Labor (2009).

the humanities. When English language and literature is compared to chemistry, computer science, and psychology—three fields within the traditional liberal arts on American campuses—the salary premium for natural scientists (chemistry and computer science) over literature professors is found to be about 15 per cent, much more modest but not insignificant, and that for social science faculty is under 10 per cent. Taken together, these data suggest substantial disparities between the traditional liberal arts and the professions in the United States. Moreover, within the traditional liberal arts, there remain more modest but consistent differences, favoring the natural sciences.

It is significant to note that inter-field differences persist across both the public and private sectors at roughly the same magnitude with two notable exceptions: in both engineering and the health professions, the salary premiums are somewhat greater in the private than in the public sector.

Academic rank

Within institutions and academic fields, the prime determinant of salary is academic rank. Almost all institutions—private as well as public—have a type of salary scale organized by academic rank. There is typically a floor and a ceiling for the ranks of assistant, associate, and full professors and several steps—perhaps between four and six—within each rank. Promotion to the next higher rank commonly entails a substantial salary increase from the then-current step within the previous rank to the lowest step on the next higher rank. For tenure-eligible academic staff in the United States, this policy typically involves promotion to associate professor with tenure after the six-or-seven-year probationary period. The available evidence suggests that over the last quarter century, the salaries of both assistant professors and associate professors, as a percentage of the salaries of full professors, have actually declined slightly: from 73.4 per cent to 68.2 per cent for associate professors and from 60 per cent to 58.2 per cent for assistant professors. This evidence means that the salary premium for attaining the highest academic rank has actually increased on average over this period[16] (Schuster and Finkelstein 2006). The data in Table 6.3 suggest that the increased premium for senior ranks varies considerably by academic field—ranging from a low level of 61 per cent in architecture and language and literatures to close to 87 per cent in business (where salary compression between ranks is the greatest), 71 per cent in computer science, and close to 70 per cent in agriculture, engineering, law, and the health professions—wherein academia must compete with business and industry in order to recruit new talent.

Within academic ranks, salary is determined primarily by seniority, although some evidence reveals that performance factors enter into the equation. Annual increases at most institutions tend to be across the board, cost-of-living increases (Perna 2001). Where there is merit pay, it usually constitutes only a small or secondary component of annual increments for faculty. This factor is more likely to be based on research productivity, as reflected in peer-reviewed publications, than on teaching performance, as reflected in student end-of-the-semester course evaluations.

Gender discrepancies

Two other possible determinants of salary merit attention. The first factor is gender. Historically, female academic staff have earned about 80 per cent of the salaries of male academic staff, with similar qualifications/credentials and performance records—controlling for institutional type, academic field, and academic rank (Schuster and Finkelstein 2006). To some extent, that gap has closed—to roughly 90 per cent between 2001 and 2011—as sex discrimination litigation and the results of

Table 6.3   Salaries by academic field and rank, 2009

Discipline	Full professor (US$)	Associate professor (US$)	Assistant professor (US$)	New assistant professor (US$)	New assistant professor—% of full professor
Agriculture, operations, and related sciences	90,053	71,583	61,645	62,589	69.5
Architecture and related services	95,723	73,319	60,181	58,935	61.6
Communication, journalism, and related programs	83,656	65,006	53,599	54,424	65.1
Computer and information sciences and support services	101,219	82,230	70,791	72,199	71.3
Education	82,919	65,182	54,953	54,009	65.1
Engineering	112,679	86,031	75,226	75,450	67.0
Foreign languages, literatures, and linguistics	85,620	65,129	53,529	52,271	61.0
Legal professions and studies	134,146	101,045	83,991	92,033	68.6
English language and literature/letters	79,372	61,684	51,502	51,204	64.5
Biological and biomedical sciences	91,184	68,294	57,545	57,021	62.5
Mathematics and statistics	84,324	66,012	55,765	55,186	65.4

180

Table 6.3 (Continued)

Discipline	Full professor (US$)	Associate professor (US$)	Assistant professor (US$)	New assistant professor (US$)	New assistant professor—% of full professor
Philosophy and religious studies	84,621	63,460	53,018	53,668	63.4
Physical sciences	88,147	66,898	56,720	56,483	64.1
Psychology	83,840	64,461	54,850	54,584	65.1
Public administration and social service professions	89,342	68,896	56,572	57,873	64.8
Visual and performing arts	79,098	62,197	51,480	50,762	64.2
Health professions and related clinical sciences	94,610	74,162	62,704	64,296	68.0
Business, management, marketing, and related support services	109,919	92,573	85,996	95,822	87.2

Source: College and University Professional Association for Human Resources (2010).

Table 6.4 Salaries of male and female academic staff by institutional type and rank, 2009

Academic rank		Public			Private		
		Men	Women	Women's disadvantage (%)	Men	Women	Women's disadvantage (%)
Institutional type	Doctoral Professor	119,255	107,918	9.51	155,952	143,630	7.90
	Assistant	71,217	65,820	7.58	86,904	79,132	8.94
	Master's Professor	90,766	87,281	3.84	102,311	94,772	7.37
	Assistant	60,986	58,968	3.31	64,656	61,537	4.83
	Baccalaureate Professor	85,681	82,345	3.89	100,008	94,362	5.65
	Assistant	58,123	55,819	3.97	59,622	57,969	2.78

Source: American Association of University Professors (2010).

gender equity, salary studies have documented "residual" gender differences. It appears that at the entry level, these differences are diminishing even further (Perna 2001).

The data in Table 6.4 provide the latest evidence of shrinking gender disparities by institutional type and academic rank. This table suggests first that gender differences are greatest at the doctoral institutions and smaller in the public than in the private sector. Moreover, the distinctions appear smaller (virtually negligible) at the entry-level ranks—except at the doctoral institutions.

Academic unions

The upcoming discussion looks at collective bargaining and the unionization of academic staff. Approximately one-quarter of academic staff in US higher education—both full and part-time—are unionized (Schuster and Finkelstein 2006), closer to 30 per cent among academic staff in the four-year collegiate and university sector (Rhoades 1998). Following an explosion of such activity in the late 1960s and 1970s permitted by federal and subsequent state enabling legislation, the pace of academic unionization has atrophied—as it has in the general US economy, where about 15 per cent of workers are represented by a union. Most of the unionized faculty in American higher education are represented by the American Federation of Teachers. About 10 per cent of its 1.4 million members are in higher education, predominantly in the public sector and evenly divided between two-year and four-year institutions. The remaining unionized teachers are in public elementary and secondary education. The National Education Association (about 100,000 in higher education out of 2.7 million members) and the American Association of University Professors (about 44,000 members, all in higher education, evenly split between public and private, mostly four-year institutions—but not all associated with an American Association of University Professors collective bargaining unit) constitute the remainder of unionized faculty. These academic staff are primarily located in the public sector. Because unionization is higher in states where incomes (and living costs) tend to be greater, it is hard to isolate the effects of collective bargaining on salaries. Moreover, in states wherein legislation has enabled unionization among public-sector employees, nearly all public-sector faculty are unionized. Thus, it is difficult to identify, for comparison purposes, subgroups of relatively comparable institutions, in which some faculty are unionized and others are not.

Mean salary by field of teaching for union and non-union members

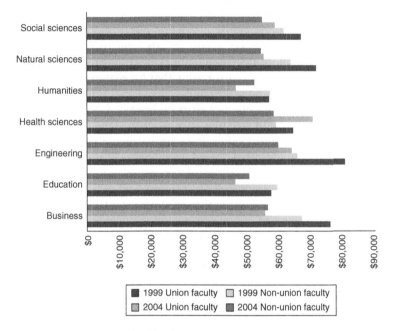

Figure 6.1   Full-time faculty salary by union status, 1999 and 2004.
Source: US Department of Education (2003 and 2008).

With those caveats in mind, it was found that the salaries of faculty respondents to the 1999 National Study of Postsecondary Faculty, who were union members, varied from salaries of those who were not (Schuster and Finkelstein 2006). Unionization was associated with somewhat higher salaries in most fields. The analysis, however, included both part-time and full-time faculty. When the analysis is restricted to full-time faculty only and expanded to include the more recent (2004) National Study of Postsecondary Faculty data (see Figure 6.1), the union salary advantage largely disappears. Among full-timers, unionized faculty show a modest salary boost only in the humanities and in education, both relatively low-demand fields, and actually show a slight disadvantage in most other, and relatively high demand, fields. To the extent that collective bargaining may be a factor in academic compensation, it seems clear that the impact is restricted to part-time faculty and among full timers—only those in low-demand fields.

Point of clarification: the typical monthly contract

It is important to clarify that most academic staff in the United States are employed on nine or ten month (academic year) rather than 12-month (calendar year) contracts—so salary reports refer to base salaries for a maximum ten month, or academic year, contract (Clark and Ma 2005). Practically speaking, this means that base-salary figures tend to underestimate actual academic staff compensation. Many faculty teach additional courses in the summer, work on research grants, or engage in other income-producing activities that result in supplemental support from their employing institution (Bair 2003). They may also engage in overload teaching and other special assignments during the academic year, for which they receive supplementary payment from their employing institution. The point is that most faculty earn at least 5 per cent of their base salary in summer or other remuneration from their employing institution—beyond any supplemental employment derived from outside their employing institution.

Academic salaries compared to those of other professionals

In 1999, academic staff in the United States earned 74.5 per cent of the weighted average salary of other "highly educated" professionals, ranging from about half in the case of lawyers and physicians, to about 90 per cent in the case of engineers and computer scientists. By 2003, the US Bureau of Labor Statistics reported that the academic "salary disadvantage" had increased slightly from 25.5 per cent to 27.7 per cent (Schuster and Finkelstein 2006). Focusing on the point of career entry, the case of the newly hired assistant professor, the market is viewed as signaling a long-standing salary disadvantage for at least the last quarter century. In 1975, entry-level salaries for assistant professors exceeded the median family income in the United States, as a whole, by 3 per cent. By 2000, entry-level assistant professor salaries had declined to about 92 per cent of median family income.[17]

Those entry-level differences tend to widen—even considerably—at the more advanced career stages when attorneys are moving into partnerships and physicians into group practices. Over the past two decades, the average faculty salary for all ranks has lagged about 30 per cent behind the average salaries of a comparison group of well-educated professionals, holding at least a master's degree (Schuster and Finkelstein 2006).

As another lens through which to view trends in the competitiveness of academic staff's compensation, the salaries of postsecondary academic staff was compared to that of teachers in public elementary and secondary schools (Schuster and Finkelstein 2006). In 1970, the ratio of average salaries for assistant professors to elementary/secondary school teachers was 1.2:1—assistant professors earning, on average, 1.2 times the salary of public school teachers. By 2000, that ratio had shrunk to 1.09 times—in spite of the relative slowing in the 1990s of teachers' salary increases, relative to those for all workers.

Finally, Table 6.5 provides yet another lens, through which to view the compensation of academic staff comparatively, and it yields a slightly more mixed and nuanced picture. It displays the average (and 75th percentile) salaries of professionals in various fields employed outside academe, with those of professionals in the same fields employed as academic staff in universities. It is found that the average salary of academic staff in engineering and computer science is roughly equivalent to that of professionals in similar fields employed in the public sector outside academe and even to those employed in the private sector as well, although there is clearly more variation at the upper end in the private sector. In the case of business, academic staff may be at somewhat of a disadvantage, compared to their non-academic professional peers; but that depends on the subfield or type of job in which those outside academe are employed (accountants are decidedly not at a disadvantage). Academic staff in law, however, actually enjoy a premium in average salary over lawyers practicing in the public sector, albeit somewhat of a disadvantage vis-à-vis counterparts in private practice. Only in medicine are the salaries of academic staff dwarfed by those in private practice. However, these comparisons require considerable caution, since academic staff in the health professions include those in nursing and other allied health fields (physical therapy and pharmacy), as well as academic medicine. The lowest academic salaries are located in the traditional liberal arts fields. While many of these liberal arts fields do not offer ready equivalents in business and industry, three such fields—English, psychology, and chemistry—do provide significant employment opportunities outside academe and Table 6.5 compares average and 75th percentile salaries within fields across sectors.[18] The results are revealing. In English and literature occupations, among the lowest-paid occupational group in the liberal arts fields, academics fare well in terms of average and median salary, although less well at the lower end of the distribution (the 25th percentile). At the highest end of the distribution, however, academic staff are actually the highest earners. In psychology, academic staff tend to do better than psychologists in private practice or in public school systems but not as well as those in

Table 6.5 Salaries (average and 75th percentile) of other US professionals and academic staff in the public and private sector by field, 2009

Discipline		Public		Private	
		Average salary (US$)	75th percentile (US$)	Average salary (US$)	75th percentile (US$)
Business	Financial managers	93,330	115,540	116,030	142,070
	Accountants and auditors	61,560	74,120	68,200	80,090
	General and operations managers	94,760	118,440	111,840	142,140
	Sales managers	80,950	96,460	111,650	141,560
	Human resources managers, all other	92,880	111,940	108,570	130,840
	Business operations specialists, all other	67,110	81,130	65,370	81,370
	Financial analysts	67,980	79,480	85,810	99,720
	Business teachers, postsecondary	82,970	104,760	84,940	106,620
Computer Science	Computer software engineers, applications	71,660	85,810	90,860	108,450
	Computer systems analysts	67,520	81,710	82,020	99,540
	Network and computer systems administrators	62,470	75,130	72,190	87,480
	Computer support specialists	45,320	54,340	47,720	57,930
	Computer science teachers, postsecondary	75,670	94,070	76,260	96,180

Engineering	Civil engineers	78,920	94,180	82,080	98,250
	Electrical engineers	83,400	101,820	86,410	104,210
	Industrial engineers	83,450	97,660	77,030	92,010
	Mechanical engineers	87,200	104,510	80,180	96,040
	Engineering teachers, postsecondary	89,920	110,760	101,690	123,650
Chemistry	Chemists	77,640	99,350	71,780	90,260
	Chemical technicians	41,700	50,730	44,020	53,650
	Chemistry teachers, postsecondary	77,230	93,660	77,580	92,460
Psychology	Clinical, counseling, and school psychologists	70,810	84,070	74,200	87,700
	Industrial-organizational psychologists	73,460	87,970	108,940	134,490
	Psychologists, all other	83,310	102,580	86,150	105,360
	Psychology teachers, postsecondary	72,500	88,210	71,570	87,030

Table 6.5 (Continued)

		Public		Private	
		Average salary (US$)	75th percentile (US$)	Average salary (US$)	75th percentile (US$)
Applied English Language/Literature Occupations	Editors	49,670	57,760	58,670	71,570
	Technical writers	64,640	78,880	65,660	80,560
	Writers and authors	65,890	82,830	64,470	75,190
	English language and literature teachers, postsecondary	65,150	$81,150	67,460	$80,350
Legal	Lawyers	98,360	127,890	137,540	#
	Arbitrators, mediators, and conciliators	87,620	114,730	60,790	70,920
	Law teachers, postsecondary	110,160	141,360	108,440	138,960
Medicine	Family and general practitioners	147,150	#	170,790	#
	Internists, general	161,940	#	185,360	#
	Pediatricians, general	150,070	#	162,030	#
	Surgeons	193,650	#	221,290	#
	Physicians and surgeons, all other	144,200	#	180,600	#
	Health specialties teachers, postsecondary	99,750	127,810	107,380	143,540

Note: # = indicates a salary greater than US$166,400 per year.
Source: US Department of Labor (2009).

the business/industrial sector. Yet, in chemistry, academic staff actually outearn chemists outside academe across the salary distribution—albeit by no more than 5 per cent.

This analysis suggests that, at least in part, the comparison of average salaries between academics (a plurality of whom reside in the traditional liberal arts) and other professionals outside academe may lead to somewhat biased—or, at least, insufficiently nuanced—conclusions. When academic staff in the professional fields—and in chemistry—are compared directly to their counterparts in the public sector and private business and industry, the salary differential is less extreme and, in some cases, may actually involve an academic salary premium—at least over the public sector. Even within the liberal arts fields, the salary differentials are not always large or in favor of the non-academic sector (as, once again, in chemistry).

One further layer of nuance is provided by the columns including data on salaries at the 75th percentile—the higher end salaries at the more advanced career stages. These data provide inferences about comparative salary differentials, at later career stages. Once again, academic engineers and computer scientists fare relatively well, vis-à-vis their counterparts outside academe. At the other extreme, academic staff and private industry differentials clearly swell at the more senior level in law and medicine. Business falls somewhere in between.

While the salaries of academic staff in the United States are good, regarding those of academic staff in many other nations, their position in terms of payment in their own national context may be less favorable—at least in the aggregate, a function of the plurality of faculty in academic fields with limited employment markets outside academe. However, academic staff in several of the professions (who are, after all, at the higher end of the academic salary distribution) compare favorably with their counterparts in the public sector and, in several cases, with those in the private sector, as well. Primarily at the more advanced careers stages, and primarily in law and medicine, academic/private-sector differentials swell considerably.

Fringe benefits of academic staff

In addition to salary, all institutions in the United States provide their full-time academic staff with an array of non-salary compensation, typically referred to as "fringe benefits."[19] These almost always include health insurance for the staff member and his/her family (to which the staff member may be required to contribute a portion) and an institutional contribution to a retirement plan (which usually requires a matching individual contribution) (Clark and Ma 2005). There are actually two components to institutional contributions to retirement: there is a cash contribution to either a private annuity plan (such as the Teacher's Insurance Annuity Association, usually referred to simply as "TIAA") or a "local" public plan (usually the state pension system for public employees including academic staff in the public sector). Also, there is a mandated institutional contribution on behalf of the individual to the US Social Security fund, as well as a requirement for all businesses with more than 50 employees that provides a federal retirement annuity for all workers (Bair 2003). Beyond these basics, many institutions include some kind of tuition benefit for academic staff, their spouses, and children. Given the costs of higher education in the United States, especially in the private sector, such a benefit can amount to a substantial portion of annual salary for years in which it is used by a staff member or his or her immediate family.

While salary is nearly always the primary component of compensation, certainly health insurance, retirement contribution, and tuition benefits are key aspects of the overall package. In 2011, most institutions estimated the actual costs to them of fringe benefits as about 30 per cent of an academic staff member's base salary, compared to about 20 per cent a decade ago. Many of these benefits, however, are largely invisible to an individual faculty member, since the increased benefits have primarily involved areas such as increased health insurance premiums and/or Social Security contributions that do not materially improve his or her current economic status (i.e., individual purchasing power) (Chronsiter 2001).

The available evidence suggests that the fringe benefits available to full-time tenure-eligible faculty are, at most institutions also extended to full-time, limited-term faculty. It has been reported that 93 per cent of the cross-section of 86 four-year colleges and universities have extended full-fringe benefits to full-time, non-tenure-track faculty, with little difference between public and private institutions (Baldwin and Chronister 2001). Such benefits were spelled out in greatest detail in unionized campuses. Part-time faculty, on the other hand, are typically not eligible for most fringe benefits at most institutions. There may be a variation for those part-time appointees who are not paid by the course, but as a percentage of a full-time equivalent appointment.

Supplementary employment

Data from the 2004 National Study of Postsecondary Faculty (US Department of Education 2008) show the following:

1. Just over half of all full-time faculty (whether term appointees or tenure eligible) report receiving supplementary salary from their employing institution, beyond their contractual base salary—usually in form of overload or summer teaching, special administrative stipends, or pass-through funds from external grants.
2. Only about one-eighth of academic staff receive supplemental income from another institution of higher education (usually teaching part-time on another campus).
3. Nearly one-third of academic staff report receiving income from consulting or freelance work in their academic field—presumably, including royalties and other income from intellectual property.
4. About one-fifth of academic faculty report receiving income from other (presumably non-academic) employment outside their home institution.
5. About one-third of academic staff report other sources of income—such as investment income from the ownership of stocks, bonds, and real estate.

Although there are not significant differences in the proportion of academic staff earning these different categories of income in the public vs. the private sector, there is some public–private difference in the actual amounts of outside income earned. Academic staff in the public sector earn an average of about 11 per cent of their institutional salary in total outside income and about 6 per cent of their institutional salary from outside employment income (including consulting). The corresponding figures for academic staff in the private sector are 14 per cent and 7 per cent, respectively, of institutional salaries, which are 20 per cent higher to begin with.

Within sectors, however, there is some evidence that supplemental employment income varies by institutional type. Academic staff at research universities are slightly less likely to report supplementary income from their employing institution (48% vs. 55%) or from another college or university (9% vs. 13%), and are slightly more likely to report income from consulting/freelance work (38% vs. 30%)

and other employment (25% vs. 21%). A significant difference, however, does not appear in the outside income they earn from such activities as a percentage of their institutional salary vis-à-vis non-research university staff (14% and 11%, respectively).[20]

An examination of differences among academic staff by discipline shows that academic staff in engineering and the fine arts were much more likely (at about 45% each) than other academic staff to earn income from consulting and freelance work, while academic staff in the humanities were least likely (23%) compared to the overall 30 per cent average. Academic staff in business (67%) and education (62%) were more likely than those in other academic fields (51%, overall) to report income from their employing institution beyond their base salary. There were minor differences by field in the percentage reporting income from other academic institutions (although the range across all fields fell between 9% and 15%).

All in all, these data clearly suggest that, in the United States, institutional base salary is by far the major component of academic compensation, especially when fringe benefits are included. While income from outside sources varies by the type of institution and academic field, nonetheless it remains a minor component of the total professional income of academic staff.

Conclusions

In the second half of the 20th century, academic staff in the United States consummated something of a spectacular rise onto the world stage. Their career prospects improved substantially in terms of the emergence of a predictable, regularized career track and an expanding academic job market capable of absorbing new recruits, almost as fast as the graduate schools produced them (in some cases, in the 1950s and 1960s, even faster). The 1970s began a process of erosion, as the growth of the academic job market slowed and economic conditions, especially inflation, robbed steadily growing academic salaries of most of the gains in purchasing power. In the late 1980s and the 1990s a period began where compensation losses recovered steadily but in which both the job market continued to deteriorate and the predictability and regularity of the career track was threatened by new types of academic appointment practices. Since then, growing marketization of higher education has fueled a widening stratification of the system across a variety of dimensions—including institutional type, academic field, and, now, type of appointment. The internal differences within the system are now wider than at almost any point in the past; and it becomes difficult, if not impossible, to hazard generalizations at the system level.

At the top of the system, at research universities, career tracks remain predictable structurally, although the competition for shrinking federal research funds makes it difficult to operationally graft an individual career path on that frame. A growing gap is emerging between the private and public sectors, as state government disinvestment in higher education continues apace and as the public sector itself struggles to diversify its revenue base. The market has introduced larger and growing disparities among the disciplines and professional fields—producing gaping disparities between resources and opportunities among the liberal arts and the professions and, within the liberal arts, between the natural sciences, the humanities, and social sciences. The development of a system of limited-term academic appointments has weakened the traditional tenure system and introduced clear lines of stratification. In effect, what had been a relatively homogeneous professional group has been transitioned into a highly differentiated workforce, playing multiple roles and progressing on multiple-career tracks.

Working conditions, employment prospects, and salary depend almost entirely on where an individual academic staff member is located, along the system's lines of stratification. Faculty members in the professional schools and in the natural sciences at research universities, especially private research universities, boast excellent career opportunities and compensation that affords them a middle-class—if not upper-middle-class—lifestyle. Faculty members in the humanities, and those outside the research university sector, have much more precarious career prospects and economic opportunities. Another case involves the large and growing contingent of the workforce—the new majority—and those full-time faculty who make careers off any prescribed institutional career track. The career opportunities and payment available to them may be less attractive objectively but may nonetheless provide a satisfactory set of trade-offs for young parents or for early retirees transitioning from lucrative first careers in business or the military.

Irrespective of location in the newly emerging stratification system, the prospects for new entrants to the academic staff are among the most precarious in the past half century. Of the 40 per cent of newly minted PhDs entering the academic workforce annually, less than half will land tenure-track, full-time appointments; and the majority of these faculty will be outside the research university sector. While possessing the requisite doctoral degree, their compensation will not compare favorably to that of a newly minted baccalaureate degree in nursing, physical therapy, finance, or accounting; and will be about half that of a newly minted attorney taking a first full-time position in a large, prestigious law firm. It will not likely permit a middle-class lifestyle—at least, not yet. The extent to which individuals can find their way to a research university, especially a private one, and manage to successfully compete for extramural research funds, then a subsequent promotion to a full professorship and opportunities for career mobility and an upper middle-class lifestyle may be promising. For those aspiring academics in the humanities and the less-quantitative social sciences (e.g., history, anthropology, sociology, and geography), prospects for either a predictable career track or reasonable economic prosperity are more tenuous; and certainly, institutional life is less accommodating and working conditions are less attractive.

Within the context of the last half century in the United States, current developments signal a clear decline in the collective fortunes of American academic professions. In absolute terms of career opportunity and compensation, these professions do still compare favorably with their counterparts in most other nations. However, for the moment, the trajectory is no longer above the horizontal level and is gradually but ineluctably declining. At the same time—as the key point—the fortunes of the academic professions in other rapidly developing economies, especially the BRIC countries, are on the rise. Thus, the threats to the continued hegemony of the American research university and academic profession are sufficiently real. Certainly, in the next half century, a gradual realignment may be seen in the global scientific pecking order—a development that may be all to the global good.

Notes

1. Contingent faculty appointments cannot always be directly attributed to financial pressure. Indeed, colleges and universities fill many different needs by short-term hiring. This trend allows them to pilot new, untested academic programs without making long-term commitments; to tap into the unique expertise of professionals in the field who do not aspire to academic research careers; to replace permanent faculty who are on research or personal leaves; as well as other factors (see Cross and Goldenberg 2009). Nonetheless, US Department of Education data show quite conclusively that from a curiosity and a largely peripheral phenomenon in the mid-1980s, these appointments became within a single decade the modal type of appointment for newly hired faculty entering the system. The precipitousness and rapidity of this trend—and its nearly perfect parallelism with deteriorating fiscal conditions—suggest, at the least, a non-spurious correlation.

2. That was the year that the American Association of University Professors, in consultation with the American Council on Education, first promulgated its classic Statement on Academic Freedom and Tenure, in which it specified the six-to-seven-year probationary period and the subsequent "up-or-out" decision as the modal organizing principal for academic appointments (AAUP 2006).

3. This tends to be especially true for academic women, who are much more likely than men to move from a tenure-track to a fixed-term appointment, even prior to tenure review—usually for purposes of reducing work demands and restoring a healthier work–family-life balance.

4. It should be noted that some four-year institutions are placing increased emphasis on teaching ability and experience in hiring all faculty.

5. Ehrenberg reported that a plurality of humanities doctoral graduates of a dozen prestigious universities, taking first full-time position on a limited-term contract, were eventually able to land a full-time, tenure-track position—suggesting that in the humanities, at least, non-tenure eligible appointments may have become a new entry step on the academic career ladder.

6. There is an exception in the humanities, where fixed-term contracts may provide a new kind of temporary entry-level holding station to the tenure track, not unlike the postdoc in the physical and life sciences and engineering.

7. About two-thirds of the headcount faculty at the two-year institutions are part-time and around about one-third are full-time.

8. For four-year public comprehensive institutions, the proportion of part-time faculty approaches 40 per cent. Since they rarely employ graduate teaching assistants, for practical purposes, such institutions do not differ significantly from research universities.

9. Since the great recession of 2008, however, progress has abruptly stopped and may have actually receded.

10. This study did not, most notably, include Hong Kong. The countries represented included: United States, United Kingdom, Australia, New Zealand, Canada, Japan, Germany, France, Saudi Arabia, South Africa, Malaysia, Argentina, Columbia, India, and China.

11. Part-time faculty on appointments that are a portion of full-time are frequently in longer-term situations: some may be professional school faculty (architects or engineers) with tenure, but substantial outside commitments (about 10% of all part-time faculty in the United States are tenured or tenure eligible); others may be female tenure-track or tenured faculty who move to part-time during early childrearing years.

12. Nearly 3 per cent earn more than US$100,000 annually (US Department of Education 2008).

13. However, we must remember that in most institutions, full-time tenured and tenure-track faculty members have significant responsibilities outside of the classroom. As a result, it may not be accurate to count classroom teaching as constituting 100 per cent of the salaries of full-time tenured and tenure-track faculty members. These responsibilities may include research, committee work, and community service. Full-time tenured and tenure-track faculty members also receive support to perform other functions—i.e., working with

student groups, being available to help with special student projects, and being available to students outside of class.

14. A systematic comparative study is currently under way in the United States of differences between salaries of tenure eligible vs. contingent faculty, including both full-time, limited-term appointees, and part-time appointees—according to John Curtis, Director of Research, American Association of University Professors. The survey, sponsored by the Coalition on the Academic Workforce, a group including several disciplinary associations and faculty unions, is scheduled to go into the field in November 2010, and a preliminary report is tentatively scheduled for late spring, 2011.

15. What follows is based on the 2008 AAUP Annual Survey of the Economic Status of the Profession (AAUP 2009).

16. There has been much discussion of salary compression in American higher education, wherein the salaries of new faculty recruits are perceived as gaining ground in a percentage of the salaries of senior faculty—narrowing the gap among academic ranks. While in a few, select high-demand fields—e.g., business, engineering, computer science, and nursing—wherein new recruits must be paid relative to the current industry norms rather than to salaries of senior academic staff—this may be the case, the available data suggest that it is not true in the aggregate.

17. To some extent, of course, a portion of that decline may be attributable to the rise in the proportion of two-income families, effectively inflating median family income (and deflating entry-level salaries as a proportion of same).

18. While many PhD psychologists practice outside academe, they tend to be employed in private practice or in public-sector health and welfare agencies, where compensation is relatively modest as compared to private business and industry.

19. Part-time academic staff almost never receive fringe benefits of any kind—except for benefits mandated by the federal government for all employees of all large employers (e.g., contributions to social security).

20. Yet, of course, their average institutional base salaries are considerably higher.

References

Adams, J. A. 2010. Is the United States losing its preeminence in higher education? In *American universities in a global market*, ed. C. Clotfelter, 33–68. Chicago: University of Chicago Press.

American Association of University Professors. 2006. *Policy documents and reports*, 10th ed. Washington, DC: American Association of University Professors.

———. 2009. On the brink: The annual report on the economic status of the profession. *Academe* 95 (2).

———. 2010. No refuge: The annual report on the economic status of the profession. *Academe* 96 (2).

———. 2011. It's not over yet: The Annual report on the economic status of the profession. *Academe* 96 (2): 4–80.

Bair, J. 2003. Hiring practices in finance education: Linkages among top-ranked graduate programs. *Journal of Economics & Sociology* 62 (2): 429–443.

Baldwin, R., and J. Chronister. 2001. *Teaching without tenure: Policies and practices for a new era*. Baltimore, MD: Johns Hopkins University Press.

Bhandari, R., and S. Laughlin, eds. 2009. *Higher education on the move: New developments in global mobility*. New York: Institute for International Education.

Black, J. N. 2004. *The freefall of the American university: How our colleges are corrupting the minds and morals of the next generation*. Nashville, TN: WorldNetDaily Books.

Bowen, H. R., and J. H. Schuster. 1986. *American professors: A national resource imperiled*. New York: Oxford University Press.

Burke, D. 1988. *The academic marketplace revisited*. New York: Basic Books.

Caplow, T., and R. McGee. 1958. *The academic marketplace*. New York: Basic Books.

Carter, R. G., and J. M. Scott. 1998. Navigating the academic job market minefield. *PS: Political Science and Politics* 31 (3): 615–622.

Chait, R., and C. Trower. 1997. *Where tenure does not reign: Colleges with contract systems*. New Pathways in Academic Careers, no. 3. Washington, DC: American Association for Higher Education.

Chronister, J. 2001. *Faculty fringe benefits. Almanac of Higher Education*. Washington, DC: National Education Association.

Clark, R., and J. Ma, eds. 2005. *Recruitment, retention, and retirement in higher education: Building and managing the faculty of the future*. Northampton, MA: Edward Elgar.

Clotfelter, C. T., ed. 2010. *American Universities in a Global Market*. Chicago: University of Chicago Press.

College and University Professional Association for Human Resources. 2010. *2010 executive summary for the national faculty salary survey for four-year institutions*. Knoxville, TN: CUPA-HR.

Cross, J. C., and E. N. Goldenberg. 2009. *Off-track profs: Non-tenured teachers in higher education*. Cambridge, MA: Massachusetts Institute of Technology Press.

Cummings, William K. 2008. The context for the changing academic profession: A survey of international indicators. In *The changing academic profession in international comparative and quantitative perspectives*, 33–56. Hiroshima, Japan: Research Institute for Higher Education, Hiroshima University.

Curtis, J. W., and M. F. Jacobe. 2006. AAUP contingent faculty index 2006. Washington, DC: American Association of University Professors.

Dooris, M. J., and L. E. Sandmeyer. 2006. *Planning for improvement in the academic department, Effective practices for academic leaders*, vol. 1. Herndon, VA: Stylus Publishing.

Ehrenberg, R. 2010. *The education of scholars*. Princeton, NJ: Princeton University Press.

Geiger, R. 2010. Impact of the financial crisis on higher education in the United States. *International Higher Education* 59 (Spring): 9–11.

Goodwin, C. D., and M. Nacht. 1991. *Missing the boat: The failure to internationalize American higher education*. Cambridge: Cambridge University Press.

Goonen, N. M., and R. S. Blechman. 1999. *Higher education administration: A guide to legal, ethical and practical issues*. Westport, CT: Greenwood Press.

Gumport, P. 2000. Academic restructuring: Organizational change and institutional imperatives. *Higher Education* 39: 67–91.

JBL Associates. 2008. *Reversing course: The troubled state of academic staffing and a path forward*. Washington, DC: American Federation of Teachers.

Leslie, L., and S. Slaughter. 1995. The development and current status of market mechanisms in United States postsecondary education. *Higher Education Policy* 10: 239–252.

Marginson, S., and G. Rhoades. 2002. Beyond national states, markets, and the systems of higher education: A glonacal agency heuristic. *Higher Education* 43: 281–309.

Matler, M. 1991. Recruiting faculty: Complementary tales from 2 campuses. *Research in Higher Education* 32 (1): 31–44.

Modern Language Association. 2008. *Education in the balance: A report on the academic workforce in English*. Washington, DC: Modern Language Association.

Organization for Economic Cooperation and Development. 2010. Biennial Conference on Higher Education. Paris, September 13–15 as cited by Doug Lederman, Commonality across countries. Inside Higher Ed, September 16, 2010.

Perna, L. W. 2001. Sex and race differences in faculty tenure and promotion. *Research in Higher Education* 42 (5): 541–567.

Rhoades, G. 1998. *Managed professionals: Unionized faculty and restructuring academic labor*. Albany, NY: State University of New York Press.

Rumbley, L. E., I. F. Pacheco, and P. G. Altbach. 2009. *International comparison of academic salaries: An exploratory study*. Chestnut Hill, MA: Center for International Higher Education, Boston College.

Ruml, B., and S. Tickton. 1955. *Teaching salaries then and now: A 50 year comparison with other occupations*. New York: Fund for the Advancement of Education, Ford Foundation.

Schuster, J., and M. Finkelstein. 2006. *The American faculty: The restructuring of academic work and careers*. Baltimore, MD: Johns Hopkins University Press.

Slaughter, S., and G. Rhoades. 2004. *Academic capitalism and the new economy: Markets, state, and higher education*. Baltimore, MD: Johns Hopkins University Press.

Twombly, S. B. 2005. Values, policies and practices affecting the hiring process for full-time arts and sciences faculty in community colleges. *Journal of Higher Education* 76: 423–447.

US Department of Education. 2003. *The national study of postsecondary faculty 1999*. Washington, DC: National Center for Education Statistics.

———. 2008. *The national study of postsecondary faculty 2004*. Washington, DC: National Center for Education Statistics.

———. 2009. Integrated Postsecondary Education Data System, Fall Staff Survey (Data file). http://nces.ed.gov/ipeds/datacenter/ (accessed October 6, 2010).

US Department of Labor. 2009. *May 2009 occupational employment and wage estimates*. Washington, DC: Bureau of Labor Statistics. http://www.bls.gov/oes/oes_dl.htm (accessed March 14, 2011).

Zakaria, F. 2008. *The post-American world*. New York: W. W. Norton.

Zumeta, W. 2009. State support of higher education: The roller coaster plunges downward yet again. In *The NEA 2009 almanac of higher education*, 29–44. Washington, DC: National Education Association.

Index

Lightning Source UK Ltd.
Milton Keynes UK
UKOW06f2223290315

248738UK00004B/30/P